"It's a cynical, outrageous, politically and absolutely hilarious modern-day ***Walden***. — Douglas Preston (author of ***Lost City of the Monkey God***).

"David is my favorite curmudgeon. I thoroughly enjoyed every page!" — Wonderhussy (Las Vegas Showgirl)

"Hysterically funny, but in a 'twisted genius' way." — Nadia Teeze (Exotic Dancer and Contortionist)

Desert Soliloquy

A Perfectly Sane Misanthrope Hides in the Desert

By David Rice

Smashwords eBOOK ISBN 978-0-463-13326-2
Paperback Version ISBN 978-1-728-96431-7

Desertphile Publishing, David Rice
General Delivery
Abiquiu, New Mexico 87510

davidmichaelrice.com

DEDICATION

For my brother. Obviously.

ACKNOWLEDGMENTS

"How vain it is to sit down to write when you have not stood up to live." -- Henry David Thoreau

Andrew and Elizabeth Sebastian, for providing a refuge from the noise and horror of the human world.

Captain Ron, for showing me it is okay let go of the helm and drift now and then. You can trust Ron with your beer can and wallet, because I guarantee you will get your wallet back unmolested.

Douglas Preston, for showing us all how to tell a story well and for telling me to stop thinking when I write.

David Morrell, for the advice in **THE SUCCESSFUL NOVELIST** and explaining why writers write instead of make an easier living.

Henry David Thoreau and Edward Paul Abbey, for the correct attitude.

Carl Sagan, for being a candle in the darkness in this demon haunted world.

TABLE OF CONTENTS

BACKGROUND

Bronson: "Oh, I don't know. Wherever I end up, I guess."
Driver: "Man, I wish I was you." **--- Then Came Bronson**

The icy west wind flowed over the Sierra Nevada mountains, across Death Valley, and around the peaks of the Avawatz Mountain Range. One corner of the plywood barrier that covered my cave's entrance had shaken loose, exposing my numb face to the bleak gray winter night. Buried beneath my winter survival blankets, sweat poolcd under me as my waking movements sent rills trickling off my chest and down my sides. The night sweats, which I am prone to during winter months, had become a nightly event; I lifted the edge of my blankets with my right hand, letting icy cold air in to dry the sweat.

I thought about connecting the light bulb's alligator clip to Mister Fusion (a spare car battery), but the dim light might disturb my roommate: a rat named "Hey Rat!" that lived tucked away in a rocky crack surrounded by used toilet paper that she had scrounged after I was done wiping my ass with it. If I had light, perhaps I could make breakfast for us both. Hey Rat! had a way of displaying her displeasure at breakfast being served too slowly: she would stand at her water tin (a lid from a jar of pickles, inverted) and rock back and forth glaring up at me. Stale bread and raisins usually calmed her down.

Thoughts of my own breakfast brought depression as heavy as my damp blankets. If I heated some water, I could rehydrate some mashed potatoes, brown gravy, and instant coffee. With cold water I could prepare some artificially colored powdered "orange drink" which never quite convinced me it tasted like orange juice. It all seems more work than it was worth.

Laying in the dark, shivering, I flapped my blankets while my sweat dried. Worse than the night sweats, which left me nauseated and as dehydrated as my remaining food stores, were the recurring nightmares.

In my dreams, enraged mobs of club-wielding urbanites chased me through book stores and chemistry labs, knocking over shelves and glassware in their zeal to seize me in their blood-soaked hands. From an aloof height I would watch as my naked body flung itself over card catalogs and Bunsen burners while sniveling and whimpering in terror, mere inches ahead of the ravening murderous horde. While my dream self fled, Carl Sagan chanted over and over and over again, "The universe seems neither benign nor hostile, merely indifferent."

Fearing my dreams, I reached out with my left hand, groped for the light's alligator clip, fumbled with it in the dark, and found the battery lug. Above my head, a tiny ten-watt light bulb glowed dimly with enough illumination to dispel some of the dark.

I looked over to the sock I had nailed into the rock wall a few feet to my right. The sock remained empty this fine Christmas morning: no walnuts and candies and no lumps of coal. Santa Claus had either forgotten me, or didn't see the stocking in the dark after prying open my plywood wall and peering inside. I felt foolish for having placed it there: an act of regression back into infancy, too powerful to resist.

Fighting the overwhelming desire to cry, feeling sorry for myself for no reasons I could name, I detached the light from the battery, pulled my damp blankets around me tightly, and lay on my side staring into the cold yet womb-like darkness of my cave home.

I had been living in the cave for eleven months.

INTRODUCTION

***"But they seem to know where they are going, the ones who walk away from Omelas."* -- Ursula K. LeGuin**

At the start of year 2000 I lived in a cave on the southeast edge of Death Valley alone for 29 months. The plan was for me to live somewhere in the desert, on public land, for three or four months. One of my goals was to write about the experience so that other people considering doing the same will have an idea on what it will be like; my other goal was to avoid humanity. If anyone had told me at the time, in the planning stages, that my adventure would stretch into two and a half years, I would never have considered the project.

If you have thought about leaving society for a brief time, this book is a warning as much as an encouragement. There are times when it is healthy for a person to go off and live alone for a brief time, and it seems to me every human being should do so at least once in her or his life when mentally and physically prepared. The danger is in lingering outside modern society too long, fearful and yet wishful of reentering, and losing the part of you that can tolerate your own species and its endless number of flaws. Emotional self-sufficiency taken to extremes can become unhealthy, limiting your options and could put your very survival at risk.

If at any time in your life you discover you can live by yourself, with little or no contact among other members of your "kind" (humanity), you might have lost more than you have gained, if anything. Beware you never come to that horrifying abyss, let alone step into it.

Two notes here about this book. The first is that I think it is the duty of a writer to be honest in her or his writing, since the readers deserve honesty in exchange for their time. By "honesty" I mean it is the writer's job to put down the words and phrases correctly and without censoring what she or he sees in her or his head; the genre does not matter---- fiction, romance, western, speculative fiction, biographical: the honest writer will treat readers as adults, and share with them the clearest mental picture that prose can achieve. Just like in painting, or poetry, or singing, or dancing, there must be no "shoulds and should nots" in writing except one: narration, description, and dialog should be faithfully moved from the writer's brain to the sheet of paper, with the writer as a sort of conduit or pipeline, without any thought to what is politically correct, or personally shameful, or socially taboo.

In this book I have been honest with the reader, even when fidelity to the truth made me look less than the law-abiding and ethical person I would like to be. "Speak the truth, but not to punish," Thich Nhat Hanh said, but some times the truth can sting.

The second note is that this book is the result of rendering six notebooks filled with my personal journal which I kept during my time in the East Mojave Desert. Each notebook was 50 sheets thick, labeled with the season and the year on the cover. I originally filled nine notebooks but three of them were destroyed by rain and mold. At times my entries in my journal were in tedious detail, coldly emotionless; at times my entries were wild, confused, irrational, and incomprehensible. I have done my best to "fill in" the events in chronological order as they appear in my journal.

WHY THE DESERT CHOSE ME

"I feel I stand in a desert with my hands outstretched, and you are raining down upon me." **-- Patricia Highsmith**

I was thirteen years old when my mother's new spouse hauled me and my family away to Indian Springs Auxiliary Air Force Base in Nevada to be daily beaten, humiliated, demeaned, defiled, brutalized, and sexually molested by strange men. Nobody had to tell me why most of the women in town wore more bruises than clean clothing, and had terrified, wounded eyes. Subservient, low-hierarchy males abuse anyone and everyone they consider lower than they are. The worse offenders either went to the one and only bar in the center of town every night to drink, or to the Mormon Church every Sunday, Tuesday, and Thursday nights to be praised by their community for being ideal husbands and fathers. If you ever visit Indian Springs, Nevada, be sure to pack something to kill yourself with.

The town of Indian Springs had only one positive trait: walk in any direction for 30 minutes or so, and one will be completely alone in the desert. After another 30 minutes one leaves the trash behind, and the noise of the highway, and the automobile stink. The desert is pure and clean and uncluttered, out there in the creosote and rabbit brush. If one is lucky, there's nobody else around for miles---and that is more precious than gold.

I spent my free time exploring the desert around Indian Springs with my brother, looking for old mines, seeking out sources of water, and enjoying the lack of people. The only fond memories I have of my youth are of being in the desert, far from monstrous, brutish, odious humanity.

Life in Indian Springs in year 1974 was just as suicide-inducing as it is now, and my brother and I found that any adventure was worth pursuing. Running naked across the field during a football match ("streaking") was popular at the time, and all us kids who had nothing to hide did it. We also had the yearly Air Show, when the Indian Springs Thunderbirds performed low-altitude stunts up to the day they all followed their leader into the ground at 400 miles per hour with hardly a flinch at all: an event hailed as "a beautiful act of obedience to leadership" by the Air Force captain who told me about the heroic and manly slaughter.

One evening, the day before an air show, the lone woman at Cactus Springs asked my brother and me to shoot a raccoon that had been harassing her hens: the pay would be $5, which was a huge sum at the time. Her daughter attended the same school we did, and even with the girl's "duck when you kiss her" over-bite she was still prettier than most Indian Springs girls, so of course my brother and I agreed. Late that night we walked west four miles, his Sears & Roebuck bolt-action .22 caliber rim-fire over his shoulder, and lay down to sleep in ambush a few dozen yards from the woman's hen house. The raccoon showed up at early dawn, and my brother sent a bullet through the raccoon's left eye. We packed the dead raccoon in a pillow case and trudged back to Indian Springs.

Back in town, the cafe on the highway was open for breakfast. The cafe was quickly filling with tourists from Las Vegas there to attend the air show, but my sibling and I got a table near the door. The pillow case with the raccoon was shoved under the table; we asked for pancakes; my brother took apart the rifle and started to clean it on the dining table like any civilized savage would. A fat, ancient, bald tourist sitting at the table nearest us loudly objected, apparently yelling at the cook, "There's a child with a gun in here!" He sounded outraged, not alarmed.

My brother's eyes locked with mine. A "silent understanding" passed between us, then my brother slowly pivoted the chair he was sitting in until he was facing the irate man. I drew in a breath slowly, held it a bit, and exhaled: I felt a tiny stab of pity for the tourist, as I know how much like a force of nature my brother can be when he turns into Cletus The Hillbilly. When my brother turns the full might of his wit against a victim, it is often spectacular and always frightening.

"Why, sheeer there iz!" my brother said. "How elzz could ah shoo' this 'er varm-mit?" My brother used one booted foot to shove the pillow case with the dead raccoon in it out from under the table.

Slowly, making no sudden moves, I started to reassemble the rifle because I might need it soon.

"Iz a' gunna make ah hat owtah 'em," my brother said, reaching down and opening the pillow case. He rummaged around and pulled the dead raccoon out of the sack by the tail and one leg.

The tourist turned purple, and there was a great disturbance among his eating companions.

"Ack! Eark! Ork!" strangled the tourist, turning the most amazing shade of violet. He managed to find enough breath to yell, "You can't bring that thing in here!"

"Why not? They dun let yerself in 'er, ain't they?" my brother said. My brother set the dead raccoon down at his feet, reached for the pillow case, and said "Wud hew like tuh see muh dead rat'ler? He gots nine rat'ls on 'iz tail." My brother put one arm into the empty pillow case, and everyone who was not his brother flinched in horror and dread.

The annoying tourist leaped to his feet and wailed, "We're leaving!" The people with him stood up also and as a herd they stomped out the door. My brother put the raccoon back in the sack just as the waitress came out of the kitchen with the food the tourists had ordered.

"Where'd the people go?" she asked.

"Went looking for a diner that doesn't serve raccoon, I overheard," I told her. She looked puzzled.

-0-

When my brother and I were twenty-one years old we went exploring the Valjean Valley, looking for a place called Rabbit Holes Spring in the East Mojave Desert. The route in to the valley is along the T&T railroad right of way.

We drove into Valjean Valley on the railroad right of way (the rails and ties were long gone, "high graded" as building materials for other tasks), in my pickup early one morning, and we walked the final three miles or so to the spring. There is no surface water there, but if one is willing to dig five or six feet into the sand and gravel one will reach water. There was nothing of interest to see, and the morning was very warm, but the hike beat anything else we could think of to do.

When we hiked back to our vehicle at about 10:00 AM, we had just put our back packs and other gear into the pickup when we heard what sounded like a train coming at us from the west. We looked westward and saw a tall, wide curtain of dirt blotting out the sky. It looked like a biblical apocalypse sent by an angry god was thundering down upon us. We got into the pickup, rolled up the windows, and braced ourselves.

A mighty blast of furnace-hot wind struck the pickup, along with an astounding amount of dirt, sand, brush, leaves, items of clothing, rusty tin cans, plastic bags, a trash can lid, pieces of barbed wire--- anything and everything in the desert that was not nailed down came our way at high speed. The heat inside of the pickup became unbearable, so we climbed out on the leeward side and hunkered down with our backs against the wheels, hands cupped in front of our faces to help keep the dirt out of our eyes and sinuses. Visibility plunged from miles to mere feet, when we could open our eyes at all.

The desert eventually ran out of trash to throw at us, so it settled down to just dirt and the occasional creosote plant. It kept coming and coming and coming, and the stinging dirt itself felt so hot it was like being sprayed with droplets of oil from a deep fryer.

Every few minutes one of us would ask the other if he was still alive. The dust got into our eyes, and our ears, and between our teeth, and in every conceivable nook and cranny and orifice. The wind got even hotter as the day dragged tediously into the afternoon. Our sinuses dried out until they were in agony; our mouths dried out, and our tongues felt like dry sticks in our mouths.

The entire day passed in a pandemonium of dirt-filled hot wind. The sun, which was an ugly burnt orange color, set behind the hills to the west, and still the dust storm hammered us relentlessly.

About an hour after the sun had set, the wind suddenly and abruptly ceased blowing. It was like someone had thrown a switch, and the mighty fans of Hell had powered down. Our ears rang from the quiet. Our lips were cracked and split open, but the sores were so dry they didn't bleed. Old defensive knife wounds on my dessicated hands and arms, that had healed years ago, had mysteriously reopened. The amount of filth that clung to our bodies and clothing could only be seen to be believed, and not adequately imagined.

My brother and I stared at each other in the dwindling twilight like survivors of an atomic bomb blast. How he managed to speak, I still have no idea, but my brother parted his withered and blistered lips and asked, "What! The! Fuck!?"

The block of ice in our Coleman ice chest had completely

melted. We filled our water containers and drank the rest, though I had to use one hand to pry my mouth open wide enough to get water in there. When I drank, the hot water washed over the dry, dusty cracks in my mouth and tongue and it was agonizing but in a refreshing way.

Around 9:00 PM that evening, as we were laying on our filthy, gritty blankets and trying to sleep, we heard what sounded like a train coming at us from the east.

“No....” my brother said in the dark somewhere to my left. We could not see it coming, but we heard the howling wind coming back at us in the dark. My brother mentioned something about “But this only happens in the movies!” as we raced to hide behind the vehicle on its western side.

For much of that night the east wind threw back westward the trash and dirt and gravel and brush and shit that it had blown eastward during the day. Now and then the hot blasting wind would have an inexplicable gust of frigid air within it, and I would shiver with the cold for a few minutes, then the cruel hot wind would return.

The sun rose that morning blood red. Within a few minutes of its rising, the terrible wind fell silent and the airborne dirt settled to the desert floor. My brother and I once again shook the dirt off of us, as we struggled to stand.

I would have shed massive tears, but my body had no moisture left. I stammered at my brother phrases like, “I... I... I’ve suffered enough!” and, “Please! No more!” and, “Make it stop!” We had no more drinking water, and every breath brought agony to my chest. My brother agreed that maybe the vacation should end early. We had enjoyed the desert enough.

Then he got the bright idea of visiting Soda Spring, to bathe naked in the ecologically sensitive micro environment while the scientists and the college students watched us in disgust and horror. Which we did, maybe setting off the latest mass extinction event in the area.

The desert was good times, and comprised my fondest memories. That is why, when I felt the need to divorce myself from society for a few months, I chose the desert to spend it in. Or one could say the desert chose me, since even when it was being hostile to me, it never meant to be. The desert has always offered to me refuge when my people-wearied mind needs it.

Many times I have feared the desert. When we were about 30 years old my brother called me on the telephone and told me he was driving into the wilderness to the northwest of Ibex Spring for one night. I was anxious when he did not return after three nights. I know my brother was as savvy as a coyote in the desert, and he could be dropped off anywhere in that area with just a belt knife, a tin cup, and decent boots and he is good for a week or three. But I was anxious to go look for him.

There was no sign of my brother at Ibex Spring, nor at Horse Thief Spring, Pachalka Spring, Kingston Spring, Coyote Hole, Tecopa, and a half dozen other seeps and springs I checked. In many places I had to park my pickup and walk to a seep to see if my brother was there, as my car cannot travel over soft sand.

After a weary three days of searching, six nights having past with my brother in the wilderness, I found his car about two miles from a seep in the area east of Bad Water, with the front right wheel hanging awkwardly by its broken axle. I walked to the seep and found that the brush around and in the seep was dead and worn down by wind, suggesting the seep had been dry for many years.

My brother was squatting over a large rock, with a small rock in his right hand, pounding what appeared to be a tiny chipmunk or kangaroo rat into paste. It was obvious that he planned on eating the entire thing eyebrows and all. With the tiny bones crushed, it would make a disgusting meal but perhaps better than no chipmunk at all. I walked up to my brother, vastly relieved to see him alive and apparently well, and when he saw me he said, "Oh, what in the world are you doing here?" I pretended surprise at finding him there also, as if I had just happened to be passing by. He went on smashing the chipmunk, trying to out-cool me with placid disinterest at his being stranded in the desolate wasteland with no food and no water. When I asked him if I could eat half of his raw chipmunk paste (brains, bones, eyes, toe nails), he looked at me with shock that I would ask, considering how hungry he must have been.

"Gosh, Martha Steward, you ain't really gonna eat that thing, are you?" I was horrified. It seemed to me that even a tiny bit of chipmunk goo is worse than none at all, no matter what the FOXFIRE books say.

"Damn right I am! It took me four ass-fucking days to snare this little son of a bitch!" He then licked the small rock in his hand, dropped it, and with his fingers scraped the revolting slime off the big rock and stuck his fingers in his mouth.

"Gosh!" I was fighting to not vomit. "Is it as good as Ma always used to make it?"

"Even better!" my brother insisted, looking a bit green in the face. But he ate the whole thing, which impressed the bloody shit out of me. He then told me to hand over all of my water.

"Water? What water? I was just now going to ask ***you*** for some water."

The problem with joking about my brother almost dying of thirst, with my brother, is that he can hit people much harder than I can. The fist, when it promptly came my way, was covered with bits of tiny mammal paste and brother spit: for sure I did not want it against my face. I blocked it with my shoulder, unslung my back pack, and handed over my water.

I love the desert: it is mindlessly unforgiving; one day it will kill me, and that's okay.

ONE HUMAN OUT OF A HUNDRED IS SANE.

***"Maybe this world is another planet's hell."* -- Aldous Huxley**

Life is often ugly, painful, and brutal at times--- and at times perhaps it should be: personal struggles often teach empathy, and that trait is vitally important for a healthy human society. A complete life also means digging in the dirt; climbing walls, trees, cliffs and other risky shit; getting burned by the sun while hiking; picking off the mold from parts of food that are still good; drinking from a muddy puddle because there's no other water available; building your own shelter; risking injury in the pursuit of beauty; cutting down a few billboards; scrubbing someone else's piss and shit off a public toilet seat; wearing rags and be happy you have them instead of nothing; stealing a car or two from a wealthy person; riding the "B" platform of a hopper car on a freight train with a flat wheel under you.

When someone's life becomes too clean, too peaceful, too sanitized, too pretty, and too easy, she or he ceases being fully human. Being human means bleeding a little now and then.

Thus we come back to me. At the end of the 1990s I found myself a mere cog in the vast industrial social machinery known as "Corporate America." Nay, I was more like a lone Light Emitting Diode shining dimly within a seemingly infinite dehumanizing billion-cogged contrivance whose purpose is to force poor people to create wealth for the already-wealthy. The infernal engine that controls humanity (aka "modern society") had me laboring all day, every day, at a tedious job for no personal benefit greater than feeding me so that I could continue to labor. Like hundreds of millions of other people, I worked for the sake of working, with no time for anything else. My days were spent in a large room partitioned into little cubicles, within which I toiled at Accounts Receivable, General Ledgers, Inventory Management, and Payroll. In the dim, hellish glow of a computer screen I longed for either a long vacation or death; any ending was preferable.

One day at work during a lunch break I discovered that I could not get out of my chair. I was taken to the hospital in Irvine, California, within which the emergency room doctor told me my blood pressure was so high that I "should already be dead." It was the first time in several years that I smiled. Instead of medication, I bought a pre-paid "funeral package" complete with cremation and plastic jar to hold my ashes: the cost of being dead was a tiny fraction of what it cost to stay alive, and a bargain at $2,200.

Life at work was all bad; it was enough to turn Carl Jung into a thumb-sucking mother-lusting father-blaming neurotic Freudian. But as bad as work was, there was also all of the rest of humanity I dealt with every day.

THAT DIDN'T HURT!

"Numbing the pain for a while will make it worse when you finally feel it."
-- J.K. Rowling

Like everyone else on the planet, most of the people I met (and meet) in the world are "just folks" and on the whole harmless (though I never forget the "humans are apes with hand guns" paradigm). That still leaves the 10% or 15% who seem to have stopped evolving some where down there among the banana slug, or eggplant, on the Tree Of Life.

My life among humanity was typical: comedy followed tragedy in a relentless and constant cycle, from birth to (so far not yet) death. Perhaps an example will be appropriate now.

I paid cash for my new Toyota pickup. By "cash" I mean I had many thousands of dollars in USA Treasury Notes, in $20s and $50s, crammed into the two front pockets of my faded, hole strewn pants, which I handed over to the Toyota dealer in the show room after I had signed the papers. That was before car dealers called the Drug Enforcement Agency, or Scientology Inc., when a customer did this.

The 1992 pickup had 15 miles on the odometer, "sport accessories" such as fancy wheels, five speeds, six cylinders, and an "air dam" mounted on the back of the camper shell. It was evening when I drove it off the car dealership lot in Long Beach, California, to my residence in Dana Point, California. It was fully dark when I passed through Irvine, California, on my way home.

At a stop sign on a dark, quiet street, with nobody else around, the woman driving the car in front of me stopped at the street intersection, then inexplicably put her car in reverse and gunned her engine. The rear of her car slammed into the front of mine. The Toyota's front bumper was peeled upward effortlessly, and then the hood crumpled inward, reaching for my throat.

The woman jumped out of her car and tried to explain that she had not seen my car behind hers, but she was incoherent and all I could extract from the babble was "You were invisible!" Like I had a super power I didn't know about. I suppose my cold, dead, zombie-like eyes must have been visible in the dark because her stammer trailed off to a low mumble and then stopped with a shudder. A look of fearful dread descended upon her like a death shroud.

Naturally the best way to deal with the issue was with sarcasm, with which I am a born genius. I apologized to her profusely and eloquently for my carelessly waiting behind her, at a stop sign, when she wanted to back up; I begged her to forgive me for not knowing the word "STOP" meant "PUT YOUR CAR IN REVERSE AND MAIM THE WOMEN AND CHILDREN BEHIND YOU."

I then bent over, got on my hands and knees, and vomited. The contents of my stomach pooled around me as I asked her if perhaps she would like to run me over and finish the job.

Oddly enough, she leaped into her car and fled at very high speed. Was it something I said?

Later I discovered a huge bruise across my face, just above my nose; I must have slammed my face against the steering wheel when she backed into me, but I had no recollection of doing so, and I didn't feel the pain until a few hours later.

I mentioned this event for one reason: I have come to expect humans to act unpredictably and irrationally, and to not have great expectations regarding people. It seems to me that far too many people are unhappy with life because what they expect from other people (and themselves) is vastly better than what humans are capable of, or willing to strive for. When one lowers ones standards for human behavior, one is not as shocked and dismayed at what humans do and fail to do. It's a form of mental and emotional self-defense; I am convinced that humanity is already doing its best. Scary thought, eh?

COMPETITION FOR MY AFFECTION

***"You realize that trying to keep your distance from me will not lessen my affection for you. All efforts to save me from you will fail."* -- John Green**

My first girlfriend was Marla Carol who lived up the street from me in El Toro, California. There were two houses between us: the Bates, and a married couple who never came out of their house except at night and whom I suspected at the time (and perhaps suspect now, come to think of it) might have been vampires. Marla's parents were both emergency medical care team members who owned their own ambulance, which they kept parked outside and on the street, facing down hill, apparently for "fast get-aways." The guest's bathroom in Marla's house had wall paper with images of naked men and women in various copulative positions, of which Marla and I were great fans and which we worked hard to mimic. Marla used to dance for me naked under the freeway underpass, and I still get all flushed and tingly when I drive over a bridge. All was fun and games for a year, until she and her parents moved away in the same month my parents divorced. The divorce was good news; Marla's absence was an emotional disaster. We were both ten years old at the time.

My love life went "down hill" from there, and has never recovered.

I've lived with many women. A bloody ***Hell*** of a lot of women, always in pairs and multiplexes. This of course was by choice at first (later, by inertia and apathy): I thought it would be awesome, and sexy, and exciting, and fun to live in a house crammed full of estrogen stomping around and with me the only male to get stepped on. The horror didn't take hold for almost three years after I eventually noticed that every woman I brought home after a few dates would mysteriously forget my telephone number, and stopped returning my calls. One or more or all of my roommates would eventually accost and interrogate my date to see if she was good enough for me, or good enough to dump me and date them instead.

For example, Irene T. from where I worked came over for dinner one evening and she sat on the kitchen counter while I assembled the eggplant Parmesan, buttered the bread, and poured the wine. All was going great until, as we were sitting in the living room waiting for the casserole to bake, my roommate Melinda came home, spied Irene, rushed over and tried to sit on Irene's lap. (Such a flirt, Melinda was.) To say this was awkward is to understate the issue. It got even more awkward when Melinda started to coo and purr and whisper sweet things about how pretty Irene was.

It was a joke on Melinda's part, but nobody else was amused. For months afterward when Irene and I met at work she would blush purple at me, then avoid eye contact. Eventually, after about three years, half the young women at work were turning purple in my presence and avoiding me. The other half kept mentioning "THOSE WOMEN!" always with a slight shudder, in voices filled with pity for me.

This sabotage of my love life was very effective. The French Resistance should have had my roommates working against the Nazis: the Second World War would have ended two years sooner.

Yes, the horror of it. Another example: my roommates often asked me to scramble the eggs for breakfast, and for years I did so and for years they would smirk and giggle while I took fork to eggs in a bowl and vigorously beat the yokes. My bewilderment regarding why was finally assuaged when one roommate, Pamela, told me that my balls and penis always shook violently in my pajamas when I made scrambled eggs.

Tennessee Williams was one of many who wrote about "The tyranny of women." Nero Wolfe of course (given life by the writer Rex Stout) was by far the most eloquent on the subject.

Then there was the farting contest my roommates had one cold winter night in a cabin at Big Bear Lake, when there was noting to do but split fire wood, stare at each other, and see who could fart the loudest. The memory still brings a quiver of fright to my bowels.

The wonder isn't that I went crazy; the wonder is that I did not go crazy sooner than I did.

The "best" women, of course, came from the office areas at the corporation where I was employed: clad in pleated skirts and blouses that were actually pressed (”ironed") to get the wrinkles out. Or in other words, I preferred women who were far too good for me. The women more fitting for me, on my level, in my league, less inclined to file a restraining order against me, were those still serving time either in jail somewhere for public intoxication and lewdness, or on probation under "house arrest" with a curfew bracelet on her ankle for greater crimes.

I fell passionately and intensely in love with a bar maid, whom I could not live without, named... um... er... shit, what was her name again? Fuck. Let me check the police record... That's right: Tiff. Tiffany worked at the now-demolished "The Villa" at Dana Point, California, near the beach where there was a bar, a dining area, and a motel.

One night I stumbled through the doorway of "The Villa" for dinner and discovered a tall, golden, blond, curvy, almost-young woman of about 32 years of age blocking my ingress. She was wearing a bikini, with a flimsy sarong thing wrapped around her fertile, broad hips. My gaze started at her crotch, then to her navel, and eventually climbed her taut womanly body, pausing left and right on its journey, and up to her eyes. She had a big smile, with the ends of her mouth curved up in a kitten-like grin. I was smitten speechless.

The romance started like they do in Sweden and Denmark: the sex came first, then the "getting to know each other" part. (You know the drill: start with anal sex then slowly work up to holding hands.) She tasted like tobacco ash, from the three packs of cigarettes she smoked every day.

The romance ended like they do in Hollywood and Las Vegas: one day when I was squatting on top of her she told me she had decided to marry the man who murdered her previous boyfriend with a knife, and who would soon be serving a life sentence in prison for that murder. I climbed off of her, and then asked, "Huh?" I had not heard about this previous boyfriend, nor about the murder, nor about the lunatic with the knife. That's what one gets for not caring enough to ask about such things.

Apparently she felt guilty about the murder, and felt sorry for the killer. After all, he committed the heinous crime just to "win her back," and gosh, it worked. She said we could still see each other; I said, "Okay then!" and climbed back on top of her. But some of the spark in the romance was lost when she asked me to be a witness to the "civil marriage" ceremony in prison, and I drifted away.

That was one of my more successful romances. There were

others.

I learned how to remove a woman's Levi jeans with my feet: a job skill one can use anywhere. I learned how to tie a knot in a cherry stem with my tongue, after the girl (at the time she claimed to be a woman) stuffed one in my mouth, followed by her tongue, and showed me-- now ***THAT*** was a talented lass!

I still fondly remember one of the Pleated Skirts from work whom I dated (even knowing I belonged a dozen levels lower on the social ladder) who spent twenty minutes selecting a tomato at the grocery store, preparing for the evening's dinner date: at the time I thought it was cute; looking back it seems overly Obsessive Compulsive Disorderly.

There was a young woman in my night-time "continuing education" Marlin Spike Seamanship class. One evening after the other class mates had left, we paused under the building's floodlight, calmly and politely looking into each other's eyes, then she turned her back to me, bent over, looked at me from between her knees, pointed her to ass, and made pleading whimpering sounds. It was a hint any man couldn't fail to notice, bless her round firm heart-shaped self. On school nights after class she rocked the thirty-foot sloop I lived in, making enough noise to frighten the seagulls.

Somehow, as I got older, the women all drifted away--- they got married to other people, or ran off to distant jobs, or met other, superior, men, or just... faded below my horizon as I sailed through my life. The women roommates remained.

THE WALLS BEND INWARD

"If you think this Universe is bad, you should see some of the others." -- Philip K. Dick

My waking and sleeping hours came to be spent almost completely at my place of employment. Everything I needed to exist was within the airless, sunless, neon bright walls of the corporation in which I had been swallowed and made a part of. Some of my roommates had become tedious to be around, and I came to dread going home.

For example, the roommate I bailed out of jail early one morning because she had been arrested for failing to appear in court for various criminal offense including speeding tickets she never paid. The night court judge put her bail at $450, and I coughed it up so she would not have to spend any more time in a cage. She never has paid me back for that $450, but I never expected her to.

For example, the many nights I came home to find a roommate passed out, completely unconscious, on the living room floor, or bathroom floor, or bedroom floor, due to her excessive alcohol consumption. Dragging her by the arm pits, her feet scuffing along the carpet or floor tile, into her bed became a weekly chore that I resented. One night when I came home with a friend from the local yacht club, we found that roommate on the living room floor and my club friend thought there was a dead woman in my apartment: she was freaked out, thinking she would be my next victim. It takes the romance out of an evening when one's lady friend must step over the body of some other woman. On the plus side, the yacht club friend helped me get my roommate into bed: it's easier with help.

For example, the day I came home to find the landlord at the door demanding to know why the rent for the apartment we shared had not been paid for the past three months. I was shocked. I wondered where the bloody hell the money I handed over to my roommates as my part of the rent had gone. I paid the entire back rent, and then later asked my roommates about the rent not being paid: none of them could explain why.

By far the worse agony I was subjected to by my roommates was late at night when they were fucking each other. It is astounding how much noise two or three women make when they are doing... well, whatever they do to each other during sex. Hours and hours and hours of screeching and wailing and what sounded like the bed's headboard being kicked by a mule (followed by half a minute of silence, then more very loud moaning). The noise kept me and the neighbors awake all night; many nights I went and slept in my car because of the endless orgasms shaking the walls. To the boys and men who have had the infantile fantasy of living with lesbians: you have no fucking clue how distressing, depressing, and deleterious to the soul it is to hear them "going at it" all night, every night, when you are single and sleeping alone.

Heterosexual roommates were just as neuroses-inducing. My other roommate, Donna, found a new boyfriend; for six weeks he only left her bed to eat and poop, and during that time span I saw her rarely and briefly now and then in the kitchen we shared, looking haggard, deprived of sleep, and pale from lack of sun light. The poor thing only had time to eat when he, Brad, was on the toilet.

Their first night together I was peeling potatoes at the kitchen sink when they thundered through the door in a rush and sprinted to her bedroom. She sent a quick blush my way, then slammed the bedroom door behind her by kicking it shut, as her hands were already busy unbuttoning her skirt.

About 20 seconds later I heard, yelled through the walls, "Oh god! It's too big!" in a tone of dismay; she sounded a little frightened, perhaps, yet still eager. A few seconds later, "Agh! Ea! Ooooh!" wailed through the walls, followed by, "I! I! I can't! It's too! Too! Buh, buh, buh, big!" I abandoned the potatoes, half unpeeled, and crammed my thumbs in my ears. Though muffled, Donna's next complaint through the walls told me, "Gack! Oick! Hu, hu, huge! No! Yes! Oh! HUGH! Oh, it's ahahahahahahah MONSTER!" and then sounds I still to this day associate with a horse being drawn and quartered with a dull chain saw.

Suddenly, all was quiet. I took my thumbs out of my ears, and went back to peeling potatoes. After a half minute, Donna stepped out of her bedroom wearing panties and a tee-shirt, her pummeled body damp and flushed pink, vagina still twitching spasmodically, and asked me if maybe I would get some English muffins for her and Brad when I next went to the store. Not waiting for an answer, she went back into her bedroom.

I started sleeping at work and never went home. The day's labors would end, I'd go to a restaurant or visit a friend or go to the harbor to check my boat for clean clothes-- and then return to work to sleep. In the morning I would shower at work and get coffee from the always-full urns that lined one wall of the production assembly floor.

Then an odd thing happened: I stopped eating. I discovered that I had no interest in food; even the concept of "you need to eat to live" turned foreign to me. Other than a cup of coffee each morning, I ate nothing for almost four weeks and I lost more than 30 pounds.

One can imaging what that did to my sanity. I still performed the tasks I needed to at work, and as long as my assigned tasks were completed it didn't matter to anyone that my eyes turned hollow, my gait was reduced to a stumble, and that I was constantly fearing the odd behavior of the hallway walls when I walked down them.

The walls kept bending inward towards me as I passed within them. The left and right walls would bend inward, while the floor bent upward, and the ceiling bent downward. I managed to keep walking by ignoring the menacing behavior, until I would come to doors--- they leered at me like the mouths of ghouls, only sideways. I also had no idea where my arms were: some times I would look for my arms and hands and I couldn't find them; some times when my arms went missing I would look upwards at the ceiling and discover that my arms were raised, and I would struggle to force them back to my sides.

The worse part was the screaming in my head. There are many jokes about people who "hear voices" when they go crazy, and I am sorry to say that it is some times true. I "heard" several, all at once, most of whom (which?) were yelling and screaming different things at me.

One voice, for example, was telling me that I was very sick and that I desperately needed medical care. Another voice told me I was fine and there was nothing wrong. Another voice was reciting poetry. The loudest voice kept chanting, endlessly, "Help me! Help me! Help me! Help me!" While this cacophony was going on in my head, I still met with people, talked with them, answered their questions, and feared they could hear what I was hearing.

After I spent an entire month not eating, one day at work an irate friend of mine came into the Information Technology room, grabbed me from out of my chair, dragged me into the employee's cafeteria, and forced me to eat the dinner that she had made at her home and brought in for me to eat. I was shocked that someone cared enough about me to do that; it took me more than two hours to eat the modest meal, and she refused to leave until I had done so.

After that I started eating again.

She wasn't the only co-worker that noticed I had gone psycho. After I started eating again (but still sleeping and bathing at work), a woman who worked in "human resources" happened to mention to me in passing, as we walked down a hall in opposite directions, that the corporation's health care insurance "also covers mental health care." She was gone before I could angrily yell "Hey! Whadduyeh mean by that?!"

I did consult a psychiatrist, in a mirror-walled City of Irvine business complex, for which I paid $100 a session. I asked her why I had stopped eating; she said (paraphrasing) "If you don't know, how the bloody hell can I know?" Her diagnosis for my "presentation" (the word that is used to explain why a patient visits a psychiatrist): sexual dysfunction. That diagnosis she kept secret from me by using the code number "302.79" ("Sexual Aversion Disorder") as referenced in "The Diagnostic and Statistical Manual of Mental Disorders Five," and which I foolishly looked up.

Apparently the reason I stopped eating, and stopped going home, was, in her professional opinion, because ***I lacked interest*** in the sexuality of my lesbian roommates even though the only thing I thought about all day, every day, every second of the day, was my women roommates having sex with each other. Our doctor / patient relationship went down hill from there. She eventually told me she couldn't help me, and I agreed: at the time, I found her tedious, obnoxious, clinically sterile, and not insightful. Later I did not blame her, as I had worked very hard to my autistic behavior hidden from her (and everyone else). One would have thought that my inability to tolerate eye contact, my revulsion at being touched by humans, my walking around tables and chairs for hours at a time, and my insane rage at people who speak lazily would have given any and all clinicians a clue. Otch, well. Sound mental health is over-rated. The correct diagnostic category is 299, so she was only off by 3.79 (though some of those 302 codes I find tantalizingly, provocatively appealing).

MY REASON FOR LIVING SHUT DOWN

***"Speak softly and employ a huge man with a crowbar."* -- Terry Pratchett**

Year 2000 was fast approaching, and the Information Technology department I worked in was preparing for the event by making sure all of our software and all of our data bases could comply with the change from the two leading year digits of "19" to "20." Of course nobody in the IT profession anywhere in the world thought the date change, from 1999 to 2000, would cause any problems at all with computers-- but the USA media was crammed full of stories about the imaginary disaster. Computer-controlled air craft were to fall from the sky at the stroke of midnight; after midnight, computer-controlled trains would fail to stop (though every train car's brakes in the USA default to the "stop" position). Nobody in the airplane industry believed it; nobody in the rail transport industry believed it; but hey, we're Americans! We only fear that which ain't true.

For several days I spent all day and all night in the corporation's IT rooms, rechecking every computerized process that we had already checked throughout the previous weeks. I brought a pillow and bath towel to work and I slept behind the IBM AS400 midrange computer (and its media storage racks) at night so that I didn't have to go home. I showered at work in the morning, and ate garbage from the vending machines in the employee cafeteria. I spotted nothing at all that could in any way cause a problem after the millennial date change.

In the very early morning of December 31, 1999, I drove out of the city and northward towards the East Mojave Desert. By evening I had made my way on foot up to Kingston Peak, in the Kingston Mountain Range, and I sat with my back to a bitter cold boulder and waited for civilization to end--- just in case. The ugly lights of Sandy Valley glowed menacingly, like a cancer, far below me in the dark. As midnight approached, I muttered quietly, in the chill crisp cold air, "Die, society! Die!" as I peered down upon humanity like some chthonic mountain god.

Nothing terrible happened to humanity, much to my dismay. It went on its monstrous course as predicted.

A funny thing happened to me up there on the mountain, however, as I viewed the world and society from a lofty, emotionally divorcing height: I found out I liked it up there; I liked the feeling of judging humanity and finding it worthy of extinction. If there had been a large, red, candy-like button up there for me to push and end it all, I would have found it my duty to push it. But after a bit of time I shook off the feeling, got to my feet, and stumbled down the mountain in the dark and back to my car.

When I returned to work I was told that the division was shutting down, and that I would soon be out of a job. I was asked to help with the shut-down process, for which I would be paid handsomely.

It is a terrible thing to be told that one's previous twelve years of labor in the corporate world has resulted in nothing of any consequence in the world. The project that the corporation was working on would end immediately, without being completed; inventory would be auctioned off, or scrapped, or sold as curious junk. All computer equipment would be sent to Corporate Headquarters, and confidential information removed.

I felt like half of my life had been wasted. What the bloody fuck was I working for, 14 to 16 hours a day, five or six days a week, when it could all just end by a mandate from those higher up in the corporate hierarchy?

The process to shut down the division took a bit more than two months. My first step of course was to copy all of the confidential trade secrets from the AS400 onto a five gigabyte digital tape cassette, which I still have. That's valuable shit. My next step was to figure out where to go, and what to do, after the division closed and I was free to go.

The division closed. I went from working all day, six days a week, for over a decade, to having absolutely nothing at all to do, and about $29,000 in my pocket.

THE SECRET LIFE OF DESERT SAND'BOs

***"I'm nobody / I'm a tramp, a bum, a hobo / I'm a boxcar and a jug of wine / And a straight razor ... if you get too close to me"* -- Charles Manson**

There are many tens of thousands of American citizens living on public lands in the country. They in fact live everywhere, in huge numbers, in the poorest and the richest counties in every state. They live on what they get from Social Security, or from pensions, that pay them a few hundred dollars a month; many live on welfare, SNAP benefits ("food stamps"), and by digging in trash dumpsters for food. (Many are mentally ill, and they receive no help from the government that they spent decades paying taxes to.) If you know where to look, when to look, and what to look for, you will find them living in nearly every town, in every city, and in every national Park, Forest, Preserve, and Monument.

In the American Southwest these people move around in large groups: southward in the winter, northward in the summer. During winter months they fill the arroyos, trash dumps, rail tramp ("hobo") jungles, and culverts in places like Yuma, Arizona; the Imperial Valley of central south California; Quartzite; Indio; the Salton Sea; the Copper King of Arizona mountain range; the Chocolate Mountains; and El Centro (to name a few popular winter tramp homes). In the summer most of them head into the cities of San Diego, Los Angeles, and the massive and ugly metropolises that blight the entire coastline of California, to beg in the streets for a living: sleeping in people's back yards and vegetable gardens at night. Other homeless tramps climb in altitude into the forests of Arizona, California, and western Nevada, and come back down when they need food or medical care.

And then there are the "sand hobos:" people who live in the deserts of Mojave, Amargosa, Great Basin, and Death Valley. They live in holes they have dug in the sand, or in trailers they managed to haul into the desert, or in arroyos they have covered over with plywood or tin--- and there they live year 'round. Many of them have valid and legal mineral claims that they work on, or that they pay the yearly "assessment fee" on; many have legal mill site claims where they are allowed to live on public land to work their mineral claims. Most, however, just moved in and stayed.

For example, I know an elderly woman who lives on public land in the East Mojave Desert, at high altitude. Her house is made out of over 100 railroad ties that came from the defunct Tonopah and Tidewater rail line. The ties had been stacked and assembled to make a box, then roofed over with what looks to be a railroad boxcar floor. The entire structure was buried with dirt, and a person can walk right past it (or even over it, like I did) and not know it is there. And there she hides all day, a few hundred feet from a slightly radioactive tailings dump of viscous fluid from an abandoned uranium prospect. Perhaps as many as a dozen people in the world knows she exists, and half that number knows where she lives; there is a person in Las Vegas who brings her food and water. I bought some turquoise from her about year 1997 or 1998, when we met by chance at Mexican Hat Spring where we were both getting water. The hand gun she carried was bigger than my dog; she could not, or would not, speak. When I next talked with the owner of the Carbonate King mine about her, he told me she is Paiute and to not feel sorry for her. “She belongs there,” he told me.

But I could never, to this day, stop thinking that she was once somebody’s little sweet girl, who had perhaps loved and cherished her.

Many tramp sites in the deserts of Mojave and Amargosa have canned food sitting around in boxes, in holes dug in the dirt; in abandoned campers; in ruined cabins; and in the carcasses of burned out cars. The canned food is left by poor people for poorer people. Now and then a savvy “tourist” (desert traveler from the city) will drop off a load of canned food and other items after camping at one of these sites.

For over twenty years, in at least a dozen places within the East Mojave, I have left canned food, gasoline, kitchen matches, Coleman stoves, flashlights and batteries, and clothing for the “sandbos” (sand hobos) to use. From Cree Camp (when it still existed) to Sloan (known as “The Sewer of East Mojave” for good reason); from Riley Camp to Bob and Ward’s; from the dugouts at Yates to the (now a ruin) aircraft beacon shed in the hills above Tecopa. For homeless people traveling between Las Vegas, Nevada, and Los Angeles, California, tramp camps are convenient places to stop and sleep when it is too dark to hitch hike on the highway.

So here I found myself out of a job, with thousands of dollars in my checking account, and nothing at all I needed or wanted to do. I thought, Why don't I spend a few months living homeless in the desert? I was utterly, miserably weary of humanity and its smog and its noise. I could not think of any good reason why I should not spend the next three or four months just sitting on my ass in the desert and take a vacation from the horror that is city life. I had no idea at the time that the months would pass by until I had been out there for two and a half years.

THE FOOLISH PLAN

***"I have great faith in fools - self-confidence my friends will call it."* -- Edgar Allan Poe**

I needed a place in the desert to live that was hidden and not visited by other people. The ideal plan, to my mind, was a place at high altitude so that even when the days were blistering hot, the nights would be cool to sleep through. Summer was quickly approaching, and I needed to entrench somewhere before the brutal heat made hauling supplies and building material into some hidden, secret spot somewhere in the vast, desolate, lonely desert unbearable.

Day time temperatures in the summer where I planned to live averaged 105 degrees (40 Centigrade). At high altitude in the desert one can expect nights to be as cool as 45 degrees (7 Centigrade); at low altitude, the temperature can stay in the high 80s to low 90s. Many nights in Las Vegas, Nevada, when I was passing through stayed over 100 degrees even at midnight. At times when I had been looking for gold in the Mojave Desert the day temperatures reached 115 degrees (46 Centigrade), and I endured only by crawling under my car (the only shade available) until the brutal sun went down. I would not have electricity to run a swamp cooler; I would not even have a fan.

Clark Mountain, north of Baker, California, is at the ideal height and there are many very good places to hide and live up there. The problem with Clark Mountain was that it was (and probably still is) already occupied by a few squatters hiding up there; it is also often visited by tourists, and at times there are various government employees on the mountain checking the riparian areas and looking for homeless people. Another negative for Clark Mountain was the lack of adequate places to hide my vehicle.

There are several sources of fresh water on Clark Mountain, if one doesn't mind it being either radioactive from the uranium mines, or filled with mercury from the gold mines, or filled with arsenic from the copper mines, or filled with equine shit from the wild burros. Some transients have tried to plant crops up there (I won't mention what species) but those crops never did well. Clark

Mountain was not good enough for my needs.

I next considered the Providence Mountain Range, since it has many places a person can hide, and many high altitude peaks, and adequate sources of water. I knew of a fairly secret place in the Providence Mountains, at modest altitude, that has a fresh water spring (metered in a few drops per second, coming from an iron pipe) and a bit of shade in parts of the day. I will describe this spot for you, to give you an idea of what I was looking for. I'll call this place "Possible Site 'A'" for convenience.

Possible Site "A" is located near Foshay Pass, but hidden in a cleft in a hill and far enough away so that if I lived there for a few months I would not likely be discovered. Father Francisco Garces during one of his "Entradas" into the desert may have passed over the area in the spring of year 1776, on a visit to the Mojave Indians and eventually the Havasupai (who thought his Catholic beliefs were the product of heat stroke, for which they tried to treat him but never did affect a cure). A dirt road goes over the pass, and there are a few places along that road where I could hide my automobile from anyone driving the road.

The approach from the pass to Possible Site "A" must be crossed on foot southward, with a brief hike up a gradual incline of parched sun-baked dirt, sand, creosote brush, fine gravel, cactus, and ancient tin cans. (The whole mountain range had at one time been heavily mined, and the miners left their trash.) The route then turns to a very steep climb over rocks and through salt brush, along what was once a miner's foot path that clings to the east side of a deep arroyo that is choked with mesquite, young cottonwood trees, and boulders.

Half way up the climb to the spring there is an old, twisted piñon pine tree that has some how survived the "charcoal makers" that swept through the area 90 years earlier. When I had occasion in the past to make the climb, the tree often reminded me of the utter insanity that greed can drive some people: healthy trees would be cut down, the green wood would be fired in brick kilns with little and then no air. The charcoal was hauled to mines to fuel the ore smelters and the steam-powered ore stamps. Charcoal makers were paid around ten cents per wagon load of charcoal, and within less than a decade they had slaughtered the once-common high altitude pine tree forests of the area (and, incidentally, eradicating the chief source of winter protein for the Southern Paiutes who depended on piñon pine nuts to survive).

Nearly at the top, on the left (east) there is a level and grassy bench that is about twenty-five feet long and about eight feet wide. There is a pine tree at each end, apparently planted by a human long ago. This grassy bench has been leveled by someone having stacked flat rocks on top of each other on the downhill slope, then filling in the lower areas with dirt and sand. This has created a wall on the slope of about 16 inches in height. When the hiker steps off the rough trail and on to this bench, she or he must also step around the eastern pine tree, or walk a few more feet and then approach the bench from the north edge.

Once on the bench one will find that there is a foot path along the east edge, leading southward to a second, larger bench with a spring at the southeast end. This walkway has also been lined with rocks on the down-hill side, with dirt filling in the path to make it level. There is a mine shaft, hidden in narrowleaf goldenbush, shrubby ragwort, Tanglewood, and cottonwoods, several feet north of the spring.

If one does not step onto the little man-made grassy bench, but continues climbing the miner's trail along the edge of the deep arroyo, one will come to an old rock-walled cabin. Most of the walls have fallen in, plunging into the arroyo that it hangs above, though two corners are still intact; for many years when I visited the site a Sears & Roebuck wood-fired tin stove used to sit in one of the corners, but some time around year 2010 someone took it--- it is no longer there. A few Juniper trees are scattered around the area.

Hiking past the ruin of the rock house, one comes to the top of the arroyo where there is a mine tailings dump of gravel, and the larger grassy bench I mentioned above.

Once one is standing on the larger bench, to the left one will see the spring; its water seeps from the base of a sharp cleft between hills (the cleft is called a "weap" in the Shoshone language, not to be confused with "weep," nor with a water seep). The weap is choked with cottonwood trees, scrub oak, salt brush, bayonet cactus, and other plants. On the bench itself someone had planted three trees, which were about nine feet high, with spiny leafless branches; the trees were alive many years ago when I first visited the area, but they are now dead. The elevation is 4,583 feet (1.4

kilometers) above mean sea level.

The southwest edge of the bench has a large, healthy, beautiful cottonwood tree growing. A very dim foot path passes to the right of the tree, and climbs the ridge to the top of the mountain range 1,437 feet higher. The west edge of the bench contains a steep hill face, with a mostly buried stock tank at its base. A rusted steel pipe drips water from the spring and into this stock tank. The top edge of the stock tank is level to the ground, though decades ago it used to be higher: the ground has silted upward, and the tank has sunken downward.

At the northeast edge, from which the miner's trail enters the area, there is a tall pinnacle of rock, looking like two giant fingers pointing skyward. These rocky fingers cast early morning shadows on the southwestern edge of the bench, and also upon the three trees that once grew (and still stand, dead) there. From the tailings dump on the north edge a person can look northwestward across the desert and see Kelso Dunes in the distance.

Therefore when I dismissed living as a squatter on Clark Mountain, my mind turned to this Possible Site "A" for good reasons: I had a "look out" spot (the small grassy bench, where I could watch anyone hiking up the trail) and a larger, better-hidden bench where there is water and at times shade.

But was it good enough to live there for three or four months? I thought I would try it for a week first, then if I liked the spot I would come back with all of my gear, building materials, and assorted bare essentials: I wanted to be sure I liked the place before I hauled everything up that very steep trail.

TEST DRIVE THE LOCATION FOR A WEEK

***"Jem spoke with enormous care; talking to Will about anything personal was like trying not to startle away a wild animal."* -- Cassandra Clare**

The mornings in the first week or two of March in the East Mojave Desert are very cold. I arrived at Foshay Pass as the sun was just below the eastern horizon, in a hurry to haul my camping gear to the hidden spot. My gear consisted of a huge nylon tent that weighed 47 pounds (21 kilograms); three blankets; two pillows; a gasoline fueled camp stove; sauce pan; frying pan; fork; spoon; butane lighter; toilet paper; water jug; Army trenching tool ("shovel" to us civilians); solar oven made out of tin-clad cardboard; binoculars; tennis shoes; spare clothing; plastic sheet; kitchen matches; belt knife; spare hat; dehydrated potatoes; dehydrated cheese; a spool of twine; canned soup; and a plush toy lion. This was a great deal of cargo for me to haul up the trail, and it all took three trips and several hours.

The toy lion was for putting outside my tent at night to frighten away the skunks, since I did not want them to come and steal any shit I left outside.

I pitched my tent along the southern edge of the large bench, under the giant rocky fingers, between two of the three still-living (at the time) trees. The doorway faced north, which put the spring to my left and stock tank to my right; looking out the tent's door I could watch the beautiful cottonwood tree do whatever trees do.

The tailings dump was a good place to set up the solar oven, so I unfolded it, perforated a can of soup, and put the soup can in the oven to heat. The oven's reflector I faced southward, towards Kelso Dunes. Even in March the days get very warm in the desert, and direct sunlight will heat a can of soup even without a solar oven, but when I'm hungry I don't want to wait an hour. The soup was hot within about 20 minutes: I took it to the cottonwood tree, with a can opener and spoon, and had my first meal at what I thought perhaps would be my home for four months.

There is an ancient wooden post up there, near the big old cottonwood tree; perhaps it was used to tie a horse to, or to anchor mining equipment. I placed a few dollars' worth of coins on top for someone to find some day. Odds are very good they are still there.

That night I lay on my plastic sheet outside the tent, plush toy lion by my side, and enjoyed the night as the heat of the day fled into outer space. The night turned cool. The night turned cold. The night turned very cold. The night turned bitter, biting cold. I climbed into the tent, put my long underwear on, and wrapped my three blankets around me.

The moon came up, and I heard it do so. Or I heard something outside, but I had no idea what it was. It sounded like rocks being hammered together. Whatever it was, I hoped the toy lion outside would frighten it away. The sound occurred several times during the night: a clattering of rocks, violently slammed against each other, a few dozen feet away. What the bloody hell was it? I wondered if whatever was out there was deciding if I was good to eat. I heard a mourning dove calling from the cottonwood tree, sounding more like a burrowing owl than a dove; what ever was lurking out there didn't eat birds, or the dove would have kept silent.

Morning came, and the sun chinned itself up above the eastern edge of the Providence Mountain Range, then wandered southward (no, really) above The Giant Fingers. Within minutes the inside of my tent turned from icy cold into blistering hot, so I agreed with the sun that it was time to get out of bed.

That day I thought I would spend visiting my distant human neighbors, optically, with my binoculars. The ridge of the mountain range in the area I was camped is at an altitude of 6,020 feet (1.83 kilometers), and the hike to the top is a rough one. Fortunately there is an animal trail that leads from the spring to the top of the mountain, and though the heat of the day made the climb a chore, I managed it in less than one hour.

Down there somewhere below me, on the east-facing slope of the mountain, there is "Warm Springs" (a seep of cold water) that I have never had the time to visit. A desert rat told me that around 55 years ago a well was dug there, and there was once a wind-driven pump that has since been "high graded" (perpetually borrowed). In fact I think the person who told me that now "owns" the wind mill and the pump... but the less said about that, the better. I asked him why the seep was called, first, "warm," and second, "springs" since neither word actually fit the reality. He looked at me as if I were crazy, and asked "Why the bloody Hell should they?" I had no good answer. But then, a genius is just a crazy person who makes sense.

Northward of my perch was Fountain Peak. Below that peak I could make out, with the aid of binoculars, the human-made structures near the "state recreational area" of the Providence Mountains: specifically, I assume, the Mitchell Caverns. Granite Peak, far to the southwest, was just barely visible through the haze: it stood alone, separate from the Providence Mountain range. The very faint trail of Highway 40 was blocked from view when looking southward, but to the southeast sections were visible with binoculars. The entire Lanfair Valley stretched eastward, with perhaps the bump of the Dead Mountains far off in the distance of about 35 miles (56 kilometers). In fact Earth's surface curves enough that I suspect I was imagining looking that far.

Some of the desert's "points of interest" were hidden from my god-like view by parts of the mountain range: the ugly, highly polluted trash heap known as the "Vulcan Iron Mine" for one example. Kelso Depot was also hidden, as was the Union Pacific railroad. Kelso Dunes stood out like a scar to the east, and with binoculars I could see the high power line maintenance facility wavering and dancing in the heat. If night had fallen, I would have seen the ugly glow of Barstow to the west and Huukyampve to the east. The town of Needles is named after "The Needles" in English, but is known as "*The Place Where They Fought*" in the Yuman (that is, Mojave Indian) language.

The air was dead still. The silence was complete: the only sound I heard was my labored breathing. It was bloody hot up there, and my body was spewing sweat like a gunny sack filled with water. At my feet were the remains of a camp fire, with blackened stones in a rough circle. Pieces of partially burned juniper littered the area, along with an ancient pull-tab aluminum soda can, an aluminum sardine can, and pieces of a plastic chlorine bleach bottle. Sounds like one hell of a lunch someone had there.

After voiding my bladder, I ran out of things to do up there. It actually seemed a shame to have struggled up the side of the mountain just to look around a bit and then descend. I feared that if I stayed up there too long I would become enlightened (a dreadful thought), so I hurried back down to camp.

Most of the way back to camp I noticed that several dozen flying insects were following me. With every few steps I took, their numbers increased exponentially. By the time I reached my tent the flying, biting, stinging horde was a thick black cloud that sought to enter my nose, ears, eyes, perhaps the anus (I didn't want to look), and every other bodily orifice. Every exposed skin surface was caked in tiny insects. I fled into my tent to get away from them, but a few hundred followed me in before I could get the zipper closed.

I hunted down and murdered the intruders. It was their blood or mine, and fuck them: I'm bigger. They can take it up with Charles Darwin in Heaven if they want.

Some how I had forgotten that the seep I was camped near would draw insects when the day warms. In fact it is one of the best ways to find water in the desert: look for where honey bees (for example) are coming from or going towards. (Second hint: remember the Alamo, by looking for cottonwood trees, i.e. "poplars," known as ***Populus fremontii*** for the species found in the East Mojave Desert.) I did not want to spend the next four months hiding in terror from the insects, and I contemplated where else I could stay.

That night, as the evening cooled and the insects went away or died, I emerged from my tent and fixed a dinner of soup, heated in its can on the gasoline stove. I wondered if maybe I could rush into town and get some insect repellent, but that seemed unfair to me because it was their seep first: I was the intruder. Plus, I would need several huge shipping containers full of the stuff to do an adequate job.

I stretched out on my plastic sheet, two pillows under my head, plush toy lion at my side to keep the mourning doves from attacking me, and I slept.

The moon came up, later than the previous night, and with it came the same odd rock clashing sounds I had heard 26 hours previously. In the glow of the moon I saw a large (actually a massive gigantic monster of a) Bighorn Sheep running away from me in terror, kicking rocks and dirt as it ran. I was very glad to see it running away from me rather than towards me.

It was the second most important thing I had forgotten about camping near water in the desert: ***NEVER DO IT***, since it disturbs the animals that depend upon that water as their only source for many miles.

That morning, understanding I was intruding, I packed up and left the site. It was the only place in the mountain range that I knew had shade, so I crossed the Providence Mountains off my list of possible places to live.

NO LAW DAWG IS MAN ENOUGH TO OUT SMART ME

"The police called it 'choking,' but I called it 'a two-handed neck hug.' That's how I knew she really loved me." **--- Jarod Kintz**

The roads around (and in parts through) the Providence Mountains region are fun to drive at very great speed due to the humps in the roads. If one's automobile is going fast enough, one can get the wheels to leave the pavement and feel one's stomach lurch upward in free fall; the physics involved means the vehicle and its occupants are actually in orbit, for a very brief moment, around the center of the Earth. Or in other words, if you have always wanted to be an astronaut, you can visit the area and take my advice: drive from Cima, on Cima Road, to Highway 15 heading northward as fast as you can. (Hell, do it in the car I told you to steal a dozen pages back.)

Start at the railroad crossing at Cima, point your mechanical beast northwestward, and stomp on the gas pedal. If you are lucky enough to stay on the road around the curve near Kessler Peak (it's on your right), you will need to hold down your car's horn to warn the hikers near Sunrise Rock (on your right), and perhaps warn anyone standing at the Teutonia Peak Trail Trail-head (on your left), to get off the road and flee into the desert. Just past that trail-head, on your left, you will pass a Sheriff's deputy in a parked hot-pursuit vehicle laying in ambush looking for speeders.

On the morning I packed up and abandoned Proposed Site "A" I figured I would check out parts of the Kingston Mountain Range to see if I could find a spot at high altitude and with shade, and give it a try-out as a place to spend the next few months. I drove past Kelso Depot, then north to Cima, then took the left turn at Cima, and crossed the rails. I stomped on the gas pedal.

All was fun and games until I flashed past the Sheriff's deputy's parked car. I was going so fast that all I saw was an indistinct white and gold blur that had wheels under it. Perhaps the lettering on the side looked sort of like "SH#####" but I was going far too fast to make it out. When I saw in the rear view mirror that the Sheriff's car was pulling on to the road in pursuit of me, some of the fun left my brain, to be replaced with worry.

I had some options available to me. Since Cima road twists and turns, with a gradual turn before approaching Highway 15, the Sheriff's deputy could not know if and when I might turn off the road. I could continue to race towards the highway, and choose to go northward towards Las Vegas and hope the Sheriff's deputy thought I went south. I could go south on the highway and hope the deputy went north. I could continue across the bridge of the highway and get on Excelsior Mine Road heading west, and hope the deputy didn't see me and instead he would go north or south.

Funny, but slowing down, stopping, and waiting for the Sheriff's deputy to fine me for speeding never entered my mind. Ever since I was a wee tyke I felt that I was fated to die at the hands of those who rode for law and order. I figured I may as well hurry that destiny along.

I looked in the rear view mirror again, and now and then as the road straightened I could see the deputy gaining on me; then a curve of the road would hide me from his view. I decided to fly over the bridge and head west: I had not only the deputy to think about, but all of his deputy friends within radio distance to worry about also, and I assumed they would be looking for me on the highway, not on the mine road.

The gasoline station flashed by me on the right, then I was over the bridge. Up ahead was a sharp bend in the road to the right which I had to slow down for. I touched the brakes, made the turn, and stomped on the gas again. After the bend in the road there is a hill the road climbs, after which on the other side I would be out of sight, hopefully, of the deputy.

Another glance in the rear view mirror showed an odd thing: a cloud of dust hanging in the air far behind me, as if maybe the deputy's car hadn't made the sharp curve at high speed. It made me wonder if I would have to pay for the damage after they caught me. But never mind, I kept the gas pedal to the floor and I looked for a hole to hide in.

Excelsior Mine Road is hilly: it is also straight in long sections; it also goes up hill, which worked against me (or I should say it worked against my Toyota pickup). Looking behind me, via the mirror, I saw way behind me the deputy still in hot pursuit, and gaining on me.

Fuck. No, I mean fuckfuckfuckfuck. In my mind I pictured the deputy finally stopping me, hand gun drawn, angry as shit, to drag me out of my pickup and beat the crap out of me just for sport, shits, and giggles.

Nearing Tecopa Pass the road gets rough, and it gets tight on the bends; it then gets ugly, rocky, broken, and dangerous to drive on even slowly. Through a series of stomping on the brakes, twisting the steering wheel, stomping on the gas, twisting the steering wheel, and stomping on the brakes again, I negotiated the section of road past where Deputy Dawg could not see me, and where anyone not familiar with the road would be crazy to drive it at high speed. As it was, I ran off the road and over several clumps of rabbitbrush ("Chamisa") plants which stayed in the pickup's grill for weeks until I remembered to remove it.

Just past the water tank (on the left) the road got slightly better, and I gunned the engine until I was nearly at Beck Mine. Looking again in my rear view mirror I saw the Sheriff's deputy car negotiating the twists and turns near the water tank at a slower speed than I had managed--- but he was still after me.

If I continued over the pass, and down to Tecopa, there would likely be other Law Dawgs down there waiting for me, having been notified of my pending and much welcomed arrival via radio. I disliked that option. In fact I rather hated it. The problem was, there was no other way to go but over the pass.

Just before reaching Beck Mine, the road makes a sharp bend to the right. A bit farther, past the bend, there is a large tailings dump of rocks and gravel on the left. The sharp bend hid me from view of the deputy, so naturally after I reached the tailings dump I slammed on the brakes and made a hard left turn to tuck myself behind the pile of gravel. I shut off the engine, and waited.

The sound of a high-powered engine filled the desert air. It reached me; it past me; it kept on going; it faded over the pass, northward somewhere.

Yes, I was feeling god-like, but my problem didn't end there. Once over the pass, and over some very rough ground (Beck Spring washes over the dirt road, and there are deep trenches a car must deal with), the road straightens out and heads down hill: the view of the road from the top is miles long, and the deputy would soon learn he had passed me.

Imagine how happy and pleased he would be with me after finding that out, and then catching up with me. It would be quite a party. I was beginning to wish I had stopped and accepted the fine, many miles back when it was still fun.

The only choice left to me was to race back the way we had come, and hope I could find a hole before the deputy crossed over the pass, crawled over the rough ground that followed, then got a look down the road and discovered I had vanished.

On the way down the mountain, going back the way we have just raced up, my Toyota's speedometer pegged at 110 miles per hour (177 kilometers per hour). The poor engine screamed and wailed but, on the straight sections, I showed it no mercy. When I reached the gravel road going to the old Kingston town site (on the left), I slowed down and leisurely drove that grave road about eight miles and eventually came to Sandy Valley where I found a ruined camper trailer to park and hide behind.

Then, and only then, did I feel smug. Strangely, I also felt a little guilty. A tiny bit ashamed, too. But yeah, mostly smug. Mostly "Fuck you, Deputy, in the eye! With a stick!" But the wee bit of guilt still remains.

BURN, BABY, BURN

***"Jesus was a strange hobo who walked on water"* -- Jack Kerouac**

I made my way into Baker, since I figured maybe some irate law enforcement officers might still be looking for me among the Kingston Mountain Range. The last place, I reasoned, they would look for me is at or near the Sheriff's substation in town. Nobody would be stupid enough to evade arrest for over an hour, then go get a burrito across the street from the would-be arresting officer's office... right?

Twilight came upon me as I ate my burritos while I was in my pickup, which was parked across from the Sheriff's substation. I kept a wary eye on them just in case I had to make a run for it, but I was left unmolested.

There is a place to park on Kelbaker Road 13 miles from Baker where there are ancient petroglyphs on the lava rocks on the side of the road. It is near Seventeen Mile Point (yet another mysteriously named place in the desert that doesn't match reality), and I thought I would spend the night there; a rock wall there hides cars from view when approached from the south, and after dark there is very little traffic.

I left Baker and turned on to Kelbaker Road, drove across the bridge, and saw a camp fire burning on the left, about 100 feet (30 meters) into the desert. It was very dark by then, and the night was cold. I parked, grabbed my shovel, and went to investigate the fire.

Laying in a blanket near the fire there was an old man. He may have been maybe twenty years old, but what ever life had done to him had aged him far beyond his years, and he looked ***OLD***. He did not move as I walked up to him, though I made noise so I would not startle him. I came only to check the fire: not to get shot, nor to bother anyone.

The fire was made from burning trash. The red glow lit up the old (or young) man's face, turning his opened eyes a hellish bloody red. Baker's trash dump was across the road, with a high fence around it, but somehow the man had managed to drag out enough trash to light it and keep warm. He watched me silently as I looked over the fire to see if there was any danger the fire would spread to the creosote and other brush in the area. It looked safe enough to me, so I walked back to my pickup.

I drove back into Baker and stopped at “Country Store:” the first convenience store on the right as one enters Baker. I bought a bag of corn chips and a fifth of whiskey, then drove back to the man’s fire and brought those items there for him. I figured come morning he could use a hearty breakfast. Nobody said anything as I left these items next to the fire. I then drove to Seventeen Mile Point and spent the night.

BUT THEN THEY SNUCK UP ON ME

***"What have you gotten yourself into? Couldn't I have just picked you up at the police station for underage drinking, like most fathers?"* -- Richelle Mead**

Before you ask, "SNUCK: a past tense and a past participle of 'sneak.'" I mention this because there is no other way I can describe what happened: the police ***snuck*** up on me!

I spent most of the day in Baker looking over topographic maps, eating burritos, and resting from my harrowing flight from justice the previous day. It was well into evening when I again headed north on Highway 15.

My next stop to find a place to live in the desert was to look in the hills on and around Turquoise Mountain. There is decent water to be had at Halloran Spring if one is used to drinking large amounts of bacteria with one's water. As I drove past the spring I was once again accosted by the road sign on the right that read "PRIVATE ROAD." It was in front of another sign "PRIVATE!" which was in turn followed by the sign that said "KEEP OUT!"

Those signs have been there for more than twenty years, on a public road, on public land, and finally I could not bear the insult any longer. I was bloody fucking tired of reading those signs every time I passed them in the past two decades. I'm a citizen of the USA, therefore I own that road, that land, that clump of dirt, that rock over there--- and no sign is going to tell me differently. Why, if I were also a tax payer I would have complained to my State Representative in Congress.

I parked at the first sign, and leaped out of my pickup while clutching a hack saw, crescent wrench, Vice Grips, and hammer. I aimed the car's headlights at the signs so that I could see well enough to do my civic duty.

It was a cool night, but I was kept warm by righteous indignation and by sawing at the bolts and nuts that held the signs to their steel posts. The bolts were rusty, and the nuts on the bolts were rusty. The heads of the bolts were flush with the faces of the signs, which left no space to get a grip on them. I could not twist the nuts off because the bolts just turned. It was hard work sawing through the bolts, but someone had to do it.

I was just starting on the second bolt of the third sign when from out of the dark night someone spoke behind me. I jumped, squeaking like a little girl. I looked behind my left elbow and there, inexplicably, was a California Highway Patrol car with two troopers inside, one of whom was leaning out of the passenger side window and talking to me.

It was quite a surprise. I did not hear the car drive up behind me. I did not see the light from the patrol car's headlights. If I had been in the Serengeti, and if they had been lions and me a gazelle, I would be blushing in front of Charles Darwin in Heaven right now. I stood there with a hack saw in my right hand, Vice Grips clamped to the road sign and my left hand holding it steady, and stared into the light like a deer caught in the beam of a search light.

The trooper asked me if I had seen a car pass me, on the road I was on, in the past few minutes. I told him, "No," which was true, and then told him that nobody had passed on the road in more than two hours, which was also true. I then gestured with the hack saw towards the spring and said "I've been camped over there for the past four hours or so, and nobody has been through here---" waiving the hack saw northward and southward to roughly demarcate the entire stretch of desolate desert through which the road passed. The trooper thanked me, the driver turned the car around, and they left me to my work.

I kept all three signs, to be used as building material for my shelter once I found a place in the desert to live. And golly, I really needed to get my hearing checked.

LORD! GIVE ME A SIGN!

***"All masculine, hard-bodied and sensual, he was a deadly weapon sent by the gods to drive women mad, and a walking billboard for all things wicked and carnal. Orgasms! Get your orgasms here. Hot and juicy! Just how you like 'em!"* -- Lisa Sanchez**

In most counties in most states in the United States of America it is against the law for people to place signs ("bills") along the right of way of roads. Election signs are generally allowed when a permit is applied for and granted for those signs, when the signs do not block road visibility.

In the East Mojave Desert, the San Bernardino County Municipal Code Title 12 Section 12.03 covers signs people illegally place on the right of way along public streets. Each placement of a sign is an "encroachment" and subject to a $100 fine. It is therefore the duty of citizens to remove signs along the right of ways of public streets, and thus save the person who put them there a fine of $100 for each sign: it's the Christian thing to do.

The town of Baker used to be buried in illegally-placed commercial signs littering the main street at the three routes in and out of town. Dozens of plywood boards, propped up with 2x4 pine studs, crowded every on-ramp and off-ramp. These illegal signs looked perfect, to me, to use as building material. Here was a fine natural resource just waiting for me to put to better use. In the early morning hours I collected the thoughtfully-provided plywood and hauled it away to a secret cache north of town along highway 127; it took me several trips to get all of it, but after the job was done I had enough plywood and 2x4 studs to build a soccer stadium. Or maybe a decent lean-to shed, any how.

A funny thing: a week later another dozen signs showed up, illegally placed on the main street's right of way. Thank you, whoever provided the additional plywood for me. Thank you, thank you. I figured I saved you over $3,000 in fines by the county's code enforcement agency. You're welcome.

THE OLD MORMON'S TERRIFYING NUT SACK

"Carpe Scrotum. *Seize life by the testicles*" -- Rowena Cherry

Some people have stated authoritatively, "The name '*Avawatz*' is derived from the Mohave Indian term '*Avi-Ahwat*', or 'red rock.'" The Yuman (Mohave / Mojave) word *'ahwat* (with the apostrophe) means "to be red." However, this is not where the name *Avawatz* comes from: the Mohave did not name the mountain range *Avi-Ahwat*. The Southern Paiutes gave the mountain range the name. The Numic name is from the word "*aviwats*" or "*avawats,*" which means "gypsum" (white clay). The Yuman and Numic words are coincidentally similar.

The name issue is complicated by two problems: early maps, dating to year 1891, show the Avawatz range being named "Ivawatch." The Southern Paiutes were probably describing the Kingston Mountain Range, not the Avawatz Mountain Range, when telling early Americans what they called various geographic places. That is, the 1891 map named the wrong mountain range: the Kingston mountains are the *aviwats*, not the Avawatz mountains.

Several topographic maps of the East Mojave Desert show "Old Mormon Spring" located on the east face of the Avawatz Mountain Range. Some maps do not show the location of the spring. I stopped in Baker to talk to one of the turquoise miners who had a shop there, and we discussed my plan of spending several months in the desert: he suggested I look over the Avawatz Mountain Range near Old Mormon Spring. He said that at times the old spring had water, but last he heard it was dry. I liked the idea.

The dirt road to the spring is easy to spot if one knows the general location of the turn-off along Highway 127, and if one approaches the turn while driving slowly down the highway. Like most dirt roads in the desert, at ground level the brush completely hides the road until one is on top of the road. Most desert roads can be seen after one climbs a hill to get a bird's eye view of the area. Heading northward on Highway 127, it's a left-hand turn close to where the town of Renoville used to be.

Renoville is the place where Charlie Reno used to live, way back in the T&T Railroad era. The "town" had a population of two humans (Charlie and his spouse), until one day Charlie came home from working on the railroad sooner than expected and discovered his spouse having vigorous sex with another man. (So I guess one could say the town's population briefly increased by a third.) Charlie was displeased and he said so; the other man, noticing Charlie's displeasure, produced a hand gun and politely asked Charlie Reno to leave town... and leave his spouse behind. The town's population promptly slumped back to two humans (Reno's spouse and her lover), as Charlie agreed it was time for him to move on.

Two things about Renoville to mention: first, the topographic maps place it in the incorrect position; second, to this day the package delivery business "FedEx" still lists the "town" as a place where they deliver packages, even though all that is left of the "town" are a few rusty tin cans and some broken glass.

I parked my pickup on the dirt road that goes to Old Mormon Spring, at the left turn off Highway 127. The hike up to the spring isn't long as desert distances go: about six miles (9.6 kilometers) in a straight line, though the road makes many turns, diversions, and loops as it winds its way around, in, and over arroyos, rock ridges, and boulders. The lack of shade along the way is absolute: with the mountain's incline approached from the east, the arroyos (erosion channels) run east to west, and the sun hammers down upon the bare rocky ground without relief. I was feeling good, and in the mood for a hike; I did not know if my pickup could navigate over all of the obstacles, so I went on foot.

I put two one-liter bottles of water in my back pack, and my Army entrenching tool so that I could dig at the spring once I reached it. By 9:00 that morning, when I started out on foot, the temperature was 90 degrees Fahrenheit (32 Celsius) and steadily increasing. I figured three hours to get there, and two hours to get back to my pickup.

Step by tedious step I made my way up the side of the mountain, as the sun beat upon my back without mercy. The three hours I thought it would take for me to get there came and went; hour number four passed, and the sun was westward and frying my face and head even though my hat shaded my eyes. The fifth hour passed, and I suffered. When almost at the spring, I stopped to fish out my second bottle of water from my backpack--- and I couldn't find it.

I was shocked at not finding more drinking water in my back pack. I removed everything from the pack, and hefted it to make sure nothing was left inside. I even squashed the pack between my two hands, into a tight ball, just to be sure the second bottle of water wasn't in there somewhere.

Meanwhile, the day's temperature was well over 100 degrees (38 Celsius). To keep alive in the conditions I found myself in, I would first have to stop moving: exertion increases the loss of body moisture. Next, I would have to find shade to hide in. Then I would have to wait until dark, then move as quickly as possible down the mountain to my pickup where I had more water.

The problem was there was no shade at all, anywhere. The deepest arroyos had mere centimeters of shade, and the shade was only as long as the width of my hand. I figured the best thing to do was to keep climbing, and hope there would be shade at the spring--- even dead willows will cast shadows, and often dry springs still have brush that one can crawl in to.

At the spring I found mud, and shade. It was a great relief when I grabbed hand-fulls of mud and spread it over my arms, on my face, in my hair, and everywhere else I had exposed skin--- the mud made an excellent sun block. With my head caked in mud, I also coated my hat with mud and then put it back on my head. Unfortunately, there was no actual water there no matter how deeply I dug with my Army shovel.

The afternoon passed with me resting under thorny brush, no doubt with me looking dreadfully uncivilized.

Around six o'clock I got up, put on fresh mud, and started down the mountain at a very quick walk. It was easier going down hill than up hill, but soon I found that my vision was going dark around the edges and I was getting dizzy. Within about 20 minutes my vision had narrowed to the point where it seemed like I was walking through a tunnel, and my face felt numb.

After about 40 minutes I mysteriously found my face pressed hard against the blistering hot Earth, wondering how I had fallen on my stomach without noticing I had: the transition from being on my feet to laying on my face in the dirt and gravel of the road was instantaneous.

Dying of thirst and hyperthermia a mere four miles from a

well-traveled highway struck me as enormously funny, and I laughed for a few second. I could even see, as I sat up and gazed eastward through my tunnel of light, cars on the road. The problem with dying from hyperthermia in the East Mojave is that my carcass won't cool until late January, so I might not even know I'm dead until early February.

I got to my feet and slapped myself in the face as hard as I could, several times. Some of the darkness around the edges of my vision cleared, and I felt better. I started to trot down hill, slapping myself in the face every few jumps to keep me focused and conscious. If anyone had seen me jogging down hill, covered in dry gray mud, punching myself in the face, I'm sure they would have thought me a raving lunatic.

After roughly two hours since leaving the muddy spring I made it back to my pickup, where I lunged at my water container and I choked down the blistering hot water. I desperately needed to cool my body temperature down: my vision was still darkened, and I could only see what was directly in front of me.

The best way to cool off, I reasoned, would be to jump into a cool refreshing pool of water. Evening had come, and my poor vision was getting worse due to the loss of sun light; if I was to drive somewhere cool, I would have to get there soon before I lost vision completely.

The town of Tecopa has a bath house and pools of water. At the time, using the pools was free, and a donations box was outside for people to leave money if they wished. I got in my pickup and managed to get it on the highway headed north to Tecopa. In my imagination I pictured how it would feel to jump into a cold, delightful pool of water, to drink from its refreshing life-giving goodness. I drove while trying to keep the vehicle over the center line of the road. At times I drove off the left side of the road, and at other times I drove off the right side of the road, but on the whole I stayed on the highway until I reached the bath house.

I stumbled out of the pickup and left a trail of clothing from the still-opened door of my pickup and in to the pool house. Boots at the pickup; socks a few feet later; pants sprawled at the door of the pool house; tee-shirt at the steps to the closest pool; mud-covered hat still on my mud-encased head, over my mud-covered face.

Blindly shoving a few naked men out of my way, I plunged into the nearest of the two pools.

Then I screamed.

Some how I had forgotten that the pools at Tecopa are fed from a hot spring, and the temperature of the water is high enough to kill some people if they stay in the water too long.

My hyperthermia went hyper-hyper-hyper-hyperthermic. It felt like I was being boiled alive. I kept screaming as I struggled to the edge of the pool and flung myself onto the concrete floor. As I hit the cement I lost consciousness completely; my last thought was that I was dying, and for no other reason than because I was stupid and careless.

When I regained consciousness, I was flat on my back and my vision was clear; the dark tunnel I had been seeing through was replaced by the full vision of being in a brick walled room lit by incandescent light bulbs. But my vision, as I became aware of my surroundings, was fixed upon a horrible, dreadful, disgusting sight.

Dangling about two feet above my face was a long, thin, wrinkled, withered penis. Worse yet, two testicles, clad in an equally withered scrotum hanging nearly as low swayed loosely with it. I moved my gaze upward and found an ancient emaciated man bent over me; the man kept asking me, in a high piping girl-like voice, "Mister? Are you okay? Mister? Hey, Mister? Are you okay?"

It was a struggle to turn my eyes away from the abhorrent sight, since I didn't trust any penis to behave itself, and when I did I saw that several other naked men were also staring at me. I told the room, "I feel just fine! Why?" I figured maybe I could pretend I meant to scream, fling myself to the floor, and die. The concrete floor was nice and cool against my back and legs, and I didn't want to get up, but.... I was feeling a bit self conscious with everyone looking at me so I got to my feet, collected my shirt, fished my hat out of the edge of the pool, and walked naked into the night and to my pickup.

Outside the pool house, I collected my clothing and climbed into my pickup. I planned on getting dressed after I had made my escape--- before Someone In Authority was summoned to annoy me for my own good. I had also left a great deal of dirt in the pool: the rules dictate that people shower first.

It was a mere 40 minute drive back to Baker, where I stopped at the burrito shop, got out of my pickup, put my pants on, and wandered barefoot, shirtless, and hatless into the fast food joint for succor. My only thought was to get at the ice machine, which I headed towards with no regard to how I looked nor to who might wonder if maybe they should call the cops.

I put crushed ice on my head, which hurt like Hell but also felt great. I rubbed ice on my face, my chest, my arms, and where I could reach on my back.

People were staring at me again. Fuck, I hate it when they do that.

Avoiding eye contact with everyone, I left the burrito joint and got back in my pickup. I vowed to try again the next day, after a good night's sleep at Seventeen Mile Point, only instead of hiking up the road to Old Mormon Spring, I would drive.

Which I did. The suffocating heat of the day quickly fled, and the biting, painful cold took over.

FORT IRWIN: LOATHED BY COWBOYS AND INDIANS ALIKE

***"Whoever said the pen is mightier than the sword obviously never encountered automatic weapons."* -- Douglas MacArthur**

Fort Irwin, which blights the southwest section of the Avawatz Mountain Range, stopped having someone to legitimately kill in year 1946. Since that time their only actual, non-imaginary enemies have been the citizens of America, and the occasional harmless defenseless brown-skinned person in distant foreign lands.

The base these days exists exclusively to train terrorists to fight against democracy in the world whenever and where ever it raises its populous head. The base trains military members of the USA's allies in desert warfare. Or in other words, the base trains the USA's surrogate lunatics in how to engage in urban door-to-door killing. Don't take my word for it: take the tour. It's an ugly blight, and it infests the Southern Avawatz Mountain Range like a hostile, malignant tumor.

When I turned my interest to the Avawatz Mountain Range as my possible home for the next few months, I was interested in staying far away from the fort. The problem is that the fort is not at all interested in staying where it belongs: they have a nasty habit of illegally encroaching on land where they are not allowed, and bulldozing roads through federally protected wilderness as well as areas protected by the Native American Antiquities Act. Eventually they will take over the whole mountain range.

I headed up Old Mormon Road early, driving slowly and carefully over the very rough road, and kept an eye out for my lost water bottle--- which I never found. It was amazing how much faster and easier it is to drive up the mountain than to walk up. I parked at the spring, and examined the year 1931 topographic map I have of the area. I took land bearings, and set off on foot to the area I was interested in--- about 2.2 miles (3.54 kilometers) away.

You are now wondering in what direction I went, and what the landscape looked like. I must keep the direction a secret, since I still have equipment stored up there, and some day I might return to the location. However I will mention that there are no roads, no trails, and no hints of any human travel along the route to where I went to look as a possible desert home. There was no easy way to travel over the steep hills and into the deep arroyos along the way: it was strenuous just carrying my shovel and a gallon of water (in four separate containers).

When I arrived at the site I had in mind, it looked perfect to me. There is a seep, choked with the usual desert brush common around seeps and springs, tucked between two steep hills. A flat, sandy floor stretched about 600 feet (180 meters) between the two hills with the seep at the eastern end. Digging in the seep, under the brush, I carved out a pool of water and let the murky water clear: after about ten minutes the water looked good enough to drink, which I did.

In my back pack I always, without fail, carry a length of quarter-inch copper tubing that I use to drink through in the desert. It helps me suck up water from cracks in rocks, and it allows me to drink below the surface of the water--- below where dead insects and other unsavory carcases tend to float, belly up.

Hiking northwestward up an arroyo I came across signs of mining activity: very old timbers, splintered plywood, sheets of tin, and trash heaps now reduced to just glass and rust. A little farther, taking a turn up a side arroyo, I found a mine adit.

Or I should say “a prospect in the side of the arroyo.” It was in hard rock (cut in a Rhyolite batholith), about 18 feet (5.5 meters) deep, 7 feet (2 meters) wide, and the remains of copper ore littered the ground outside. Someone, many decades ago, had piled rocks at the base of the cave opening, and brought in dirt to make a level floor. It was almost as if the ancient miner had me in mind when hacking out the ore and making the inside comfortable.

This was the place I planned to stay for the next four months. The seep was at an altitude of 3,910 feet (1,192 meters) above mean sea level, and the cave was higher. The cave would shelter me from the sun and rain. I would move in immediately.

Fort Irwin’s main buildings lurked a mere 25 miles (40 kilometers) away.

The history of Fort Irwin started ugly and brutal, and has stayed that way to present time. Fort Irwin is located at what had once been called “Bitter Spring,” where it was said that Paiutes had murdered two European Americans (Thomas S. Williams and his brother-in-law, Jehu Jackman) at the spring on April 18th, year 1860, though it is more likely (due to several witness's accounts) that one or more members of the Church of Jesus Christ of Latter-day Saints ("Mormons") committed the murders out of lust and greed. The victims had been guiding a Mormon wagon train through the area, and various flirtations between one of the victims and a young woman were enough inducement for the murder--- so one witness said.

To punish the apparently blameless Paiutes, the USA government sent Major James H. Carleton into the area to capture and kill any and all American Indians, regardless of age, sex, tribal connection, or family band association: any Indian would do as an "example." Major Carleton had eighty men in his campaign.

The campaign against the mostly harmless, mostly defenseless, starving, weaponless Shoshone and Southern Paiutes in the area lasted three months, with the Army detachment chasing barefooted naked people over and around hills in a futile attempt to "chastise" them for the murders they did not commit. During the rapidly hotter and hotter days, the boys, girls, and young men the soldiers were chasing would taunt and laugh at them from tops of hills, at a distance, and turn their butts at the soldiers and slap themselves on the ass, laughing. During the nights, the soldiers bivouacked with their entrenching tools in case of attack (which nobody involved believed would happen, but regulations required it of them) and stewed in their ire and hatred.

Finally the day came when Carleton and his men captured a few random Indians who had been found sitting naked in the dirt, probably members of the same family. Their victims were taken to Bitter Spring, at the site where the two Americans were murdered, and Carleton ordered the victims shot to death, then decapitated; the severed heads were then hung by their hair on a pole near the spring for all of the American Indians to find and talk about. This was the "lesson" Carlton was sent to "teach" the people who lived in the East Mojave Desert.

Local newspapers at the time, from San Bernardino to San Francisco, called Carlton's terrorist act "controversial." In fact, at the time it was an uncommon, even unimaginable, thing for a USA Army officer to do to prisoners. Such acts would not be common until after the American Civil War, and during what is called "The

Indian Wars."

When I drive on Highway 15 and pass the off-ramp at Fort Irwin Road, I lift my right hand to my brow and salute: not to the Army, but to the victims of Major James H. Carleton.

PARANOIDS ARE HERE TO SERVE US

***"Paranoid? Probably. But just because you're paranoid doesn't mean there isn't an invisible demon about to eat your face."* -- Jim Butcher**

Before moving into the cave I needed supplies. There was an Army surplus store on the north end of Barstow, California, on East Main Street. The store was located half way between the off-ramp of Highway 15 and Barstow Road, near the right-hand turn at Yucca Avenue.

When I made my way down the mountain, to my pickup, I kept an eye out for an easier route to and from the cave. Hauling all of my gear would be a major chore: there was no better route than the one I had taken. I planned on hauling up the plywood sheets I had collected from the right of ways of Baker's streets, plus ammunition containers, sleeping gear, cooking gear, books, car battery, photovoltaic solar panel, hand-powered radio, and a great deal more.

I rushed to Barstow and made the right-hand turn on to East Main Street. I jumped out of my pickup and made sure my belt knife was left in the vehicle. When going into an Army surplus store, it is best to either go in fully armed with several pistols in one's belt near one's crotch, or go in unarmed: I wasn't going to give anyone an excuse to kill me.

Entering the store I found a large pile of ammo cans to my right, not stacked and cataloged by size neatly like a sane person would have them, but piled in a disorderly heap that rose higher than my head. Behind the pile, with a steel-clad glass-top hand gun display case between us, was the paranoid terrified wide-eyed Fundamentalist Christian pro-Confederacy nervous trembling proprietor. He had the pallor of someone who had lived his entire life in a damp cave, sunlight never having fallen upon his unwashed, hairy face: a mighty accomplishment, since his store was deep inside the desert. He kept both hands under the gun display case where I could not see them, and eyed me with naked, intense, overpowering fear. He was a fine, typical example of an Army surplus store owner. I made no sudden moves.

"Ah iz heer tah gets sum amoooo cay-uns," I said in a quiet, soothing (I hoped) voice, showing I spoke his native tongue and was thus not a threat. He twitched his eyes to his left (my right) to the pile of ammo cans (which I was almost standing upon) then back to my face. I spent my time looking over the cans and lids, making sure the lids had the inner rubber seals, and that the cans had both side handles sturdily attached. I set out three large cans that read "A63G Detonators 60%" on them, and one skinny 44 millimeter machine gun ammo can.

Under the Nazi soldier manikin that was hanging by its neck with a noose, and which had a bayonet stuck through one eye, I found a large bag that contained camouflage netting; I added it to my pile of goods to purchase. I also found a hard plastic canteen sturdy enough to jump on, a sewing kit, a bright orange whistle, and a "tactical ball point pen" used to stab unsuspecting autograph seekers (it was an "impulse buy"). I dragged my selections over the neurotic hiding behind the gun case.

There was what looked like half of a rocket-propelled parachute flare on the display case glass, encrusted with ancient wax. I desperately needed one of those (who doesn't?) so I asked him if I may buy it. After a very long silence, where he looked me over carefully to see how much I was worth, he said I could have it for $20. When I handed over the USA Treasury notes, Mr. *Non Compos Menti* kept one hand on either his gun or his penis under the counter (same thing), and worked the ancient cash register (a note pad and a wooden box to hold money in) and the sale was completed. The netting alone cost $70 and the cans were $15 each: the total purchase was so expensive that I felt like stabbing someone in the eye with my "tactical pen," but the mood passed and I hauled the gear outside to my pickup.

THE MAD GREEK TRAVELING PREACHER

***"As more people become more intelligent they care less for preachers and more for teachers."* -- Robert G. Ingersoll**

I drove into Victorville (known locally as "We Won By Nuking The Slant-Eyed Japs Ville") and bought a 12 volt deep cycle battery, and a 14-watt folding photovoltaic solar panel that had two parts that were hinged in the center so that I could carry it under one arm. I also wrote a letter to my brother that explained where I was going to live, how I was going to get up there, and provided the general latitude and longitude. I also bought 100 pounds (45.36 kilograms) of dehydrated refried beans.

Perhaps you have only a dim idea of what dehydrated refried beans are. First, take a large pile of Pinto Beans and boil them on the stove in water until they are soft. Then drain the water, add vegetable oil and salt. Then take a huge spoon and mash the bloody shit out of it all. Fry it in the pot until most of the moisture is gone, stirring constantly. Then take a large cookie sheet and spread the ugly gray lumpy mass on the sheet, and put it in the sun to dry. Never mind the flies and stray dogs that visit the drying mess. Finally, when it is dry, hammer the "food" off of the cookie sheet and store it in an air-tight container.

The beauty in dehydrated refried beans, if any, is that it lasts a very long time if enough salt is added, and if the container is sealed well. To eat the wonderful (disgusting) stuff, one merely adds hot water, waits a few minutes, and then stirs the vile concoction. It's tasty on saltine crackers, so I also bought ten cartons of those. I also bought 100 cans of various fruits: pineapple, peaches, apricots, and cherry pie filling. I also bought an armful of artificially flavored drink mix packets, and a bag of sugar: this was to make the water I was going to drink for the next few months easier to not gag on. I also bought four bottles of insect repellent.

My pickup had a full load, so I headed northward again to start my new life in a cave.

But first I wanted a sandwich in Baker, at The Mad Greek, because I love dry, hard, excessively crunchy unappealing falafel and wilted, brownish rubbery iceberg lettuce. The sauce was good, and it was okay as long as I didn't look at what I was eating. I had parked under the cottonwood tree next to the "Mexican" fast food place ("Fresh Menudo Every Tuesday"), next to a battered brown van, and had walked across the street for the meal.

The van I had parked my pickup next to had a stick propping open the back hatch. The two sliding side doors were opened, and an equally battered man of about 45 years sat on the floor with his feet sticking out of the door and resting on the ground. The inside of the van was filled with clothing, bedding, camping gear, a guitar, Bibles, magazines, rolled up rugs, folding chairs, and trash. I stumbled out of The Mad Greek, under a brutal sun on a hot afternoon, wishing I had just starved to death, and ended up greeted by The Traveling Preacher.

From the carpeted interior of his van he eyed me up and down. I put my hands in from of my crotch, feeling naked and uncomfortable at the examination. He spoke.

"Looks to me like you're a travelin' man!" he said. I allowed as that was true, and I told him he looked like a traveler also. He said he was a traveling preacher, and he was lit by the Fire Of The Lord to tramp from place to place, earning his meals and gasoline by telling people The Good News. He then looked at me as if I were his next meal ticket. "Let me sing you a song," he said, and he snatched up his guitar before I could warily back away from him.

I stood there politely as he sang something about a god doing something to a sinner one rainy night, in some kind of nonsexual way, the gist of which I didn't grasp but in truth I wasn't paying attention. (I had the real world to deal with instead.) When he was finished he asked me what I thought about his song, which kind of made me wish I hadn't completely blotted him and his song out of my brain at the very start.

"Um. That was, um, great." I said. "Well done." He seemed to be expecting a different answer, so I added "Fine fret work you do." I was trying to be polite.

"But what about the ***story***?! What about the ***moral***?! How did the song make you ***FEEEEEEEEL***!?" Before I had tuned out the noise I had heard the word "god," and since he said he was The Traveling Preacher, I surmised that the song was religious so I went with that.

"It seems to me," I said, "that since there is no evidence

showing that the gods exist, they must be hiding from us. Since they are hiding from us, they must be frightened of us, or they want us to think they do not exist, therefore the polite thing to do is live our lives as if they don't exist. Maybe if they discover that we suspect they exist, that would upset them and they might come here and kill us all. Best to be safe and ignore them."

There was "a pregnant pause." He looked shocked, then he looked pleased, and then a big smile came over his ragged, haggard face. He had found that which is more precious to traveling preachers than gold, or a free meal: an atheist! He put his guitar down, got to his feet, and took a few steps towards me with sheer joy on his face.

"You don't believe in god!" he said.

I then made my second horrible mistake of the day. "Well, I don't believe in any of them, actually." I wanted to be all inclusive, like a good liberal. (It was the Christian thing to do.) He took that statement as a challenge.

"But what about prophesy! What about the witnesses! What about the miracles!" That is when I made my third mistake (the first being that I had not ignored him completely). I asked:

"Uh, what prophesies?"

He was very happy that I asked. He spewed Bible verses at me, and anecdotes, and I stuck to what I know best: asking him "how do you know?"

It went on for an hour and more, as the sun beat us mercilessly like a cudgel against our heads and shoulders. Finally, as my frustration at his evasive answers grew, I kicked dirt on his feet.

"Ah, ha!" he said. "Ha ha! You can't answer that argument, so you resorted to kicking dirt on me!" He was laughing, and so was I. "Hot damn this is fun!" he yelled. He insisted on hugging me, and before he did I put my hand over my wallet's pocket so that he wouldn't steal it, and then he suggested that people usually buy a meal for him after being given The Good News. I was still waiting for that news, but apparently he was finished so I gave to him a sawbuck ($10) and a bottle of extremely warm wine. He had worked hard, for a useless preacher, and I figured he deserved it.

Funny thing about preachers: they tend to learn early that people will pay dearly for comforting lies because the demand is as great as the supply. The truth costs almost nothing because supply greatly exceeds demand.

I got in my pickup, made an illegal turn at the 127 intersection, and headed northward. Pausing at my cache of plywood sheets, I loaded eight of them in my pickup, then found the road up the mountain.

I TURN INTO A DOPE FIEND

"When the situation is hopeless, there's nothing to worry about." -- Edward Abbey

Having driven back up the mountain, I parked at Old Mormon Spring, got out of my pickup, and fished around among the gear for my binoculars. The sun had set half an hour earlier, but the glow still lit up the west-facing Kingston Mountain Range. Far to the northeast I saw the road going to Kingstone Spring (later renamed "Kingston Spring"); years ago I had hiked Kingston Wash and passed the spring on foot, and I marveled at the amazing geology of the area--- dirt spires, heavily encrusted with salt, surrounds the northern edge of the spring. A thick carpet of travertine carpets the desert floor around the spring, looking like snow. There is no good water at Kingston Spring, but there used to be: the forth (and last) Fremont expedition camped there and met "Pegleg Smith" at the spring, along with some of Smith's shall we say "horse trading business partners." I could see the road, but the spring itself was hidden by the western hill.

Pegleg Smith is said to have been a horse thief by the people who were nowhere within Smith's hearing at the time they said it. His chief route with stolen horses between Los Angeles (and the horse-populated San Joaquin Valley) and Salt Lake City is not known with high confidence, but it likely started around Agua Caliente, California (the one east of San Diego near the Anza-Borrego Desert), and loosely followed what is now Highway 10 up to what is now Highway 247. If he had stolen horses with him he would take the northern trail at what is now Barstow; if he was trading in Navajo slaves, he would head east at what is now Barstow to get them. On the northern trail he would take his horses through Kingston Wash and past the spring, and up through Tecopa Pass and past Horse Thief Spring.

From where I was standing with my binoculars I could have seen him, his business associates, and the horses making their way into the wash and out again, and see their dust hang in the sky above Tecopa Pass. Part of me wished I had been there, in the early 1850s, to see them pass.

I unloaded the camping gear from the pickup, then got in the back of the pickup with my blankets, pillow, and plush toy lion. The waning moon, now just a sliver, rose in the wee hours of morning and cast a slight silver glow across the hills. And then I heard bells. The tinkling of what may have been sleigh bells, clearly, distinctly, but way off in the distance. The sound seemed to come from no particular direction, but instead it came from every direction. Or maybe it was just in my head. I sat up and stared into the silvery night, and the sound stopped. I laid back down, and the absolute silence descended again upon the desert.

A few minutes later the sound of bells returned. I ordered myself to ignore them, thinking it must be cactus needles rubbing against rocks in the wind, or perhaps some of my camping gear contracting as it cooled in the frigid night air. But of course I couldn't ignore it: as soon as I sat up to look around, the sound stopped again.

Fearfully, I said in a quiet voice, "I am not amused," and laid back down. If the sound of bells returned afterward I do not know, as I slept until the sun was broiling me in my pickup's bed and it was early morning.

I had a bloody hell of a lot of work to do that day. First I needed to find an easier route to my cave. There was no possible route from the north that I could see: the hills and arroyos were steep, and littered with broken rocks and boulders. The lack of vegetation made the landscape look like I was on the surface of the moon, and there was nothing to hide the stark hills from my view: that was a problem, because I needed to find a place to hide my pickup. I thought I would get to the cave, then look for an easier route from there.

The Hell of it was, there was no simple way to get my gear from the road and to the cave: I would have to carry everything on my back and in my arms over ground so rocky, sharp, dangerous, and steep that most pack horses would have refused, and over which no horseman would risk taking pack horses. To prepare the cave the way I had planned, I would need to carry about sixteen plywood sheets, one or two at a time, over my head and walk over the broken ground for over two miles--- and do it eight or nine times. Then haul camping gear that in total was three times my body weight over the same ground, on my back and under my arms. Worse yet, I wanted to leave no boot tracks on the ground.

In the hot, blinding early morning light, I put three bags of dehydrated refried beans into an ammo can, grabbed some of my bedding in my left arm, picked up the full ammo can with my right hand, and I started walking into the hills. In my back pack I carried two one-liter bottles of water, my survival gear, and assorted tools. Half way there I had consumed one liter of water, and I was weary of the weight. When I got to the spring, I had consumed the rest of my water. I was glad to see that the hole I had dug on my first visit had filled with clear water, and using my thumb to block the dead bugs from entering I filled my containers.

The job went on all day, and it was brutal work. The worse part of the torture was the flying insects. When I neared the spring they would see me coming and descend upon me in a ravenous, blood-seeking mob. To mitigate the attack, I paused many strides away and freshly doused myself with insect repellent: I soaked my hat, my face, my neck, my ears, my throat, my hair--- and then, taking up my burdens again, I walked through the hellish beasts while slapping hundreds of them to death along my way (a death count only rivaled by the battle at Verdun in year 1916). Many dozens would follow me, and then lose interest as I passed on northward up the arroyo and to the cave.

(On every trip, back and forth, I carried the back pack even though I was temped to leave it behind to spare me the weight. Or in other words, I was temped to be stupid. See Appendix One for the items I kept in my pack.)

Eight plywood sheets took me four trips. The rest of my gear took me six trips. At the end of the day, as the sun was setting, I had carried a bloody hell of a lot of weight about twenty-two miles (35.4 kilometers) in seven hours and had consumed four gallons (15 liters) of water, without eating.

That night I slept on my plastic sheet outside the cave, exhausted beyond words to describe, and unable to sleep. Thoughts filled my head, racing and flowing by so fast I could barely notice them before they were gone again. Thoughts like: why am I where I am? Am I really going to live here for four months? Will I miss pizza delivery? How many books can I read before the act of reading all day drives me insane? Am I sane? Do sane people do this? Hours passed and still I didn't sleep. I stared into the night sky and noticed bats flying above, in jerky movements as they snapped up insects. I held my breath and listened, and the only sound was the blood in my veins passing under my ears. Ursa Major and Cassiopeia spun around the north star and swapped places in the sky, and I slept.

When I woke with the rising of the sun, I was in agony. I could barely move: my legs were locked rigid with the knees unbendable. My back, when I tried to move, felt like it had been doused with gasoline and set on fire. My neck and shoulders felt like my arms had been torn off. Worse of all, I desperately needed a toilet. As I lay in the hot morning sun I realized that the day before I had worked myself far beyond what was safe and sane: I was now paying for it, dearly. I managed to reach my back pack and pull it towards me, and I fished out my Ibuprofen bottle. I consumed six tablets, totaling 1.2 grams (recommended dose: 200 milligrams every 4 to 6 hours). I then laid there unmoving, in direct sunlight, frying on my plastic sheet like a side of bacon, waiting for the pills to work.

It was a bloody hell of a way to start life at my new home.

HOME IMPROVEMENTS

***"If a plant cannot live according to its nature, it dies; and so a man."* -- Henry David Thoreau**

When I could once again move, with only a massive amount of pain, I examined the opening of the cave. The cave opening faced exactly due north; the bottom of the opening was about three feet (one meter) above the flat, sandy arroyo floor, and had a row of rocks carefully placed from left to right. The arroyo ran up hill going west, with large white boulders littering the arroyo a few steps westward. Climbing above the cave, the peak of the hill it was carved out of made a sudden drop to a deeper arroyo to the south. The southern arroyo was littered with Chamisa and other water-loving brush, suggesting that there was subsurface water in the arroyo. That arroyo also ran east to west, and at its western end it joined the arroyo that had the cave in it. If I were to start at the spring and then walk westward, and make a detour into the southern arroyo, I would come up behind the hill with the cave.

Spotting the highest hill in the area, I climbed to its ridge and looked around. To the north there were more arroyos that ran east to west, and to the northeast there were arroyos that cut deeply into the Earth going north to south--- in effect connecting the ones going east to west. To the west the mountain rose high above me, with a seemingly endless series of serrations on its side as if a giant cat had raked the mountain with its claws, top to bottom.

It was a fucking maze. Anyone thinking to look for me would never, ever find me.

Back at the cave, I noticed that there were cracks in the rock above the opening that I could probably hammer nails or pikes into, and hang some 2x4 pine studs, horizontally, above the mouth of the cave. I could then add hooks to my plywood sheets and hang the plywood to those studs. Then for the lower plywood sheets I could make holes in the bottom of the sheets already hanging, and hook the second layer of plywood on to the top lay. With three horizontal layers of plywood, I would have an adequate wall closing the cave entrance, and easily unhook plywood sheets when I wanted to open the place.

The idea was to put the hanging wall in place in the morning, then take it apart in the evening. In this way, I hoped, the inside of the cave would remain cool through part of the day, and have the inside cool at night.

One problem though: I did not have spikes or long nails to drive into the rock. Bailing wire would not work; using the weight of boulders to anchor the wall would not work because the hill the cave was in was too steep.

Since I still had many sheets of plywood down the mountain in my secret cache, I had to go get them: I would get large nails or spikes at the same time. I dragged my plastic sheet into the cave, and carried all of my gear into the cave. I rolled up my sleeping gear, since blankets are beloved by rattle snakes, field mice, pack rats, tarantulas, badgers, foxes, and ring-tailed cats. I left the plush lion toy to stand guard, and made my way back to my pickup.

I tried to find large nails in Baker, California. It's as easy as finding an honest member of the USA Congress. My second plan was to find railroad spikes, perhaps by walking along the BNSF right of way and pulling them out of the ties; as it was, I knew of a mill site in the desert where there were many railroad spikes, and I didn't have to place anyone's life at risk to get them.

WHAT A FINE PLACE FOR A STOLEN CAR TO DIE

***"Like a valet who commits grand theft auto not to go for a joy ride but to open a used car lot, so do we seize upon love not to revel in its ecstasies but to haggle over its blue-book value."* -- Bauvard**

Mike's mill site consists of two camper trailers stuck at the base of a hill, with a sandy trail that some times cars can drive on if the drivers don't mind getting stuck. The mill site is there to help the mineral claim workers hammer the ore, drink beer in the shade, sleep inside where the insects find it hard to attack, and read. A few years earlier I had passed by the mill site and noticed a pile of railroad spikes amid the assorted valuable junk that litters every mill site in the desert. I hoped I could get a few of these spikes, and if they were not there then perhaps I could find something else to do the job.

When I drove to the mill site, after a nerve wracking trip over soft sand and many torturous twists and turns over the "covered wagon trail" one must drive to get to the site (and the tire-ripping booby trap at the gate, which I ran over), I found a dead car sitting in front of the larger camper. I knew it was dead because it was resting on its driver side door. It rested on its side helplessly, wheels on the passenger side about as high as my shoulders, with the wheels on the driver's side helping the car keep its balance.

The car appeared to be a rental, perhaps from the airport in Las Vegas, or perhaps from Barstow. It was new, with around 2,000 miles on the odometer. Peering inside, I noticed that the dual air bags had been removed, and when I walked around to look under the bright shiny belly of the beast I saw that the catalytic converter had been neatly cut out. In other words, it was considered "legitimate salvage" and someone had done so.

Looking around I was not able to find railroad spikes, but I found short pieces of rusty rebar that would work, so I took some of that. I then drove in to town and found Mike, and I mentioned the car to him; he was not interested in the car at his mill site--- he told me he had cancer and was expected to live only a few more months. (I later heard that he died about nine days later.)

As far as I know, the car is still there.

Filling my vehicle with gasoline (six USA dollars a gallon) I headed northward once again, collected my hidden plywood, and went back up the mountain.

MY WALL WAS WORSE THAN PINK FLOYD'S

***"I had a chronic beer-face condition; no matter what I was drinking, I ended up looking like I'd just eaten a live tarantula. It was very sophisticated."* -- Anna Jarzab**

After I drove up to Old Mormon Spring I kept on driving on the rocky, ruined dirt road northwestward, looking for a place to hide my pickup. The sun was soon to set, and the long shadows would help me find the spot I was looking for. (Hint when traveling the desert on foot: sit on a hill when the sun rises or sets, and watch the country while the sun changes position in the sky: the deep gullies and arroyos show themselves and you can plan your route to avoid some of them.) I needed a hiding place off the main road, or down a side road, where I could then drive off the road and into an arroyo or behind a hill; I would then wipe the sand and dirt where I turned off the road so that anyone passing would not see the tire tracks.

About one quarter of a mile (400 meters) I found a narrow space between two low hills that looked like I might be able to drive into. I got out of my pickup as the sun dropped behind the mountain ridge, and I went to explore the "weap." I figured I could drive over the ground by placing several sheets of plywood on the ground, then drive over the plywood, then get out of my pickup, move the plywood sheets in front of the pickup again, and drive more. Thus in a long series of moving plywood I would get the vehicle where I wanted it, and leave no trail, and also avoid the wheels getting stuck in the sand.

I got back in my pickup as the evening grew darker, and I headed southeast back to the place where I needed to start the hike to my cave. By the time I parked there, full night had fallen and it was very dark.

Could I walk to my cave in the dark? As always, without fail, I had my back pack and its emergency gear and that includes a "pen light." The light only illuminated the ground directly at my feet, and when I aimed it into the night, the darkness swallowed the light completely. Light from the stars, and the "Zodiac Light" (glowing space dust, some times visible after sunset) illuminated the ground so faintly that if I looked directly at something I could not see it; I found that if I looked "sideways," and not directly at where I was walking, I could barely make out rocks and ditches enough to avoid them in the dark.

So, was I foolish enough to walk over such a dangerous terrain, into a maze that could engulf me and hide my bones for centuries if I got lost, essentially blindfolded?

No. I spent the cold night in the cab of my pickup, in the passenger's seat, with the back folded down. I ain't crazy.... right?

The next morning, after a cold night with little sleep, I was up just before the sun came above the horizon, and I was on my way back to the cave with two plywood boards. The weary trek over the brutal, broken ground was getting "easier" after the many previous trips, as my soft flabby ancient cheese-fed body became more accustomed to the work. It was never easy walking the distance with a pack on my back and my arms above my head to hold the plywood aloft; every few minutes I paused to rest, moving the plywood to block the sun from my face, catch my breath, and then soldier onward.

At the spring I left the two sheets of plywood, to use as a shield to limit evaporation, and I went the distance again to my pickup for two more sheets.

Fuck, this was getting tedious. The second trip, with a load of rebar as well as the plywood, took longer, and expended more sweat, than the first. I passed the spring and the freshly awoken insects, and carried on to the cave.

The rebar was not easy to drive into the side of the hill using a large rock instead of the hammer I had forgotten to bring from the pickup, but I didn't feel like making a third trip. It is amazing how much extra work a human being will do (and especially a man) to avoid doing extra work. The labor involved in getting "fresh" rocks to use as hammers as the ones I used kept shattering was slight; more annoying was having to find flat surfaces on the rocks that could take a powerful enough blow to drive in the rebar. My huge clawed hammer, a mere 2.2 miles away (4.4 of course, round trip) would have taken me more than 90 minutes to fetch, but would have saved me maybe 90 minutes in effort.

Finally eight sections of rebar were pounded in, with several inches of each end sticking out above the cave opening. Next I needed to drill two holes in each of the plywood boards in which I could have the rebar rest. Golly, a nice heavy clawed hammer sure would come in handy for that, with which to gouge out the holes. I went to the spring, checked the pit I had dug, filled my water container, and hiked back to my pickup. When I got to the pickup I crouched down against the shaded side, gasping in the heat, and I asked myself if I was having fun. "Shit no," someone said out load, and I think it was me. (This was the start of a long period where I started talking out load and not realizing I was doing so (Human life itself is a breach of the fourth wall.). But it's okay: every crazy person does it.)

Since I was already there, and I needed a rest, I drove the pickup up the road to the only hiding place I had found, and I stopped just at where I wanted to turn off the road. I laid four sheets of plywood in front of the pickup. I got in and drove forward, off the road, about eight feet; I got out, went to the rear of the pickup, and moved the two sheets in the back up to the front of the pickup; I then drove another four feet or so. Into the sandy wash we crept, the pickup and I, step by step, tediously and under the tyrannical sun, until we rounded the screening hill. I left four boards on the ground, one under each wheel, set the hand brake, put the gear shift in FIRST, and turned off the engine. The pickup slumped forward, off the plywood, and promptly sank into the sand--- front left wheel much deeper than the other three. I got out and looked over the problem.

Sad. It looked fucking sad. The pickup, I mean: it looked hopelessly abandoned, like a orphaned inner city waif in a Charles Dickens story. If it could have spoken, it would have asked plaintively, "Why me?" I had to admit I had treated the loyal beast unkindly, even harshly, recently. Heartlessly, I threw the camouflage netting over the suffering mechanical creature and anchored the corners and sides with sand.

Leaving the vehicle stuck in the sand, I hiked back to the cave--- with the clawed hammer.

The rest of the few remaining hours that day I hung the wall pieces over the cave opening. Bailing wire held the lower pieces to the upper pieces, and the whole thing went together quickly. And it looked like shit. In fact there were so many gaps between the boards, which refused to lay flat because the cave opening wasn't flat, that the whole job seemed to be a wasted effort. The Big Idea was to shut the cave in the morning after the night air had cooled the inside, then open the cave again in the evenings: with all the holes and gaps, hot air could pass inside freely. What I really needed with a heavy canvas tarp to hang over the entire structure.

What I ***REALLY*** needed of course was a circular saw, saw horses, ten times the number of 2x4 pine studs than I had, an electricity generator, R60 fiberglass insulation, a bubble level, some door hinges, a door, and a refrigerator with ice maker. But I figured that out of the desired shopping list, I could at least manage to get the heavy canvas tarp on my next trip to Barstow (which, by the way, proved impossible: only plastic tarps could be found).

It was finally time for bed--- I dragged the plastic sheet out of the cave, down to the sandy floor of the arroyo, and unrolled my bedding. An astonishing number of nasty beasties, such as "stink bugs" and hornets and spiders and those spooky translucent yellowish bald-headed-man-looking segmented... THINGS... were dispossessed of their new fluffy warm home. I shook out the blankets, with a creepy skin-crawling shudder, and then I shook out my pillows. At least the tarantulas had not found the sleeping gear.

Darkness came with a thud. You will be skeptical of that statement if you have never stretched yourself out on a plastic tarp in a sandy arroyo deep in the desert wilderness, waiting for the sun to set. Night replaced day in the time it takes to snap one's fingers: with a thud. A thud.

The best part of sleeping in the desert while facing northward, when one is in the northern hemisphere, is that one can keep an eye on Polaris and keep track of the time that way. Cassiopeia (actually, ***Kassiepeia***) over there on the left (in Summer) or on the right (Winter); Ursa Major on the right (Summer) or left (Winter), looking nothing at all like a bear let alone a major one. When the night is gone, they will have swapped positions.

The American Indians of the area think of Ursa Major, if they think of it at all, as Old Man Winter--- perhaps because winter "comes from the north." The constellation looks like a plow to me, probably because I come from a long ancestral line of corn-eaters. It also looks like a wheelbarrow, only without a wheel.

Why, I wonder, does Orion's "sword" jut out of his crotch,

pendulous and lewdly, half way to his knees, in a very non-sword-like way? Dr. Freud: you're needed somewhere in Ancient Greece---and it's an emergency!

The Great Plow slowly turned counter-clockwise as I lay on the plastic sheet, deep in the inky darkness of the desert, as Cassiopeia dipped under the northern horizon.

From very close to my right ear the sound of tiny feet were making faint crinkling noises on my plastic ground sheet. The sound was getting closer, and closer, and closer. Terrified, I sat up and grabbed my pen light and fumbled at the switch. I turned the faint beam of light towards the right and behind me, where my head had been, and I saw a large "hairy" tarantula coming to visit me. It's forward "arms" located where I assumed its mouth is flailed at the air perhaps in consternation that the tasty-looking ear it had been sneaking up on had escaped.

The day's second shudder passed through me as the creepy willies made my testicles tighten in spooky terror. I gently pushed it away with the pen light, not wanting to anger it further, but as soon as I pushed it away it started back towards me again. And again. And again. It desperately wanted to examine the pillows, and the blankets, and the "new best friend" it had found and was currently spooking the bloody shit out of. Finally I put my boots on (after shaking them out and examining them inside with the pen light), and I collected the spider with a tee-shirt; I carried the "puppy-sized" horror eastward towards the spring, in darkness so complete that I may as well have been blind, and shook it off the shirt at the mouth of the southern arroyo.

Back at the mouth of the cave, I gingerly eased myself on to the plastic sheet again. I thought I was too afraid to sleep, but eventually I did.

BUT I'M THE GUY WITH THE WATER!

***"The wise and good are outnumbered a thousand to one by the brutal and stupid."* -- Douglas Preston & Lincoln Child**

Some people go into the desert for fun, and they die. That's probably not the kind of fun they had in mind, but their lack of preparation some times, in retrospect and after the local newspapers mention their inglorious (that is: stupid) deaths, one can sometimes legitimately wonder if they set out deliberately to die. Very few people, if any, have ever complained about being dead: it's the dying that's the bitch.

When driving across the Mojave Desert, temperatures typically climb to 110 degrees Fahrenheit (43.3 Celsius) during the summer months; car radiators boil and the engines shut down if they are newer models with temperature protection designed to save the engine from over heating. Radiators boil and the engines seize and die if they are older models. A more common problem is that cars pulling off paved roads onto the side, for the occupants to de-piss or to take photographs, get stuck in sand and the typical car jacks automobiles are sold with are not adequate to lift the wheels high enough to fit rocks or brush under the buried wheels.

In both cases, many Brave Souls have found themselves "carless" in the East Mojave and they have taken off on foot to hoof it back to what passes for civilization. The fact that they are almost always better off staying at their cars seems to either never occur to them, or the wait for rescue by a car that passes by (if any) is longer than their patience. It still makes me amazed at how unaware of danger millions of modern humans are when they find themselves in a situation where they have a very good chance of dying in agony, and yet they have no idea they are in that situation. In a society where a hot pizza can be delivered to one's house in 30 minutes or less, after a mere telephone call, it is probably to be expected that people living in the industrialized world have lost many survival skills that in very rare occasions they desperately need.

(A parenthetical element: yes, of course police officers take longer to arrive than pizzas after you make the phone call. Pizza drivers are better motivated to get to you when you call for help, or for a pizza. Next time you need a few police officers to rush to your home, do what I always do. Call the police and say, "I've just gunned down a police officer at [give your address] because he was talking sass at me. Golly there's a huge amount of blood. Blood! ***Blood everywhere!*** But it's stopped jetting out of his neck now so I guess he's finally dead. I think I can get away with it. Good-bye." Then hang up. Now immediately call for pizza delivery. Guess who shows up first, properly motivated.)

My careless act of not having enough water to get me to Old Mormon Spring and back was a fine example: there was no valid excuse for my losing half of my water, some where along the road. I also under estimated the amount of time necessary to climb uphill on the road to my destination--- another inexcusable mistake.

And then there are the careless bastards who wander into the desert and who should die (for the good of society) but do not. I discovered a fine example of such a person a few years previously before my life in a cave. If ever there was someone who almost died accidentally but acted like a suicide, it was the man I found stumbling on foot near Lathrop Wells (north of Death Valley Junction) in July of year 1998.

I had been prospecting for gold in what is called The Old Man Hills to the west of Lathrop Wells, and I went into "town" for gasoline. I had not found anything worth working, prospect wise, so I thought maybe a look in the sandy washes north of Lathrop Wells would produce "color" enough to work a mineral claim. There are several dirt roads that lead northward from the general area, and some of them end before they enter the area claimed by Nellis Air Force Base. There are worn, weary, faded signs at the end of the roads that warn people they are not welcome on the base, and to not enter. Some of those signs lay on the ground, blown over by the wind, and the few signs that still stand are generally too faded by the sun to read. They are about fifteen miles, on average, from the various northward turn-offs from Highway 95, between Indian Springs and Beatty.

The general landscape is that of a very flat desert, populated by dry lakes filled with dust and alkaline deposits, punctuated here and there with very low hills that seem almost like stationary waves that had been undulating under the ground and then froze in place; these hills rise about twenty or thirty feet above the flats. Liberally sprinkled over the landscape are countless washes, gullies, and arroyos that cut through the ground and go in every direction. To the far north and to the immediate east of the area there are low mountains on the horizon which the Air Force uses as a "bombing range."

On the day in question I headed northward on a faint dirt road towards Dead Horse Flat. To the northeast there is Frenchman Flat and the dry lake there, which is also on the military base. Even without bombs falling and jet fighters crashing (which some times they do there), it is not a safe place to travel through even in the best of conditions.

I was about seven miles into the desert, off Highway 94, when I saw "something" well ahead of me on the road. The heat from the desert floor made the image very indistinct and at first it would narrow to a paper-edge thinness, then it would widen to what might have been a horse staggering drunkenly. As I drove slowly closer the image resolved itself into having arms and an upright gait something like that of a human being. It appeared to be swaying left and right, standing in one spot, but that was an illusion of the shimmering air: as I crept closer the image came into focus and I saw a most wondrous thing.

It was a human being. In fact it was hatless, wearing a nice dress shirt and fine, dainty office shoes on its feet. Its pants looked like they might have cost more than what I paid for my first automobile ($300). It was not standing in place: it was stumbling, step by painful step, northward into what most sane people (even the stupid ones) would think of as "certain death." I slowed my pickup's speed to match its pace, and followed along behind him. For half a minute I marveled at the brave man's chosen method of suicide, and then I yelled out the window. "Hey there!" He jumped, startled. Perhaps his hearing, and all of his other senses, were locked on his glorious and imminent death. He stopped walking. I stopped the car.

Reaching to my car's passenger seat, I snatched a plastic bottle with very hot water in it, opened the car door on my side, and got out of the car. I approached the dusty, sun-blistered man with the bottle of water in front of me, offering it to him. His shaking hands took the water bottle and he twisted off the cap and choked down the steaming liquid. He drank all of it, which was about one liter or so. I took a step backward, then another, and another.

With a violent retching motion that bent his body double, the hot water came back out of his mouth, and his nostrils, and perhaps even his anus. It was not just disgusting to watch, but revolting to listen to. It sounded like a horse was being flogged with a bull whip, while a choir of Klingons sang opera softly, out of tune with each other. He wailed and screeched and moaned a bit, then eventually stood up. I was so glad it was over, and probably not as much as he was.

Back at my pickup, I opened the ice chest and I fished out a can of icy cold cola and I brought it to him, pulling the pop top for him first. He drank it quickly and managed to keep it down. I went and got him a second can of cola, then a third. Finally he was feeling well enough to speak.

"Thank god! Oh, thank you, god!" he screamed at me. I looked behind me to see who he was talking to, but there weren't any gods I could see. "Oh, I prayed so hard and here you are! Thank you god! Thank you lord!" I was very confused, or he was. I asked him if he would like a ride in to town: he looked at me like I was the idiot around here and said, "Of course!"

He climbed into the passenger side of the pickup, and I got behind the wheel. I looked at him closely to see if he was going to puke more any time soon, but it seemed he was done at the moment. His left ear was... melted, is the word: burned so badly from the sun that it was liquefied and did not look like a human ear any more. The back of his neck was oozing puss. Most of his face and neck was the color of a red lobster, only with suppurating blisters that I could not look at without the bile rising to my throat. While he continued thanking someone I couldn't see, I fired up the pickup's engine.

He told me he had "sojourned into the wilderness to pray." He said his automobile had become mired in deep sand, so he took what he believed to be a short cut back to the highway to fetch help. Having seen what was left of a few dead men who had done the same thing, I heaved a sigh, put my vehicle in gear, and turned around--- back to where I had come from.

"Where are you going?" he asked, with alarm in his voice. I explained to him that he would need to go in to a town and get medical help. I asked him where his car was. He pointed somewhere in the direction I had just come from, and reiterated his car was stuck in the sand. He then told me to turn around and head north. I asked him why he was walking into the military air base instead of to the highway and help, and he said he wasn't: he said he was walking away from his car and heading south to the highway.

"Er, no you weren't," I said. He had not been, but that fact did not deter him from insisting he had been. "I was headed south!" he insisted. "To Lathrop Wells!" I told him he was staggering northward into Hell and agony and misery and death. He said I was a liar, and to turn the car around and head "south" (i.e., north). My suspicion is that he had driven northward into the flats around Dead Horse on a different road, got his car stuck some place nobody will ever find, and then stumbled around until he came across the road we were currently on: he then went north instead of south.

"Look at the sun!" I yelled at him. The sun was low above the western horizon. "It's almost seven o'clock! The sun sets in the west, and it's to our right, so we're heading south!" He looked at the sun, then he looked at his right hand, then he said, "No we're not! It's impossible! I prayed and god told me south is that way!" he tossed his blistered, oozing right hand over his shoulder backwards in the direction he had been walking.

"Your god has a morbid sense of humor," I said. "He sent you in the wrong direction." He sat silently for several minutes as we continued getting closer to the highway. "He wouldn't do that to me...." he said, sounding unsure. It must have been a shock to discover one's god is a malicious killer with a fine sense of humor, I suppose. When we saw the cars on the highway in front of us passing left to right, he looked betrayed. "I was heading north!" he wailed.

I dropped him off in front of the whore house at Lathrop Wells (the only business that welcomes strangers in need) after telling him it was a restaurant. I pushed the buzzer at the gate, then drove away before the salesman inside could come out and ask him, "what's your pleasure?" (It's their job to be helpful, after all.) He never did thank me for saving him. Any remaining issues he had with his god was no concern of mine: I headed back northward and into the deadly flats, looking for gold which I never found.

WHERE TO GO, AND HOW

***"I want to write a poem about 'Truth,' 'Honor,' 'Dignity,' and whether the toilet paper should roll over or under when you pull on it."* -- Jarod Kintz**

Waking up in front of my cave, I recalled my pickup being stuck in the sand, and that reminded me of the praying man at Lathrop Wells. Did he find his car? Did he trade his god in for a magnetic compass, or at least for a more serious, or more accurate, god? As I lay on my plastic sheet, blankets pulled tightly under my chin and with the sky to my right rapidly getting lighter with the rise of the sun, I thought about why that man never thought to thank me for saving his life. He did not thank me for the cold cans of cola. He did not thank me for the ride in to Lathrop Wells. I assume it was the terrible stress his brain had been under. When I give money to beggars on the street they always thank me, without fail, even if it's just two or three dollars; did the man I saved think his life worth so little that it wasn't worth a "Thank you?"

The sun leaped up and over the eastern horizon, huge and yellow and menacing like a super villain. I gathered up my blankets, shook them vigorously, and wrapped them and the two pillows tightly in the plastic sheet.

I needed a toilet. Some people will wonder how I took care of that chore.

Usually when a person is passing on foot through the desert, or even driving and paused along the road for a nature call, it is sufficient to merely drop one's pants just about anywhere and answer the call. Since I was living in a sandy arroyo, with my source of drinking water located down hill, I had to walk about 15 minutes eastward and past the spring before I could "let loose." I could not use the southern arroyo as a toilet since the brush in there suggested to me that there was subsurface water and that the south arroyo is where my spring got its water. I could not crap on the hilltop because shit runs down hill, plus it would eventually pile up even when scattered over a large area. Think "twice a day for 120 days." When living in a confined space, sanitation becomes a concern that must be dealt with.

You may think a mere 15 minute walk is not a problem, but you're forgetting our friend Lord Diarrhea and other forms of gastrointestinal distress. At other times the night is dark, and the walk can be dangerous. The arroyo floor I was living in was rocky when continuing west (up hill), but even if there was not a danger of stumbling around in the dark and suffering injury, it is stupid to shit or piss up hill from one's drinking water in an arroyo: rain will come eventually, washing one's waste into the spring.

What I needed was a cat litter box, with me as the cat, filled with sand and dirt, near the cave in case I could not conveniently walk eastward and down hill from the spring. During the day, or on moonlit nights, I could walk the 15 or 20 minutes out of the arroyo and de-poop; when very dark, or when I could not wait that long, I could use my "litter box." For urine, of course, I had a bucket and could dispose the contents at my leisure. (By the way: in the desert heat, put that bucket down wind. Phew!)

At the spring I had left two plywood boards, to use as a shade screen to slow evaporation over my pit. I did not know if the water volume would increase or decrease over time, so I figured to keep as much as possible. But I needed one of those boards for my toilet. I went to the spring and brought back to the cave one of the boards. While at the spring I also dug out the pit again, since it was silting up.

Near the cave opening, westward and at the edge of the rocky area, I piled up some of the rocks in five places. I then rested the plywood on top of the rocks. Using my Army shovel I added dirt, sand, and gravel on top of the plywood. I then kicked the structure a few times to judge its sturdiness; its height was half-way between my knees and the ground: about 10 inches.

Time to try it out. I turned eastward, dropped my pants, bent over a bit, contracted some muscles and relaxed others.... and missed. Shit! This would take some practice. It wasn't even a moving target, and there was really no legitimate excuse.

Toilet paper I saved to burn. Some people think they should bury toilet paper: that's not the case unless they bury it three or more feet deep. Every mammal in the desert loves used toilet paper, and they will dig it up to see if it is good to eat; that paper then litters the ground for several years as it slowly degrades. In places with little rain it can last more than a decade. It is far better to increase carbon dioxide in Earth's atmosphere by burning the paper, and it makes excellent kindling for camp fires.

FIRE AND WATER

***"The camel has a big dumb ugly hump. But in the desert, where prettier, more streamlined beasts die quickly of thirst, the camel survives quite nicely."* -- Tom Robbins**

Speaking of camp fires, there is scant firewood in the East Mojave Desert, and what can be found is generally not safe to burn. When looking for wood in the desert you need to dig for it; when looking for water, you need to climb. "Climb for water; dig for wood" is the survivalist mantra in that area: it does not apply in all deserts. The wood comes from two chief sources: human structures that have fallen to ruin, and dead brush. Creosote burns quickly, and hotly, and it spews a shower of sparks that can set off near-by brush down wind. Rabbit-Brush (Chamisa) burns well, instantly, and leaves almost no coals to cook over: the same is true of sage.

To collect the "native" wood (dead brush) one needs to pull the dead roots out of the ground and then shake the dirt off. In areas where there have not been humans building fires, there is often a large amount of dead root material available--- such as in the area where I was living. Many armfuls of dead roots are needed to heat a pot of water.

There is also, in some areas of East Mojave, dead mesquite trees killed by the parasite Desert Mistletoe (***Phoradendron californicum***). There was a time, in my youth, when I traveled East Mojave on foot with a bow saw cutting dead and dying mesquite branches off the sick trees, but the Desert Mistletoe spread faster than I could keep up. The Department of the Interior had zero interest in saving the mesquite trees in the East Mojave Desert: in fact the woman who was put in charge of the Mojave Preserve actively prevented the rescue efforts by stating the Preserve should "revert to nature." Within less than a decade every mesquite tree was infected, and almost all are now dead. Mesquite Valley no longer has any mesquite living in it. This is called "natural." The fire that swept through Cedar Canyon, destroying Bob Hollimon's cabin, was called "natural" and left to burn.

The most fuel efficient way to heat a meal in East Mojave, using the available "wood," is by using a "hobo stove:" a large tin can with holes around the open end's top lip, and one large opening at the bottom. The large opening should be facing the wind, if any, and twigs are inserted there as the fire burns. It uses very little wood, and the heat is applied to the pot or pan sitting on top of the stove--- the flames do the cooking, not the coals as is the case with open camp fires.

For water, in East Mojave Desert one is more likely to find it by climbing the desert hills and mountains than finding it in valleys and arroyos. In most cases Cottonwood trees will mark the spot; in other cases the dense green brush will prevent Cottonwoods from growing, and that brush is harder to see from a distance. In most cases the water is hard to get at because of the thorny brush, and it is also filled with many kinds of water borne disease-causing organisms and it should be heated before drinking. Water should be collected as close to the source as possible.

There are a few places in East Mojave where the water gushes out of the ground in large volume, but it is very rare. In all cases, surface water has sharply decreased in the region and most historic water sources are now dry; the rest will soon cease to exist. The natural aquifers in the region took 50,000 years to fill, and humans are doing their best to pump it all dry in 200 years or less, drilling deeper and pumping faster to keep the casinos' golf courses green.

In addition to humans pumping out the ground water for landscaping and manufacturing, human-caused climate change has warmed the region by +2.35 F per century. Meanwhile, precipitation has decreased by 0.3 inch per century. This is madness, and means doom for many desert species (including humans), but people need to golf in the desert: it's our god-given right. In the American Southwest in about 70 years there will be only half the amount of fresh water available that people will need to meet basic survival amounts: that is, only half the people currently living there will get the water they need to drink to live even after ending the use of water for landscaping, manufacturing, and washing dishes: funny how nobody seems to care.

My water source was mostly harmless to drink without treating: where it came out of the ground it did so quickly, and it spread over an area (by actual measurement) 42 meters (140 feet) wide by 148 meters (486 feet) long. A Rhyolite batholith a few dozen meters to the south blocked ground water from draining in that direction. The west end had water at the surface, while the center and east end of that area had water below the surface. It was very good water, and plenty of it, but it was hard to get to at the west end due to vegetation. My sand pit, where I let the water accumulate, was at the east end and it was meant to be used for bathing instead of consumption: my plan was to get drinking water from the west end, where it came out of the ground.

After my "litter box" was in place, I set out to make a path through the spring's brush at its west end and get at where the water was coming out of the ground. My plan was to disturb the ecosystem as little as possible. Ha! That plan was impossible: the brush was very thick, and billions of thorns stood between me and the water. I could hear the faint sound of the water gurgling upward, and judging only by the sound it seemed like there was maybe 15 feet (4.5 meters) of brush I would need to shove my body through. I thought maybe I could get a length of pipe into the water and siphon it down hill, but alas I did not have any pipe: but I knew where some could be acquired (er, stolen) many miles to the east: in the Providence Mountains there were very long sections of black PVC pipe laying discarded on the ground--- but it would mean a special trip to go get some, and I might not be able to get the pipe into the water through the thick brush. I resolved to get some pipe if and when I had the time.

Then I got angry. How dare the brush stand in my way? I'm an American and a human: that water belongs to me, not to the huge number of species of desert life that depends upon it to live. I had coffee to brew, and dehydrated refried beans to rehydrate, and teeth to brush: I did not want to depend upon the water in my sand pit at the east end to be healthy to drink, even when heated to a boil (and the insects loved that pit).

I raised my left foot and stepped into the brush. When my foot found something solid to rest on, I used my right knee to push aside some brush and get my right leg into the biomass; the plants resisted but I persevered. Left leg pulled out of the brush, thrust forward, then planted again. Right leg pulled clear, pushed forward, stopped by branches and thorns--- I shoved harder, using my hands to pull the branches away. Branches and twigs grabbed at my hat and yanked it off; I struggled to reach it, grabbed it, and put it back on my head (it wasn't much of a hat, but it was good for another twenty years or the next rain which ever came first). With every painful step the brush got denser, fought back harder, and attacked me with more vehemence.

About six feet in, my forward progress was stopped; the spaces between the branches were too small, and I lacked the leverage and strength to push or pull the branches to the side of my path. Figuring I could not walk in, I thought maybe I could sort of... swim in. I leaned forward, grabbed a distant branch, and pulled my feet off the ground and went in horizontally. For another six feet that worked, using my head and shoulders to twist and turn into the brush, until I got stuck.

Not merely stuck: wedged between branches so tightly I could no longer move forward, nor leftward, nor rightward, nor upward, nor downward. It was then, and only then, that I realized the fatal flaw in my approach: after I pull myself in, how do I pull myself the fuck back out again? I had to get out the way I came in, if possible. I found branches near my shoulders, grabbed hold of them, and shoved my body backwards. I repeated the process about twenty times and finally found myself out of the brush: scratched all to hell, bleeding in a few places, and worse of all my hat was missing. I stepped back into the brush a few feet and found my hat within arm's reach.

Exhausted, I went to the east end of the spring and bathed. The brush had won.

I ENTER THE NINETEENTH CENTURY

***"I am not eccentric. It's just that I am more alive than most people. I am an unpopular electric eel set in a pond of catfish."* -- Edith Sitwell**

My spare car battery was a major pain in the ass to haul into the arroyo, then to the cave. The folding photovoltaic panel was easier since I could carry it under on arm pit. I placed the panel above the cave opening, facing southward, and I placed the car battery next to it. The wires from the PV panel were not long enough to place the battery anywhere else; I packed rocks around the battery to keep the sun off of it.

From the battery I ran a power cord into the cave, and I attached a 10 watt light bulb. To turn the light on I just twisted two wires together; to turn off the light I pulled the two wires apart. Real Men don't use switches: they either twist the wires together, or they sit in the dark because nothing frightens them. The bulb hung down the cave opening and stopped about three feet above the ground. If I had longer wire I would have moved the bulb to the back of the cave: yet another item I needed to steal from somewhere.

Since I am on the subject: yes, I "steal" (re-purpose) things I find when I'm in the desert. It would be wrong, immoral, unethical not to. The desert is filthy with ruined cabins, destroyed and flattened camper trailers, heaping piles of trash, and abandoned military bases--- this provides valuable natural resources for people to dig through. I know a trash heap in the desert, among the Turquoise Mountains, where there are over 100 paperback books rotting in the brutal desert sun because nobody thought them worth salvaging in time. The usable material out there is vast: bicycle wheels; bed springs; iron pipe; copper wire; stainless steel sinks; table legs; refrigerators; television cabinets; swamp coolers; bar stools; toilet seats; wood burning stoves, gas burning water heaters. The entire East Mojave Desert is one massive trash dump.

The night after I tried to force my way into the brush at the spring I decided to fire up the ten watt light bulb and see if I could read by its light. I ***twisted the wires together like a real man***, and a feeble light illuminated the mouth of the cave. Immediately, a ravening cloud of flying insects came "running" towards the light. It was horrible to see them just keep coming and coming and coming, thundering in like buffalo, by the thousands. It meant I would need to close the opening of the cave when I wanted to read at night, and make the closure tight enough to keep most of the insects out. I ***pulled the wires apart like a real man***, and went outside to sleep. I unfolded the plastic wrapped blankets and pillow, gave everything I mighty shake, spread the plastic sheet on the sand, and made up my bed. Somewhere my plush toy lion was hiding, but I could not find it.

GOLLY THAT WAS REVOLTING; WAS THIS HOW BENEDICT ARNOLD GOT STARTED?

"Returning home is the most difficult part of long-distance hiking; You have grown outside the puzzle and your piece no longer fits." -- Cindy Ross

My ancient Coleman gasoline-fueled stove leaked fuel, so I had to carry it carefully. If I did not pump air into the tank just right, or if I didn't get the stove resting at just the right angle, it would spit gasoline at me as well as all over itself, and ignite at unpredictable times when I was trying to cook. Some people would suggest I fix the leak, or buying a new stove, but I hate throwing something away just because it might kill me some day.

The sun stomped on my face and I knew it was morning. I filled a sauce pan with water from my sand pit and set it on the stove to boil. When it was boiling, I added a scoop of dehydrated refried beans and shut off the flame. The leak caught on fire, setting the entire stove on fire, which eventually went out when the fuel was consumed: a good sign that breakfast was ready. I stirred the mixture with a spoon, and gave it a try.

The paste wasn't bad. In fact it was quite good, since all I could taste was the salt. I got a handful of crackers and crushed them, and added it to the sauce pan. After eating, I put sand in the sauce pan and rubbed the inside clean. It was a good breakfast, but it lay heavily in my gut--- like I had eaten a bowling ball. What I wanted were pancakes, heavy with butter: next trip in to town I would get the "just add water" pancake mix, and maybe I could wrap butter inside a blanket to insulate it from the heat so it would last for a few days.

After breakfast I looked around for something to do. There was absolutely nothing that needed done, nowhere for me to go, no comfortable place to read. What I needed was a hobby. I thought about the subject, then I came up with a great hobby: I would spy on Fort Irwin, my neighbor.

The highest point in the mountain range I was in is at the elevation of 6,204 feet (1,891 meters) according to my year 1933 edition of the topographic map of the area. As the crow flies it was only a mere three miles away; following the easiest route possible, the distance would be about six times that. I rolled up a blanket and tied it to my back pack; I filled every water container I had with water; I put my binoculars into the back pack, and then I set out on foot westward up the arroyo.

The first 4,800 feet was easy: the arroyo was flat, sandy, with a slight incline. The boulder field to the west of the cave took only a few minutes to pass, then the floor was clear of the annoying hazards. Every few steps there would be a bush, but they were widely spaced and not a problem passing. I passed what looked like a sunken crater to my left: a bowl with a high cliff edge spanning about 270 degrees, with the northeast side cut off. The bottom of the crater was about 400 feet wide, and 700 feet long at the base; as I walked farther up the arroyo I came to a second crater that was very similar to the first, also on the left. At the second crater I made a right turn, northward, up another arroyo.

An odd thing about those two craters: I could not see how they could possibly have formed by erosion. As I climbed higher inside the northern arroyo, I looked back and I saw a smaller third crater much like the second, and then an even smaller crater next to it. They looked like a massive soup spoon had taken a big scoop out of the hill, and then a knife had cut off the northeast facing sides of each hole--- and the dirt removed was then taken somewhere.

Up the northern arroyo I went, and it was not as easy as the first wash. The sandy floor was narrower, and littered with rocks. Little hills had to be climbed over, and it was very slow going for 2,200 feet. I then came to a “fork” in the arroyo, and I took the left-hand turn. The arroyo became somewhat wider and easier to hike up, though the incline became steeper. There were far fewer bushes to step around, and no boulders worth mentioning, and the annoying little hills to climb over were only a few feet tall.

After another 1,000 feet I found the arroyo had opened up, east and west, into a narrow valley, with steep cliffs on both sides. The western side was a sheer drop of about 120 feet; the eastern side was just as tall, but the cliff rose gradually over the width of about 400 feet. Within this valley, as far as I could see, there were countless hills running east to west, like ribs; each hill was only about 30 or 40 feet tall, but it would take considerable effort to pass over them to the north end of the valley. Was there a better way, I wondered? The valley was only slightly longer than half a mile, but crossing it would take a few hours.

I examined the western cliff face. If I back tracked a bit, and went into a side canyon to the west, maybe I could then climb up to the ridge of that valley and walk the ridge northward. I walked back the way I had come, and then climbed a hill on my right, to the west. I then headed northward, looking for a route to the little valley's western ridge, and eventually I found a way. It was a longer distance, but less time.

Walking northward on the ridge, the eastern valley looked deeper than it had looked from the bottom looking up. I could also see across the valley and the maze that I had traveled through: some where in there my car sat, under netting and stuck in the sand. I knew it was maybe about four miles away, but looking over the terrain it seemed like hundreds of miles.

To my left, westward, a second valley lay, mostly flat inside with a depression in the southeast end that might collect water in the rare moments when rain falls. I continued walking the ridge northward for about 2,300 feet; the ridge bent to the right, and I followed it.

Across the arroyo to the northwest I saw bright green brush. I got out my binoculars and looked over that area. It looked like another spring, but with no surface water. The line of bright green brush followed the bottom of a wash for about 250 feet, and from what I could tell I would be able to visit the area without much difficulty: the ridge I was walking on ended about 500 feet farther north, to be joined on the left by the wash that had the bright green brush in it.

I walked off the north-going ridge, stepped into the western wash, and followed it westward. When I got there I saw a geological formation I had never seen before: the sandy wash with the spring in it was running along the lip of a southeast-facing cliff, for about 250 feet. There were cottonwood trees on the ridge, but no sign of water on the cliff face itself: no lush plant growth at all. It was as if the subsurface water was being held in a shallow baking pan, with some kind of rock formation acting as the pan, so that no water was getting over the ridge of the cliff.

Looking around for the source of water, I saw cottonwood trees on a hill to the north. There was also a patch of dense light green brush. It looked like the water came close to the surface on the south-facing side of that hill, went below the ground for 800 feet, then came up to just below the surface again in the south. Dense brush followed a few feet north of a ridge for 250 feet. At the end of that 250 feet, at the west end of the ridge, there was a large fissure in the hill and the tree growth ended.

It would have been an awesome place to hide from the Department of Justice, if and when necessary. But by gods! The commute to get in and out was murder. There are no direct routes through that mountain range: one is lucky if one can find a pathway that goes one mile in the desired direction for every six miles one must walk. It is almost always a mistake to climb over hills to save time: in most cases it is a better idea to walk around hills when possible, even though it is a longer distance. One can die climbing a series of steep hills in one hour that one could have walked around in three hours.

I walked eastward again, toward the north tip of the little valley, and I came to another wash that headed north. I had no idea where I was at this point, but I still had a few hours of day light so I made the left turn and up that arroyo.

That arroyo was a struggle to pass through. It ran northward about 8,000 feet and ended at a large, deep, sheer drop into another little valley. A layer of gypsum was exposed in the west cliff, and several layers of gypsum were exposed to the southeast. It was almost as barren as the surface of the moon, though a few plants grew in the dusty, rocky, sun scorched dirt. I was suddenly very weary, and I did not want to hike any more. I was too far away, and too low in altitude, to see anything of Fort Irwin: the whole point of the hike.

I backtracked about 600 feet and climbed a hill to the west. To the west I could see my desired destination: Avawatz Peak. Shit: I had gone too far north, and not far enough west. Gazing over the landscape I saw row after row after row of tall steep hills between me and the peak. I found a pile of rocks tall enough to cast some shade, and I laid down in the shade to spend the rest of the day. At sunset I wrapped my blanket around me and slept, weary and exhausted.

The next morning I awoke early and hiked back to my cave.

I BECOME LIKE LEWIS AND CLARK AND POCAHONTAS

"Twenty years from now you will be more disappointed by the things that you didn't do than by the ones you did do." -- **H. Jackson Brown Jr.**

My shortwave radio receiver ran off of re-hydrated refried beans. The Grundid FR-200 has a hand crank on the side to turn a dynamo, and a rechargeable battery some where inside. It also has a "flashlight" mounted on its face, but in the dark it was not easy to find the switch. In theory I would be able to listen to the world using this radio (3.2 - 7.6 MHz, 9.2 - 22.0 MHz, as well as the local FM and AM stations); in practice what I usually got while in the arroyo near my cave was about three hours of static for the 20 minutes of cranking necessary to recharge the battery. The static sounded better than most popular songs "climbing the charts," but I was disappointed. I kept the radio handy because the light was useful.

The days were very hot, and my chief source of entertainment (hiking) was becoming painful and dangerous. In the early mornings I would wake up, hike up the arroyo westward, climb the south ridge, and wait for the sun to rise. The sun would eventually show up, a minute or so sooner every morning, and I would climb down the ridge, pass my cave, and pass the spring to find a toilet. I would then hike back westward to my cave, heat water on the Coleman stove for coffee and refried beans, and eat a can of fruit while I waited for the water to boil.

After eating, I dragged my bedding into the cave, to hide from the sun, and I slept until evening. When the sun was setting, I would come out of the cave for dinner. I would then drag my bedding outside and go to sleep again.

This went on for about two weeks, and I lost track of the days. My radio told me what time it was (WWV time ticks), but it never bothered to tell me what day of the week, or day of the month, it was. The moon had passed from totally dark and to "new," following the sun downward later every day, becoming brighter. I did not shave my face, nor did I bother to bathe. My brain slumped into a befuddled stupor.

What I needed was a gun. A big loud hand gun. That way I could lay on my plastic sheet inside the cave, and shoot out into the sun-blasted desert. Something noisy and violent to break the monotony. But I had left my guns on my boat, and I left over 1,000 cartridges for my pistol and rifle in Capitan Ron's garage for safe keeping (to hide the cache from the FBI).

The last use I had for my .45 hand gun was to murder my television. It only took one bullet, early one morning. For about two hours I waited for the police to arrive and haul me away, but nobody came. Perhaps nobody complained. Perhaps my neighbor in the condominium, right behind the paper-thin wall, was a heavy sleeper. Weeks later my brother came to visit and he saw the dead TV with the hole in the tube, the exit wound, and the hole in the wall behind the TV. "I like what you've done to the place," he said. "Election results," I replied.

My cans of fruit ran out, and I was left with little to eat but crackers and re-hydrated once-dehydrated overly-salty sometimes-crunchy refried beans. At times the act of heating water seemed like too much work, though I had absolutely nothing else to do, so I ate the "bean gruel" dry. I started to burn body fat, even though I did almost no exercise. I constantly thought about the lone can of peaches I had left in my pickup, sitting there as a reward for making the effort to visit the sunken orphan.

Finally, one bright moon-lit night, I snapped out of my befuddled state and decided to go for a long hike: immediately. I quickly rolled up a blanket and tied it to my back pack. I filled my water containers from the sauce pan where I kept boiled water out to cool, changed my filthy socks for merely dirty ones, and I set out into the darkness, heading eastward.

I was heading into the unknown, since I had not looked over the topographic map. I had a general idea that if I went east for about a mile, I could then work my way southwest a bit, then west, northwest, and finally north. My goal was to look over the western valley where Red Lake was, and perhaps see the dirt road that went through Red Lake Pass. I would have to climb up Avawatz Peak, and I figured the best way would be to walk all the way around the southwest end, and climb up to the peak from the west: there should be a road somewhere, and I would find it. The road passes the Big Iron Mine, which worked digging up ore day and night (one can see the truck's headlights move through the desert at night), which was located far to the south: I planned on finding the road well north of the iron mine, and walk that road up to Avawatz Pass. Once at the pass I could then climb eastward up to the peak. On foot, pausing during the heat of the day, I figured it would take two days--- maybe 50 hours--- to get there. I took a little bag of dehydrated refried beans with me.

Passing the spring, I continued eastward until the arroyo ended abruptly at a series of broken hills that hid the eastern horizon. The arroyo forked at the first hill, the left hand fork heading northeast and the right turn going southwest. I turned right, and within two minutes I came to another fork in the arroyo. One turn went due south, while the other went west. I went west.

The west arroyo continued westward for about twenty minutes, then went south. The moon was low over the horizon, casting deep shadows into the arroyo bottom and with every step I found it harder to see what I was stepping on.

In about ten minutes the south arroyo dead-ended up against a tall cliff face, and I could not pass any father south, nor could I climb westward. To the east there appeared to be a deep valley but it was too dark to tell: the moon had set. I unrolled my blanket and slept for about four hours until the eastern horizon glowed with the rising of the sun.

To the east there was indeed a small valley. It was bleached white, filled with a powdery dust which would be a bitch to walk across, but I was loath to back track: I would have to stop walking in about an hour, and wait for the sun to traverse the sky, and I wanted to make as much progress as possible while the day was still cool.

The Valley of Dust was spooky. No life existed anywhere on its floor, and the sides of the valley were almost devoid of brush. I felt like an "extra" in a Mad Max movie as I headed eastward, then northeast as the valley bent that way. The northeast end of the valley narrowed into an arroyo, and headed east. I followed the arroyo and came upon another arroyo heading south. Judging by the surrounding hills, I realized I had just completed a circle and that the south-draining arroyo was the same one I had not taken five hours earlier. Shit. I would get no-fucking-where, and slowly, making circles in the desolate wilderness.

I headed south down the arroyo. It was a very good choice: it went on southward, over easy ground, going down hill, for three miles. I found myself nearly out of the mountain range, well to the south of my cave, a bit farther east than I had hoped. It was a good place to stop and wait for the sun to burn the ground for the day. There was a ridge, about six feet tall, running on the east side of the arroyo for about 500 feet. I spread my blanket in the shadow of the ridge, and I laid down.

The day got hot. The day got extremely hot. Then the day got good-gods-it's-fucking-hot hot. The sandy floor of the arroyo sucked up the sun's heat and threw it in my face: the glare was painful, and I could feel my face drying. Since the heat made it impossible for me to sleep, I got off my blanket and I hung it on the ridge over my head, anchoring it with rocks, to shield me from the glare. I then got back into the rapidly narrowing shade. It was a great relief, but it would not last long: as the sun headed westward, my shade was being swallowed up by the terrible, ruthless sun.

I endured. When the urge to pant like a dog came over me, I strangled it and forced myself to breathe through my nose. I kept my mouth shut to keep as much moisture in my body that I could. When the east edge of the arroyo lost its shade, I packed up and moved to the west edge, hanging my blanket above me, and I waited for shade to fill in around me. It seemed to take many hours, but eventually the west edge of the arroyo threw its shade over me and I suffered less.

It was a bloody Hell of a way to spend a day. While the sun was still about one hour above the western horizon I figured I had waited long enough, and I continued south and out of the mountains, and turned west. If my memory was correct, the hill I was heading towards would have a rough dirt road going over it, passing between two rocky pinnacles on its top, and once I reached that road it would be "gravy" to get to where I wanted to go. If I were where I thought I was, Silver Lake Road was not far to the south, and the iron mine was far to the east. I climbed the hill and just as the sun set I found the road. Sweet!

The road was actually a pale strip in the sand. The road ran straight as an arrow northwest for about nine miles (14.5 kilometers) up towards Grave Summit, and I set off in the dark at an easy, slow pace. The climb was not strenuous, and it felt good to be walking again after the tedious hours of waiting for the sun to set.

In about four hours I spotted light up ahead on the road. I stepped off the road, to follow it as best I could in the dark, on its northern edge. I had no idea there would be people at Grave Summit, and I did not want them to see my shoe prints. I continued walking west, and roughly 800 feet (240 meters or so) from the lights at the pass I found what I thought was the dirt road I wanted: that road headed due north. About a mile and a half later I found what I was looking for: an abandoned ranch, and shelter for the day.

Someone had told me, way down in Baker many months ago, that there would be fresh water near the abandoned ranch, in the form of a "guzzler." As the sun rose, I looked for any sign of green brush to see if I could find the water and fill my containers. A pair of hills sat to the west of the ranch house, with a low saddle between them, so I climbed the saddle and looked around. To the northwest there was an arroyo that continued northward, cutting deeply into the rocky hills; there was no sign of the water I had hoped to find. I went back to the abandoned ranch and went inside.

The inside of the building was a mess. I kicked a clear spot on the floor, laid out my blanket, and I laid on the broken concrete floor to sleep.

The building was shaped in the form of a "U" with the open end facing north. Behind the building and to the east was an outhouse, fallen into ruin. Somewhere to the northeast of me was Avawatz Pass, but I did not know how to get there. I had heard about a spring with good water on the road to the pass, and I wanted to make sure there was enough day light for me to see it; if I did not fill my water containers, I would soon be at risk of dying of thirst. I pressed my body against the cool, though broken, concrete floor trying to have the floor soak up my excess body heat. I rolled off my blanket and pressed my face against the floor. It was filthy, but the coolness felt great. Meanwhile, the inside of the building became like an oven: again I endured.

Judging the time to be about six o'clock, with three hours of day light left, I set out due east for about 2,000 feet (I counted 1,000 steps) and I came to a fork in the trail that headed northeast. I made a left turn, and after about ten minutes I came to a well-used road. I had found the pass, and the northern route out of the mountains, and hopefully to fresh water.

Walking along the road, with the sun at my back some times, on my left shoulder other times, I came to a concrete stock tank that had water in it. An iron pipe dribbled water into the tank. The relief I felt was so great, everyone around me (if there had been anyone) would have felt it wash through me. I filled my water containers, drop by drop, and then drank as much water as I could put in my gut. I took off my shirt and dunked it in the disgusting slimy water and put it on again. I then dunked my hat and put it on. For a few seconds I thought about taking a bath, but the water in the tank was vile so I declined. The water from the pipe? I did not want to look at it too closely since I had to drink it.

With still more than one hour before sunset I headed north on the road, bright moon high to my right, blood red sun low to my left. I had no idea how much farther I needed to walk, but I wanted to get the brutal “adventure” over with. As the sun set, I recognized the “back side” of Salt Basin: somewhere to the east was Sheep Creek, and excellent water. I located what I thought might be the “castle” (dirt spires) that rise high above Sheep Creek Wash, and I headed cross country eastward. In the bright moonlight I could not see the “castle” very well, but the area “felt right” so I turned northward. If I was wrong, I would end up in Anvil Canyon, and far from drinking water. I got lucky: in less than an hour I came to Sheep Creek Wash, and followed the wash to Sheep Creek Spring.

At the spring I fished out my pen light and followed the black pipe from the spring down to where there was a steel tank. Fresh, pure water gushed out of the end of the pipe, and I filled my water containers. Then I connected the water pipe to another pipe that ran into the steel tank, and I left it that way to fill.

Gods, I was fucking tired. The hike had already taken longer than I had thought, and I was far from my cave and home. It was at least 90 minutes down the wash to the road heading east, then 90 minutes to the road heading south, and another two hours to the road that went up to Old Mormon Spring, and then, if I was lucky, another five hours to the dry spring, then two hours to my cave.

I slept as the steel tank filled, and in the morning I climbed into the tank and had the best bath of my life--- wearing my clothing except for my boots. The sun came up over the east edge of the wash, and I loathed the idea of getting out of the water. I took my clothing off, still standing in the tank, and washed the grime out of them. I tossed them onto the dead Salt Cedar tree behind me to dry.

Some time around noon, as I soaked in the cool water and tried to stay awake, I opened my eyes to find that someone was standing near the tank staring at me. Some how he had driven up the wash without me noticing. He asked me if it was okay for him to look around. I feared maybe he meant my naked, lily white, unmanly body, but he meant the cabin to my left. I said "Sure!" He went inside, and I climbed out of the water tank and put my clothing on.

His name was "Hadley" or "Henry" or something like that, but who gave a shit? I declined to tell him my name, which seemed to upset him a bit. He asked me about the history of Sheep Creek Spring and the people who had lived there. I told him about the family that still owned the cabin (we were on private property, and trespassing), and about the previous family who lived there and worked the dry wash as a placer gold claim.

During the Great Depression there lived a family of three at the spring. They panned for gold the hard way: with a "dry washer" that rocked like a baby cradle, with the heavy rocks and gravel removed by hand as the sand and, hopefully, heavy gold settled to the bottom of the cradle. The cradle had to be slammed hard against its stops, left, then right, then left, then right, many times and it was hard work. The top dross would then be scraped off, and the bottom layer put in a pan to wash with water from the spring. The family took turns shoveling the sand and gravel into the cradle, working the cradle, and panning the pay dirt. On a good day they collected enough gold dust to be worth about $2.30 which was good wages for three people during the depression. On a bad day, of course, they worked all day for nothing.

I asked "Hadley" (or whateverthefuck) if he would give me a ride to the highway, and he said he would. I tossed by back pack in the rear seat, hopped into the passenger seat of his huge, new, shiny, compensating-for-something Ford and away we went northward. It was amazing how fast and easy the miles passed when not done on foot. We turned right, and some 15 minutes later came to Highway 127. He asked me where I wanted to go. "To

Baker," I said. He turned southward, and several more miles went by.

Coming up on the road that leads to Old Mormon Spring, I said, "I'll get out here." He looked at me like I was crazy. The desolate, boiling, frying-pan-hot desert stretched menacingly in every direction, unrelieved by shade or structure or.... well, fucking anything. He said, "Really? Here? Are you sure?" I told him I was almost home, and thanked him. He stopped about a half mile past the spring's road, and I grabbed my back pack, slammed the door, and waived affectionately as he drove away shaking his head.

I walked to the road that leads west with a overwhelming feeling of ***Deja vu***. Didn't I already almost die walking this road? But I had seven liters of water, and even though the sun beat on me like a homicidal Thug, I knew what to expect and I started up the road slowly, taking my time, drinking liberally. My best speed was a little over one mile per hour, and it was well past sunset when I finally passed Old Mormon Spring and eventually reached my pickup.

In almost four days I had traveled a brutal, exhausting, painful, agonizing loop through and around some of the most hostile country in the American Southwest, and I did it on a few handfuls of salty, dried pinto beans. I felt slightly manly.

PEACHLESS

"When a man must be afraid to drink freely from his country's river and streams that country is no longer fit to live in." -- Edward Abbey

The night was warm for several hours as the desert gave up its heat. In the early morning hours I wrapped my blanket around my weary body, and placed my head against the west-facing side of the rear driver's side wheel of my pickup: nothing says "Wake the fuck up!" better than a desert sun kicking one in the face.

When the sun came up I headed to my cave, stopping at the spring to dig out my sand pit. At the opening to my cave I started water heating on the stove, and realized I had forgotten to get the last can of peaches I had cached in my pickup. I imagined the tangy sugary goodness I would have been enjoying, and I contemplated making the trip all the way back to my pickup: was it worth it? I was very tired of walking, so in an empty pineapple can I mixed some artificially flavored drink powder (flavor: "purple") with some hot water, added sugar, and drank that instead.

My trash was piling up. My "good food" had all been consumed. I had been at the cave one month and four days, though at the time I didn't know how long it had been. It was time to go in to town and do some shopping! But the thought of walking even two miles more than what I had just done, in the rapidly increasing heat, just to then struggle to get my pickup out of the sand, made me want to whimper. Instead, I spent the next two days and nights in the cave, bothering only to eat and then walk eastward to my "latrine area" below the spring.

Well rested, I got up and stumbled out of my cave and into the blinding, homicidal sunlight. Only one thought in my mind: peaches! Today was finally the day I would remember the last can of peaches long enough to actually eat them. I packed up my trash (a huge pile of empty tin cans), filled my water bottles from the pot of heated water I kept handy (it took many hours for the hot water to cool in the shade of the cave), slung my load on my back, and headed to my pickup.

At Old Mormon Spring I noticed two things: the damp ground around the spring had dried completely, and there was an ancient, much abused white Ford Fiesta parked nearby. The car was not occupied. I did not want to reveal myself, nor my pickup's hiding place, but I could not see anyone around. I looked into the car and I saw that it was crammed full of paperback books. I also recognized the car: I had a visitor!

I passed the spring and walked around the hill that hid my pickup.

The driver's side door of my pickup was open. The camouflage netting was pulled back from the side of the vehicle. All four wheels of the vehicle were firmly planted on plywood sheets, out of the deep sand. My brother was sitting in the driver's seat, sucking down the last of my lone, greatly desired, can of peaches. I rushed over.

"My! My! ***My PEACHES***!" I wailed. I flung down my burden of trash. He said something about skipping breakfast, and that if I had really wanted the can of peaches I should not have left a P-38 can opener on the dashboard. Apparently it was all my fault. I was glad to see him. I love my brother, most times, but other times I love canned peaches more.

"How did you know where my pickup was hidden?" I asked him.

"I found it because I knew it was hidden," he said. "The first step in finding something that has been hidden is to know that ***something has been hidden***. I looked around, and there was only one place you could hid your car. A hiding place only works if there are too many places to look."

A fucking Sherlock Holmes.

"How did you unlock the door?"

"I found your hidden spare key."

"Let me guess," I said. "There was only one place for me to hide it?"

"Only one ***logical*** place," He said.

A fucking Science Officer Spock.

"Okay, how did you get my car out of the sand it was stuck in?" He looked at me like I was an idiot.

"Lever and fulcrum," he said, pointing to an ancient, half-burned 4x4 beam he had dragged from the dry spring and over to the car.

A fucking Archimedes.

He threw the empty peach can over my shoulder and on to the

desert floor. I picked it up and added it to my trash sack. My brother went to fetch his Ford while I sat in my pickup and started the engine, to keep the battery charged. When the Ford Fiesta was as close to my pickup that it could get without going off the road, we transfered books from my brother's car to mine. I hoped the water-tight camper shell was still water-tight. It was an awesome pile of books, and appreciated. It was the best gift I had ever received: over 80 Louis L'Amour novels! Isaac Asimov! Gene Roddenberry! "The Mists of Avalon!" Two books written by David Morrell! Even a book written by that ne're-do-well Douglas Preston, whom nobody loves nor reads, ever. There were hundreds, enough to last for months of reading. Even "I, The Jury" by Mickey Spillane, which I used later to wipe my anus. Note to Mike Hammer: you are so far "in the closet" that you're in danger of becoming an overnight bag.

I asked my brother if he wanted to see my cave. He suggested we go shopping for food instead, maybe because I was looking thin and haggard. We loaded my trash into his tiny, battered car, and he got into the passenger side. "You can drive," he said.

The Fiesta's wheels are tiny; the ground clearance is mere inches. I declined to drive, since I was not used to going over such a rough road in such a wimpy car. He relented.

Down we went, loud banging noises from under the car as we encountered rocks with great vigor. I yelled often, warning about boulders in the way, and the louder I yelled the more my brother aimed at them so I stopped yelling. Once again, after reaching the highway about 25 minutes later, I marveled at how much easier and faster it is to travel in a car than on foot. We survived the deep patch of sand that lays just in front of the highway, turned right, and headed to Baker.

The town of Baker has many charms. It is the garden spot of the East Mojave, and thousands of tourists flock there every summer to bask in its beauty and culture. The opera house is full of beautiful women in dazzling dresses every weekend night, handsome tuxedoed men hanging onto their arms, as great plays like "Othello" and "Paint Your Wagon" premier, followed by rave reviews in the Hollywood press the next day.

Well, I lied. Baker sucks limes, but it's better than no Baker at all. We stopped at a taco place, and I grabbed my water bottles and went to the water spigot that sticks out of the south wall: the only working, non-locked source of water I have ever been able to find in Baker without invading someone's kitchen. I filled my eight one-liter bottles with clean water, and each one took mere second instead of the several minutes I was used to. I held a full bottle up to the sun.

"Good god!" I said. "I can actually see through it! There's no dirt! There's no bugs! And, ***IT WAS SO EASY!***" It made me wish I had a plumbing system back at the cave, and a filtration system, and a purification system, and that ice cube maker I was constantly dreaming about. When I loaded the filled bottles into the Fiesta, my brother and I walked up to the taco shop's door.

"Okay, then," my brother said in a low, menacing, but loud voice. "We'll do this, but remember: ***NOBODY*** leaves this place alive. No witnesses this time!" I looked around to see if anyone had heard. There was nobody around. We went in.

The people serving fast food inside knew us, and they knew what to expect.

"Six large orders of French fries, please! To go," my brother said. The person at the counter didn't blush. My brother forked over the cash, then stepped aside. I stepped up.

"I would like six orders of large French fries to go, please, and a small fountain drink: I'm on a diet." My brother giggled.

"It'll take a few minutes," Counter Guy said, still without a blush. The woman at the drive-up window said "Howdy" at me, and asked me how the turquoise hunting was going. I fished into my front left pocket and pulled out a pale brown rock that had a zero-quality (worthless) streak of turquoise and I gave it to her. She has been working that drive-up service window for over ten years, and I wondered at how she has managed to not shotgun her brains out, while standing in a bathtub in some motel, from the angst and despair such a "career" must cause. She was pleased with the rock.

Our heavy bags of highly-salted deep-fried starch were ready. I got a cup of ice from the soda fountain, and we left.

Nobody died.

"You drive," my brother said. We got in the Fiesta and I drove across the main road and under the shade of a Salt Cedar. We dug into the deep fried potato goodness with both hands, stuffing handfuls into our mouths like elephants eating carrots with their nostrils: barely pausing to chew. I started on my third serving of

French fries.

"I wish I could pay someone to stop me from making such a disgusting pig of myself," I said between handfuls. Suddenly an arm shot out from my right, snatched up my bag of three remaining French fries orders, and threw it out the right front window.

"Ahhh!" I yelled.

"That will be twenty dollars," my brother said.

"Shit!" I said. I jumped out of the driver's seat, raced around the car, and grabbed the greasy sack of French fries before the ravens could grab it and fly away. I got back in the car, glaring at my brother.

"Do I still get my twenty bucks?" Instead of answering I hunched my body over my fried salted grease, protecting it from further assault.

It is amazing how disgusting a human mouth feels after eating six large orders of deep fried potatoes, heavily salted. My cheeks felt stiff, and the inside of my mouth was burning from the salt; my tongue felt like it had licked a grease trap clean.

"Good shit," I said. I fired up the car's engine and we headed south to Barstow to get food and other supplies.

I recalled my first road trip to Gallup, New Mexico. I had stopped at the McDonald's on the main road (left turn when heading east), went in, and asked if I may please have six orders of French fries. The emaciated, milk-white, highly freckled, greasy-haired junior high school girl at the counter said, "No," with dead, dull, bovine eyes looking at something way off in the distance past my shoulder. She offered no explanation. I asked if maybe I could have five. She said, "No." I asked if maybe three or four would be allowed. She said, "No." Still no explanation.

"Look," I said, being reasonable, "I'm a USA citizen! It is our birthright to suffer and die from obesity and diabetes! May I at least have one order of French fries?!" She agreed, I may. She punched a few buttons on her plastic electronic cash register thing, and then asked me what else I wanted.

"Five more orders of French fries," I said.

"No. Anything else?" she asked.

"No, thank you." She told me what I owed her and I paid it and she handed over the lone, single, only order of French fries. To this day I have no idea why I was allowed only one.

A man; a real man; a real American man would have gone to his car, got out his Glock 18c, then gone back in and ask politely again for more French fries.

(Later the next day I drove to Window Rock and along the way I saw a sign that read "FAT SHEEP $80." I stopped at the sign, as any sane person would, and I talked to the Navajo man sitting next to the sign. I asked him if he had any skinny, pretty sheep for sale: I was willing to pay extra. He told me to go away.)

The east side of Barstow is a nicer place than the west side. The slum is on the east side, and all of the decent, good, hard-working people live there. The east side is where the hobos, tramps, bums, and homeless live: people like me. Every time a flop house or strip joint shuts down on the east side, it's like a star has fallen from the sky: the universe becomes that much dimmer and sad. Scary, filthy, babbling people with open sores on their faces need places to go, too, damn it, but the City Council still believes the place needs to be "cleaned up." Here's an idea: replace the City Council with bums, tax the churches, and shut off the water to the fucking golf courses--- the improvement would be instant, and everyone wins. Who the ***Hell*** do they think they are, anyhow?

We took the off-ramp for East Main Street, went a few miles into the better (that is, shabby) part of town, and pulled into the parking lot for the supermarket. I drove around the back to the large trash dumpster, unloaded my trash, and drove around to the front.

I turned in my seat and faced my brother. "No witnesses! Agreed?" He nodded. We got out of the car and stepped into the hot early afternoon sun.

Since I was wearing filthy rags, I felt a little embarrassed in the brightly lit, neat, clean store. Entering the store, the merchandise stretched left and right in neat tall rows, clearly labeled with signs hanging from the ceiling, the hum of air-cooling machines up there somewhere. It was a store one would find on the west side, not the east side: bright, sterilized, bulging with wealth. As vast as the store was, only a handful of customers were shopping. Other than the hum of fans, it was dead quiet inside.

"It's like the west side!" I told my brother. "You be the Jets and I'll be the Sharks!" I pretended to stab my brother with a switchblade knife, then I flung my arm to my forehead and yelled, with great angst, "Maria!"

"Stop that," my brother said. We got a shopping cart and went strolling through the towering racks of canned, plastic-wrapped, gaudy prosperity that almost none of the neighbors within three miles could afford to buy.

I loaded every can of peaches the store had into the shopping cart, three different brands, in heavy sugar and in juice: it was all good. Also a hell of a lot of other canned fruits. Pancake mix; instant (dehydrated) mashed potatoes; dried minced onions in a plastic can; powdered garlic; cocoa mix; six boxes of raisins; a dozen cans of green olives; several jars of salsa; a dozen jars of red pasta sauce; pasta noodles; dried grated Parmesan cheese in a plastic can; corn flakes; jars of dill pickles; cheese crackers; vegetable oil; bags of corn tortilla chips; a wall calendar; a can of stove fuel from the "picnic supplies" section; kitchen matches; a bag of russet potatoes; several bags of chocolate chip cookies; dozens and dozens of other food items, until the shopping cart was fully loaded and then some.

Now I needed toilet paper. I hunted for the "paper products" and found them in aisle six. Shit (no pun intended), there were dozens of different types, from a half-dozen manufactures: why the bloody Hell does The United States of America produce more choices in paper to wipe the shit off our asses than it has choices of politicians? (Choice One: openly, flagrantly, proudly corrupt. Choice Two: corrupt and tries to hide the fact.) The different selections of toilet paper stretched 30 feet down the aisle, six feet high, three feet deep: a sure sign of a declining, doomed civilization.

There was a woman of about 50 years old, dark skin weathered by the sun, in the aisle looking over the toilet paper, trying to decide which offered the best ass wiping for the best price. I stood a few feet away trying to make the same decision, but the options were just too many--- so I thought I would ask the woman for advice. Instead this came out of my mouth, without my knowing it would:

"Golly, I wish I were a dog. That way instead of having to buy toilet paper, I could just drag my poop-rimmed ass on the carpet. Think of the money that would save!"

A flirt. I was flirting. This is how I flirt. A charming, well-breed flirtation.

The startled look in her eyes kind of gave me the sense that she suddenly wished she had not left the pepper spray in her car. Then her face lit up in a big smile, which was nearly as bright as the store's glaring florescent neon lighting. She giggled, then blushed. I grabbed two packages of the nearest toilet paper and fled.

Every single brand of toilet paper emphasized that their paper was "soft." As if softness in a asswipe is of vital importance. But what about those of us who like it rough? What if one's pooper pucker requires a bit of internal scrubbing to mitigate that last, final, dry and nasty itch?

We made our way to the check-out counter, and looked around for a cashier. The store seemed devoid of employees, but we waited quietly and patiently, looking around to see if any human beings would notice us waiting. The silent, unpeopled, depopulated wait continued for several minutes.

"Maybe they finally dropped the neutron bomb," I suggested to my brother.

"Maybe they want us to haul our stolen goods out the door without paying," my brother said. A cholera epidemic was suggested; armed robbery and hostage taking was suggested; space alien abduction. The emptiness of the massive store, in the middle of the day, was eerie. My brother stepped away from the check-out lane, spread his arms out, tilted his head back, and started to pirouette like Julie Andrews.

"THE HILLS ARE ALIVE! WITH THE SOUND OF MUSIC! THE SONG THEY HAVE SUNG! FOR A THOUSAND YEARS!" he bellowed, rotating swiftly clockwise. I was just about to join him, going counter-clockwise for an ascetic symmetry, when an employee rushed over looking angry.

"How are you?" Her inquiry's tone and inflections, added to her unfocused eyes, suggested to me that maybe she did not much care how I are.

"Autistic," I said. "How be you?" The fabricated smile on her face, that had been beaming itself at my brother and me, went from "strained" to "if I don't drop this grimace soon I fear significant face injury." She "rung up" our purchases. The staggering sum was full explanation for why the place was nearly void of customers.

Our next stop was in the worse (i.e., most affluent, rhymes

with "effluent," i.e., wealthy) side of town and a massive sporting goods store. While driving around town I marveled at the green lawns, the swimming pools, the car washes, the lawn fountains, the tropical ornamental plants everywhere by the hundreds of thousands. What, did these stupid shits believe water just comes falling out of the sky? It's the fucking desert, and they were consuming fresh water at such a furious rate that their thirty-year mortgages would last longer than the Colorado River and the subsurface aquifer. In thirty years they will once again be shooting each other over the rights to the last remaining mud holes. Tens of thousands of people ignorant about their own history (and the California Water Wars), and utterly unconcerned about their future. I expressed my amazement at my brother.

"Look at these insane fucks," I implored him. He ignored me, of course: he's heard it from me thousands of times before. "Year 1934! Arizona National Guard! Owens Valley! Mulholland! What the bloody Hell is wrong with these people!?" I was getting warmed up. "More than half the springs in the area have gone dry in the past twenty years! What are they going to drink after they've pissed away what's left?!" Then my brother came up with a new angle that I had never thought of before.

"When they run out of water here, I want a monopoly selling them guns and ammunition."

Why, I wish I had thought of that! Instantly I saw the massive, ugly, water-sucking city in a new, fresh light: there's profit to be made here when the water runs out, and everyone's houses become uninhabitable and unsellable.

At the sporting goods store I bought a folding reclining camp chair, good enough to tilt backwards and rest my feet up. I looked over an assortment of water filters, water strainers, and water purifiers, but the best of the lot was vastly more expensive than I could afford. Then a fine idea came into my head: solar still!

We raced to a hardware store and I bought a clear plastic shower curtain, two one-gallon buckets, and twenty feet of flexible clear plastic tubing. Instead of protecting my sand pit from evaporation, I would cover the pit and let the sun clean my drinking water for me. I also bought a spool of insulated wire to extend my reading light farther in to the cave.

HE JUST STARTED PUNCHING RANDOM FACES

***"The emotional, sexual, and psychological stereotyping of females begins when the doctor says: 'It's a girl.'"* -- Shirley Chisholm**

When shopping was done, I suggested that we looked for "a family restaurant" to visit for dinner. My brother suggested we go to a "fast food" place or a truck stop instead of "a family restaurant" because he did not want to get punched in the face again. Sheeeish. Just how many times did I have to apologize? That was ancient history, and besides it wasn't my fault. I told him, "I'm better now: I'm on muh-muh-muh-medication." I will tell the story once again, and apologize in print, and I hope this will be the end of his complaints.

There are times when I have no idea I am talking out loud (known as "delayed echolalia"). At other times I think I said something out loud when the words remained only in my head (known as "this dude's nuts!"). One can imaging how confusing the latter is for other people, and how problematic the former is for me.

In August of the year 1995 my brother and I drove from Southern California to the Denver, Colorado, area to attend a large group camp out, and we passed through Nevada and Utah along the way. When we stopped at Beaver, Utah, for dinner I wanted a "sit down dinner" instead of the usual "fast food" garbage, so we stopped at the one and only Mexican food restaurant in the town. We parked in the dirt parking lot, got out of my pickup, and stretched the kinks out of our car-cramped bodies. We stumbled to the restaurant's vestibule and got in the queue of customers waiting for a table; the place was not crowded, but the "hostess" insisted on showing people which tables to sit at, and she was a lethargic beast with sore feet. We waited patiently to be seated, standing in line with the other road-weary white trash.

Unfortunately, there was a very beautiful young woman (I mean "girl") in the queue in front of us. She was tall, and wore cut-off Levi jeans that were so short I suspect the poor lass had felt a terrible draft in her nether, austral regions when we opened the door to walk in. Her long, sand-colored hair fell in a cascading tumble down past her butt, and when she tilted her head forward a bit, her hair would flow like water forward to block her feline-like green ice colored eyes; when that happened she would tilt her head backwards and give it a little becoming, fetching shake, and the hair would flow backwards again. Her full, pouting lips turned down slightly at the corners, giving her an aloof, slightly cruel look. Her womanly foudroyant breasts lifted exuberantly upward in healthy good humor. She might have been as old as 16 years, to be liberal with the guess.

"Oh, ***good gods***! Look at her! Argh, she is soooooo hot!" someone said, loudly. A few backward glaces from the crowd were aimed at me, for no reason I could think of. Then the same person said, "That ass, it's so flawless, and heart shaped, and the perfect ending to amazing legs!"

Then another, different voice spoke up.

"Hey! That's my ***daughter***!" A man of about fifty years of age, and wearing several years of food debris on his shirt from previous meals, was stomping towards me, and that was when I thought maybe the first voice had been mine. Oh, shit--- not again! He shoved his face forward, inches from mine, and started splattering my face with spit when he said, "You don't talk about my daughter like that!" I tried to explain myself.

"But, ***she's so fucking hot!***" Truth would be my defense.

His face went from merely purple to dark purple, as he took a step backward and then sent his right fist in a leisurely, round arc towards my face. While I was waiting for it to get to me, I took a step backwards, into the racks of tourist advertisements, and I ducked. His right fist swept past me and around to his left side, making him bend slightly forward. He straightened and sent his left fist, again in a slow arc, towards my face. I stepped to my left and ducked, and his fist swept past me harmlessly. If it had been a fight between him and Bambi, this guy would have got his ass kicked.

My brother, my hero, stepped in to save me. "What he meant was...." he began. He was interrupted by a fist landing solidly against his mouth. How the Hell he didn't see it coming, considering how long it took the man to get it there, is a question my brother and I have been arguing over ever since. "What did you hit ***me*** for?!" he yelled. "I didn't say anything!" The man turned around, walked away from us, collected his daughter by putting an arm around her, and pushed her into the dining area.

As she walked away, she briefly turned her head to look at me over her right shoulder, her right eyebrow raised, mouth opened slightly, not in the least bit looking surprised that her father had just punched some random stranger in the face for no reason at all.

My brother was rubbing his face, looking confused. A half-dozen people were staring at us. I began to feel kind of guilty, like maybe it was my fault somehow. Suddenly I wanted to go some place else to eat.

"Let's go some place else," I said.

"What just happened?" my brother asked.

"Maybe a burrito across the street," I said.

"Did someone just punch me in the face?" my brother asked.

"Or we could go to a store and get stuff to make sandwiches," I said.

"Did someone just now mistake my face for yours?" my brother asked.

"Or hey, let's just skip dinner and get back on the road," I said.

"A fist, meant for you... did I imagine that?" my brother asked.

I was desperate to change the subject, but he just kept going on and on and on about ancient history. I turned around and walked out the door. A few seconds later my brother followed. We climbed into my pickup, got back on the highway, and drove half a mile in the direction we had come to find another place to eat. Every five seconds, I apologized. All the way to Grand Junction, which I tried to drive around because I hate the place, I apologized. All the way to Denver, I apologized.

THE BLIND DRIVING THE BLIND

"Fate is like a strange, unpopular restaurant filled with odd little waiters who bring you things you never asked for and don't always like." -- Lemony Snicket

So now here I was in Barstow, hoping to find a restaurant only to eat in and not get punched in, and my brother had the ill grace to mention his face-punching again. I had lied about me "being on medication," since I'm not crazy. He said, "Okay, but if there are any women at all in the place, I'm leaving."

There is a good place to eat in Barstow, in the better part of town, that serves what it calls "Mexican food," but I knew my brother would not eat there if he saw it from the outside in bright day light, or even by candle light once inside. Dead flies on the window sills just means the people doing the cleaning spent extra time on the dishes... right? As the sun set we drove west into the blood red light down East Main a few seconds, then took a left turn into the restaurant parking lot.

My brother turned to face me; I turned to face my brother.

"No witnesses this time!" we both told each other at the same time. We got out of the Fiesta and invaded the restaurant, telling the host we had a reservation which, when he looked, he could not find: I pretended to be outraged, but since the place was almost completely empty of customers we got a table immediately. While walking to the table I kept telling my brother that the restaurant was a great place to eat.

"Looks kind of.... dirty in here," he said.

"It's just the candle light," I said. "It's great food!"

"Is the waitress over there really wearing a knife in her belt?"

"Excellent food in fact! Good salsa!"

"There's electrical wiring duct taped to the carpet, running everywhere to trip people, and the carpet seems to be sopping wet. And what is that urine smell?"

"The guacamole is tangy and spicy! You'll love it!"

"I don't like it in here. Let's go some place else." That was the final straw, and I couldn't stand any more complaints about my choice in where to eat. I looked around for an attractive woman so that I could get someone to punch my brother in the mouth again. The waitress with the deer-skinning blade strapped to her hip didn't qualify (if the cholesterol doesn't kill you, the waitress will). We followed the host to a table, and my brother examined the chair, which of course had an assortment of food debris on it. He made an ugly face.

All of this was vastly baffling to me, because I have seen him drink, and gladly, from a mud hole that had just recently been visited by a cow with a serious dysentery affliction (better than no water at all).

The waitress came over and asked what we would like to drink. I asked for iced tea. "I'd like a bucket of hot water and a mop," my brother said. The waitress looked confused.

"It's the name of a drink they serve in Key West gay bars. Get him a Margaretta, please" I told her. She went away, her boots making sucking squishing noises on the water-logged duct-taped carpet, and I continued looking for someone attractive. Drinks came, and I asked for a plate of cheese enchiladas; my brother asked for a plate of French fried potatoes. My brother looked at my glass of iced tea. "You'd better check that with a urinometer," he said.

Dinner came; I immediately took half the French fries; he immediately took half the cheese enchiladas. It was good fodder, and better than I had eaten in over 30 days. He paid the bill; I left the tip, and we both rushed out of the building. To tell the truth, the urine stench was getting to me.

Night had enveloped Barstow, and that meant I couldn't see well enough to drive. The problem was, neither could my brother. Without my eye glasses, I am lucky to see the hood of the car I'm driving at night, and I left my glasses at the cave. My brother's night vision is worse: even when standing next to his own car, a mere five feet away, he asked me, "Where's the fucking car?" I told him I had better drive.

The trick to driving when blind is to remember where the turns are, and hope there is a car in front of you going in the same direction: then just follow the blurry tail lights. We got in, I fired up the Fiesta's engine, and I made what I hopped was a graceful right turn out of the parking lot and on to East Main Street, heading towards the freeway. When I counted two stop lights, I followed blurry tail lights down a right-hand turn and on to what I hoped was Highway 15 headed north. It "felt right," though I would not know until the lights of Midway came into view (correct direction), or if Los Angeles appeared (wrong way).

We saw the lights of Midway. It was a lucky guess.

It takes me 65 minutes driving from Barstow to Baker when I can see. When I cannot see it takes me about 45 minutes, since all fear leaves me. In record time we reached Baker, where we paused at the lone stop sign. In the distance we saw the burrito place was still open for business. Without asking my brother, I drove straight instead of turning left, turned right, parked in the parking lot of the fast foot joint, and we went in.

"Six large orders of French fries, please," he told the counter guy.

"I'd like six orders of large French fries, please," I told the counter guy.

Gods, we're disgusting.

PLEASE LET ME FINISH EATING BEFORE YOU KILL ME

***"And I'm sure than in Poland, or somewhere, it is considered cool to drive a Porsche and wear necklaces and black silk, but at least back in Brooklyn if you did those things you were either a drug dealer or from New Jersey."* -- Meg Cabot**

Restaurants are so dangerous that I hate going inside one without a body guard like my brother. It is not only because I am paranoid; it's not only the irate fathers: it's also the drug dealers and the enraged little cowboys I fear.

There is a burrito store in El Centro, California, I visited after a trip through Yuma, Arizona (August 10th, 1997). I was sitting at a table eating a disgusting burrito with one hand, holding the book I was reading with the other hand, when someone I had never seen before sat down at the table across from me. I looked up, wondering what the person wanted, and he pushed a paperback book at me, sliding it across the table top. Ah, I thought: my new friend wanted to exchange books, or talk books, or something. So I slid my book over to him, and I picked up his book.

At least a dozen $100 bills fell out of his book onto the table in front of me. I stared at the currency, baffled a wee bit, not too concerned yet, and then I looked at him a second, then over his shoulder at a person sitting alone in the opposite corner. The guy in the corner had a hat that looked like mine, and generally speaking he looked like me--- none of which concerned me: it was the carnivore, eyes-of-death stare Meat Eater was giving me that greatly concerned me.

My new friend turned a bit and looked over his shoulder at the killer I was looking at. He then turned back around slowly, collected his $100 bills, gave me a "you're dead meat" look, and then walked over to the guy in the corner. The whole ballet of pending death took maybe ten seconds at most. They both then sat there quietly staring at me.

Shit. Shit, shit, shit, shit, ***shit!*** I had no idea what they were planning on doing to me, but I assumed it was a drug deal and some how I had been misidentified as the seller by Book Guy.

Would they let me live to testify against them? Would they let me live long enough to finish eating my burrito? Out of the corner of my eye, pretending to give them no attention at all, I saw Book Guy hand over the book with the money in it, and Meat Eater passed over something compact and about the size of his hand. Then they just sat there, doing absolutely nothing but watching me.

I picked up the book I had been reading, and pretended to read; in reality I was thinking furiously, looking over my escape routes. I ate the remainder of my burrito, put the book down on the table, and slowly stood up. I walked to the food order counter, and in a very loud voice I asked for another burrito. I made a show of paying for it, loudly thanking the counter guy, and then I loudly asked where the toilet was located. Without waiting for an answer I loudly said, "Thank you!" and I walked to the right side of the counter, made a left turn, shoved open the "Employees Only" door on the left, walked through the doorway and through the cooking area and out the back door. Then I ran like bloody Hell, and hid behind a brick wall that sheltered a convalescent center.

It was no more than five minutes when Meat Eater and Book Guy came out to look for me, but the wait seemed like hours. They got into a car and headed east. When they were out of sight, I ran to my pickup, got in, turned the ignition key with a trembling hand, and headed west. I suppose eventually someone found the book I was reading and took it home, or threw it away.

Later that night I telephoned my brother and told him, "Hey! Today in El Centro someone tried to give me over a thousand dollars!"

"What did you have to do to get it?" he asked.

"Pretend I was someone else," I said.

"Shit, man, you have to join the Actor's Union for that. Did you take the job?"

I told him, "Nobody would ever believe me being me, let alone me being someone else," and let him stew in that Zen-like conundrum when I hung up.

As inelegant as my exit from the burrito joint in El Centro was (running for my life like a coward pissing in his pants), my act of fleeing a restaurant in Grand Junction, Colorado, was ignoble. It was fear of the police that prompted my hasty retreat from the field of battle.

My opponent was a very short cowboy who took offense, for some reason, at my answering the simple question he had asked of me.

It was August (again), in the year 1989. I was on my way to the Denver area to attend Dragonfest: my first year to do so. I had never been on the highways from the San Diego area up to Denver, and it was all brand new to me: the Virgin River Gorge; Beaver, Utah; Green River, Utah; the Fremont Indian museum and camp site; Highway 70 which spans most of the country from east to west.

It was extremely hot when I drove through Grand Junction. It was in fact so hot that I decided to stop at the town and spend the afternoon in some place cool and wait for the sun to set before I continued eastward. I made the right turn at the off-ramp, made a death-defying left turn across the highway, and looked around for some place to eat. After driving around in a circle for many minutes I saw a restaurant that doubled as a bar on the left side and a whore house on the right side: the food was in the center, more or less--- the place appeared to cater to every hunger, so I stopped and went in.

It was cool inside, and the food was served a few feet from the bar itself so that the bartender could be yelled at for more drinks if needed. I was greeted by a woman after I spent a few seconds inside the door, and I told her I would like some lunch. She showed me to a table against the wall and to the left of the dining area. She handed to me a menu and asked what I would like to drink.

It is extremely rare for me to drink alcohol: I dislike the taste, but I had heard about how cool and refreshing Margarettas are so I asked for one. She gave me a “measuring look,” so I fished out a $20 bill from my wallet and put it on the table. (People constantly mistake me for being a homeless street person, so I always pay up front.) The menu included an item called “Six Enchiladas Pick Your Meat,” and in the fine print I saw that one could skip “Your Meat” and just ask for cheese enchiladas. When the Margaretta arrived, I asked for the six cheese enchiladas, and a second Margaretta. Again she gave me the “measuring look,” so I fished out a second $20 bill and placed it on the table with the first.

The food came, the second drink came, the sun outside tried to murder tourists, and inside the cool restaurant life was good. I quickly ate the enchiladas, drank the Margaretta, and made eye contact with the waitress. She came over and I asked for another Margaretta, another plate of six cheese enchiladas, and then I asked her when the "live music" (a sign was at the door) would start. She said the night's band would show up around 9:00 PM, which was still about seven hours away. It seemed like a very long time for me to stay there and wait, but I considered it. After she asked me, "Do you really want another plate of enchiladas?" and I assured her I did, she wandered off to fetch them and another Margaretta. The third Margaretta arrived first, and I drank it before the second plate of enchiladas arrived. I asked for a forth Margaretta.

I had made good progress on the second plate of food, feeling rather dizzy and not able to wield my fork precisely due to the booze, when the door opened and an angel stepped into the room. Well, perhaps angels don't wear skin tight jeans tucked into cowgirl boots; angels maybe don't wear tight pink tee-shirts over a healthy, plump, ample, bra-less set of boobs; perhaps they don't have awe-inspiring, fertile, full hips packed inside blue denim; I suppose angels don't have embroidered butterflies on each side of their crotch zippers, that seemed to flap their wings amorously when she walked. This woman.... and by gods, what a woman!... was all these things, and more. I barely noticed the cowboy that walked in behind her. The light of her blinding sexiness was like a stab through my drunken, tequila-soaked heart. Wow! I kept my eyes on the butterflies, while shoveling cheesy goodness into my drooling mouth.

Her hair seemed to be made out of spun honey, cut short all around her head except for a tuft, like a duck's tail, over her eyes. When she reached the bar and turned right a bit, I could see the left half of a large butterfly embroidered on the seat of her pants. My heart fluttered.

Madam Butterfly sat at the bar, and her cowboy friend sat next to her. I noticed he was diminutive, and he had to slump forward on his barstool so his boots could rest on the boot rail. She giggled at something the bartender was saying to her, while she squirmed on the barstool to get comfortable. The top part of the right butterfly wing on her ass joined its left partner in a very appealing dance, and I was mesmerized. I stared, and I didn't know

I was doing so: the blood had left my brain and headed south, leaving only tequila up there. I imagined how happy and joyful the two zipper butterflies were flying around her labia, major and minor. I imagined big grins on their faces. I suspected there was a big grin on my face too, but the tequila had numbed everything from the neck upward.

Abruptly my vision of Madam Butterfly was interrupted by something that interposed itself between her and my optic nerves; my eyes struggled to refocus, but it was quite a tussle due to the alcohol interfering with my ciliary muscles. Fortunately my ears were still working, and I heard the visual obstruction speak:

"What the ***HELL*** are you staring at!" it asked me, more like an accusation than a query. Ever so slowly, my eyes focused from fifteen feet away to twelve, then to nine, then to seven, then to five. By golly, it was the half-sized cowboy blocking my gaze, and he appeared very irate. He was probably about my age (thirty years), but he looked older. Hard years and harsh sunlight had creased his face, and deep lines from the corners of his eyes stretched ear-ward from wind and rough labor. He was skinny, and looked made of weathered iron.

I was not sure what the question was, so I sought clarification.

"What?"

"I said, 'What the ***fuck*** are you staring at!'" he said. I was certain that wasn't what he had said, but I am always polite to people so I did not contradict him. Being polite also meant being honest, so I started to tell him, in graphic detail, what I was staring at, only he didn't let me finish. When I was in the middle of my second sentence he gave out a high pitched squeal of rage and he launched himself at me, hands extended, over the dining table.

His two hands latched onto my throat, as he leaned against the edge of the table to get a better grip. I was shocked at his behavior, but I was also confused. I was not used to having strangers attack and batter me, especially when I was going out of my way to answer their question, and for a few seconds I could not fully comprehend someone was harming me with serious, even fatal intent. When it finally occurred to me that I was being assaulted, I did what any rational, food-oriented American will do: I grabbed my dinner plate with my left hand so that it wouldn't get knocked off the table and on to the floor. Then I struggled to my feet.

Somewhere near the bar a woman was yelling, "Craig! Stop it Craig! Stop it! Stop it, Craig!"

In getting to my feet, I had also pulled Half-poke off his feet and he fell stomach and face on to the table, which jerked my upper body downward. I felt the dinner plate, with at least three enchiladas still waiting for consumption, tilt and slip between my fingers, so I grabbed it tighter. (Saving lunch was my alcohol-speaking priority.) With great effort I straightened my back and took half a step backwards, and the hands mercifully released my throat. It was a huge relief.

The relief was short lived, though. Half-poke flung himself off the table, shoved the table aside, did an amazing feat of levitation, and latched onto my throat again with both hands, still apparently upset. Regretfully, my plate of food crashed to the floor. Suddenly I realized I was in a "fight," and that I had one hand free and empty. I took my left hand and slapped it ineffectually against his right arm, trying to knock his hand from my throat. After a few slaps I realized that I could not breathe; I also realized my right hand was not empty: it still held my dinner fork, ready for either finishing my cheese enchiladas, or for sticking into Half-poke's upper left arm.

Surprising both of us, I used the fork on his arm, and not gently. It was like sticking a fork in a baked potato to see if it was done. He yelped, and both hands flew from my throat as he jerked his body away from me. He clutched his left arm with his right hand, bellowing in pain and rage. He took a few backward steps, suddenly peaceful and apparently no longer wanting (or willing) to strangle me. It appeared this baked potato was done.

I was horrified. I had never forked anyone before (or since); I explained that it was my first forking and as I rule I do not fork people. In fact I had never hit anyone before, or kicked anyone before, or even yelled at anyone in anger before. It was shocking to see how effective violence is in solving problems. It briefly made me wonder what other problems in life I could have solved with violence.

Then guilt took over and I started to apologize to everyone. I wanted to explain that I had not meant to fork anyone, and that I was a good person, but I didn't want to spend the time: fear of the police replaced the guilt, and I made my way drunkenly to the door.

The outside heat was like a mighty blow to my face, and the

glare was blinding. My throat was in agony, and my shoulders were stiff from the unfamiliar weight of lifting a human being off a table by my neck. I started to shake from fear and dread, terrified Half-poke would come outside and beat the bloody shit out of me. Even worse was the fear that someone was calling the pigs as I stood at the restaurant's door, blinking at the brutal blazing sunlight. With a whimper of wide-eyed terror, I stumbled to my vehicle, dropped my dinner fork and fumbled the key into the door lock and yanked the door open. In an alcohol-befuddled haze I fell onto the driver's seat, smacking my forehead against the gear shifter. Pain lanced through my head, and my neck felt like I had been decapitated.

I crawled out of the vehicle on my knees, got to my feet, and climbed into the driver's seat. Hand shaking with fear, I got the key into the ignition after several stuttering attempts and fired up the engine. Letting my ears guide me to the highway, I raced at high speed across the highway, down the "frontage road" that parallels the highway, and took a right turn into the city's trash dump. Amid a sea of trash, with broken glass glittering in the sunlight, I found a place to park behind a pile of dirt and between bed mattresses and broken chairs. I climbed out of my car, crawled under it for the shade, and rubbed my aching throat with both hands, whimpering.

The sun seemed to take a week to climb down from the sky, and as the evening cooled I slept, my hands covering my throat protectively, laying on trash and shards of glass, until morning.

THE DEPARTMENT OF POWER AND WATER

"You smell good, too," said Patch

"It's called a shower." I was staring straight ahead. When he didn't answer, I turned sideways. "Soap. Shampoo. Hot water. Naked. I know the drill." -- Becca Fitzpatrick

Now I was living in a cave on the border of Death Valley, with my brother driving us up the mountain in the dark, blinded with the complete lack of anything resembling night vision. The Fiesta encountered boulders along the way, and deep trenches, and it made terrible noises as my brother mercilessly compelled it to climb up the brutal, rocky dirt road. The contents of the car scattered liberally and vigorously inside, with paper bags ripping and fluids gurgling. A few times the immovable objects the car encountered in the inky blackness would halt our progress completely, and the car would be flung backwards a few feet: my brother would then randomly pick either right or left, swing the steering wheel that way, and attempt to proceed again. It was harrowing. Carrowing.

With a mighty, puissant thump from out of the gloomy night, the car came to a sudden stop, the headlights went out, and the dashboard lights went dark. The inky night engulfed us. It was as lacking in light as being in a coal mine deep within the Mariana Trench while blind folded at midnight during a total solar eclipse after the Solar System had been swallowed by a black hole.

"I guess we have arrived," my brother said.

"Can you see anything?"

"'See?' What is 'see?'"

"There's this thing most eye balls do when photons have their promiscuous way with them," I explained. "It allows humans to navigate automobiles."

We sat in the dark, thinking. Presently I heard noises coming from a few inches in front of me, as if a glove box had been opened and a human hand was fumbling around inside. The noise stopped, and a few seconds later a flame flared up in front of my brother's face. He waved the burning kitchen match down near his feet, found the hood release, and pulled the lever. The flame went out and we were once again plunged into total blackness. I blinked my eyes, half believing I only imagined the brief light. My brother struck another match.

"You stay here, I'll go fix the problem."

"Don't we have, like, a token black man to send out into the monster-infested night?" The match went out; the complete darkness was like a blow to the face.

Ignoring me, my brother opened the driver's side door and I heard him climb out of the Fiesta.

"I'll be right back!" he said, like in all of the teen splatter movies. After a few seconds of grunting and cursing, the sound of the car's hood being raised came to me from out of the sinister night. A thought then occurred to me.

"Smell for leaking gasoline before you light another match!" I yelled, a second before a bright flare showed under the hood. The light moved to my left, illuminating my brother's face, which said, "What?"

"Never mind," I said. My brother's face, floating disembodied in the otherwise impenetrable ink, returned to what ever it was doing under the hood. Kitchen matches were struck, burned, and went out, to be followed by more matches. Grunts and pounding and curses filled the night, and now and then the car would rock gently as The Struggle Under The Hood was fought.

Just as I was contemplating going outside to help, once again just like in all of the teen splatter movies but without torrid sex first, the car's headlights went on and the interior dashboard lights went on. The car's hood slammed, and I watched my brother climb off of the boulder he had slammed the car in to. He climbed into the car.

"We stopped here, but the battery kept going another nine inches," he explained. "Start, youfuckingmudderfucker!" he said while turning the ignition key. The headlights dimmed, the engine started, and the boulder in front of us was once again lit up.

"How the fuck did you not see that?!" I was mystified.

"Why didn't you fucking tell me it was there?!"

"I didn't fucking see it!"

"But it's right fucking there! A blind man could fucking see it!" he replied, even though he was the one who had been driving the vehicle. He put the car in reverse, released the clutch, and pressed down on the gas pedal six inches. The car shuddered but stayed up against the boulder.

"Get out and push," my brother said. Just like in all of the teen splatter movies. I got out, stood next to the boulder, wedged my right hip against the car's front end, and shoved. With one rear wheel spewing dirt and sand towards us, the Fiesta slowly worked its way backwards a few feet, and on to firmer ground.

Inexplicably, the car kept going backwards down the mountain, leaving me in the darkness. As I watched the Fiesta recede, the headlights seemed to be swallowed up as if the blackness was a living, voracious thing, consuming light. The distant headlights seemed to pause, then grew brighter as the car came towards me.

The car passed me, though I stood in its way while yelling and waiving my hands. Tail lights slowly crawled up the mountain, while I contemplated the risks involved of running after it in the terrible dark. The tail lights stopped, and I trotted over what I hoped was the road and up to it. I opened the door and got in.

"Oh, there you are," my brother said.

"You didn't see me?!"

"I can't fucking see fucking shit!" my brother yelled back, before putting the car in gear again and continued driving westward up the mountain.

The tortured vehicle crawled past Old Mormon Spring and the dying cottonwood trees there, and dragged its abused ***car***-cass up the hill a few hundred more yards and came to rest close to where my vehicle was hiding. The lights and engine were shut off, and a peaceful, dark silence descended upon the mountain. I was weary of my day in town, and ready for sleep. I stumbled out of the passenger side of the car, and lay of the rough rocky ground, finding a "soft rock" to use as a pillow instead of hunting for my backpack somewhere within the wreckage of the Fiesta's interior.

"Let's go for a hike," my brother said somewhere deep inside the dark, lightless void to my left.

"Bed time," I said. There was silence for another minute, then:

"A hike would be fun."

"A hike, when neither of us can see our hands in front of our faces...." I was trying to use reason and logic. The silence lasted long enough for me to get relaxed again.

"You can stay here. I'm going to go find your cave."

I sat up, and stared in the direction of his voice.

"You don't even know the direction it's in!"

"It's over that way," he said. I assume he gestured with an arm or finger, but not even Rambo with night vision goggles could have seen the movement.

"No it's not," I said, having no idea if he was right or not. "This is fucking stupid. We can hike to the cave tomorrow." I settled my rock under my head to a harder part of my skull and tried to sleep.

"I have to leave early tomorrow morning: it's a work day for me," he said. I sat up again.

"But you have to see my cave!" I yelled with dismay. He explained the economics of the situation: no work meant no job, and no job meant no pay, and no pay meant he would not have the time nor the money to come and visit me again a month from now. Like I said: a Fucking Science Officer Spock. We agreed that when he found the time he would came back and visit my cave. I laid back down and found my rock pillow.

In the morning, as the sun was turning the eastern horizon silver, we unloaded my groceries and other supplies from my brother's Fiesta, dumping everything on the ground, and I waved my arms at him as he drove away. The mount of food and gear was heaped around my feet in a wide, knee-high pile. As the sun stepped over the Providence Mountain Range, my brother drove away as I sorted what supplies to store in my vehicle and what to immediately pack to my cave for the first trip of several.

First trip included cheddar cheese and butter, which I knew would not last long even stored in the cave. Also bread, six chicken eggs, plastic shower curtain, buckets, plastic tubing, and wire spool. The bag of Russet potatoes went in my back pack; the other supplies went into the two buckets, and with a bucket in each hand I headed to my cave.

At the spring I left the shower curtain, flexible tubing, and buckets. Food I took to my cave and wrapped tightly within my blankets. I then wrapped the blankets with my plastic sheet. I then raced back to where my supplies were sitting baking in the hot sun more than two miles away, and packed what I thought I could carry: the remainder I put in my vehicle. I had learned my lesson about making too many trips in one day when the sun was doing its best to kill me (which it did with cheerful malice 14 hours a day).

Back at my spring, I dug out my sand pit at the spring again (the new silt getting less each time I did so), and I placed one of the one-gallon buckets in the water that was seeping upward, in the center of the sand pit, open-end facing up. The bucket started to float, so I found a rock, wiped the dirt off of it, and placed it inside the bucket. The bucket stayed firmly on the sand, standing in about three inches of water. I took the flexible tubing and stuck one end in the bucket, laying it on the bottom and holding it there with the rock.

Carefully I covered the pit with the shower curtain, avoiding knocking sand into the hole or into the bucket. With my belt knife I cut the shower curtain in half and secured it over the pit with rocks on each corner. Using my hands, I scooped sand on top of the edges of the clear plastic, making a circle, around the edge of the pit. Then I placed a small rock in the center of the plastic, above the bucket inside the pit.

It did not take long for the sun to start evaporating the water from the wet sand; the clear plastic shower curtain was getting cloudy from water vapor, and when I tapped the plastic sheet water dribbled into the bucket. Success!

I carefully laid the flexible tubing on the ground, eastward, and I placed a rock where the end of the tube lay. I then went back to my cave for my Army shovel and returned to my new solar water distiller with it.

I used the shovel to dig a hole in the sand large enough and deep enough to put the other bucket into, at the end of the flexible tubing. This bucket I would siphon water into by sucking on the tubing and drawing fresh water out of my still and, since eastward was down hill, it would empty the still without my needing to disturb it.

Then when all of this was done, I stood at the still and waited. It looked like it was working great, but the plastic was so wet inside that I couldn't see how well. I thumped the plastic sheet with a finger, and water streamed off the underside of the plastic and into the bucket, but I could not tell how full the bucket was getting. The urge to fiddle with it, play with it, modify it, improve it was overpowering--- it was like a new toy that was agony to force myself to leave alone. I walked away to let it do its thing.

Nearly tripping over a green iguana that had been hanging around the seep, I headed back to my rent-free residence to the west.

At the cave I rewired my little 10 watt light bulb, moving it back against the far wall. There was no simple way of hanging the wires on the ceiling, so I ran the wire along the left wall (facing inward). My plan was to fetch my new reclining / folding chair the next day, and some books, and give the little light a test to see if I could read by it that night (quickly, before the insects flooded the cave).

The rest of that day, according to my journal, I spent eating potatoes fried in butter until crispy brown, smothered in cheddar cheese, spooned between slices of toasted and buttered bread, with a fried egg in each.

At the end of the day, as the sun was setting, I went to check my solar still. I knelt at the siphon tube, sucked mightily upon the end until I tasted water, and then stuck the end of the tube into the open bucket. Water gushed into the bucket, and just kept coming, and coming, and coming. It was amazing how much water had distilled in about seven hours. The amount of fresh water was larger than I had hoped for. I poured the clean water into my bottles, then carefully moved the flexible hose to the still and laid it on the ground so that I would not step on it when visiting my toilet area.

It had been a great day: I had water and power!

IT'S ALL FUN AND GAMES UNTIL SOMEONE LOSES A BRAIN

***"As amused as I may be, I must inquire upon the particular context of this particular irony as I find myself slightly befuddled."* -- Julian Zahreal**

Over the next week I made several trips to my car to get the supplies hidden there: my new chair was the best investment, and made life at the cave vastly more comfortable. Sitting on ammunition cans had been getting tedious. During the heat of the day I fled the sun by hiding from it inside my cave, reading while reclining with my feet up. The foot rest, like the rest of the chair, was made from thin aluminum pipe, and it did not hold up well to my bare feet: I had to place a pillow on the bar to keep it from gouging into my ankles.

The 10 watt light bulb cast just enough light to read by if I draped it over my shoulder, near my ear, where the light fell on my book but not directly into my eye. It took a few seconds for insects to detect the light at night and come flooding into the cave, so I resisted the urge to use the light unless necessary.

The morning routine saw me climbing the steep hill to the north, with my radio in my hand, to listen to the morning news out of Laughlin, Nevada, about 80 miles to the east. There were radio station broadcasting antennas closer such as at Mountain Pass, but reception was not as strong. The news never failed to astonish me: not what the news was, but what was considered to be news---such as the presidential election that had happened a few months ago. What did it matter which homicidal schizophrenic lunatic owned us for the next four or eight years? I find it refreshing to see all pretense of democracy abandoned.

After what passed for "the news" came the local weather forecast, which was only accurate at the random chance level. After the weather forecast, the previous day's body count for the number of dead on the local highways was given.

It seems to me that whoever selects the 90 seconds that make up the day's "news" does so with an eight-year-old child of below-average intelligence in her or his mind as the intended audience. They leave out all of the vitally important facts and information adults need to know about what is going on, and they only put in vacuous trite stories that teach stupid people whom to hate and fear. If you ever need to know who in the USA has no political power at all, just pay attention to who the media tell us to fear.

The solar still was producing enough fresh water every day that I had more than I could store. I was drinking about one gallon of water a day, and when I moved around exploring the area I consumed at least two gallons a day. The day's temperatures hovered around 105 degrees, which slowed my hiking speed down to about two miles per hour. When temperatures were around 110 degrees I could manage one mile per hour. The few times it reached 115 degrees, I stopped where I happened to be and endured the sun as best as I could, moving as little as possible.

The terrain in which I was living and hiking is hard to describe: it has to be seen to comprehend just how hot, dry, rough, and hostile it is in the summer months. The rhyolite batholith that bordered the south edge of the arroyo I lived in, and within which the cave was carved, looked like it had been bombed from high altitude: the faint flow lines of the volcanic material was broken into razor sharp points, like medieval weaponry, which stuck out in all directions. Rhyolitic tuff lay in heaps throughout the area, through which water, wind, and moving sand had cut gullies.

Craters in the volcanic rock spanned several dozen feet, perhaps made by "lava bombs" ejected from a caldera that has now weathered away. Most of those craters were then filled in with dirt and sand, leaving vaguely round, concave impressions in the ground. Other craters had less dirt in them, and the edges that made up their sides stood out sharply in the sunlight, casting shadows from their southern edges which moved west to east as the day progressed.

Where the ground was rocks and lava, lichen and desert varnish were the chief life forms visible to my eyes. Each rock, if placed under a magnifying glass or microscope, would show a vast and complex ecosystem as dozens of species worked with and against each other to earn a living. Microorganisms that lived in the thin clay layer of the desert varnish converted the magnesium and iron into food for little beasties higher up the food chain, turning the harder rocks brown. The lichen would then move on to spots in the rock where the iron and magnesium had been completely oxidized, and set up shop over the dead bodies. It must have been a brutal, harsh life down there, living very slowly and without liquid water.

I have included desert varnish here as a "life form" because it acts like one, even though it includes organic and inorganic elements. It can be said to "eat" and it also "reproduces." Strictly speaking, it isn't itself a form of life.

In the sandy and dirt-covered areas, the dominant species is the creosote bush, then rabbit brush, then salt brush, then various forms of cactus. Each were living quiet, separate lives, spaced well apart from each other. Each receives just enough rain in the spring to last them the rest of the year; if drought conditions persists, they drop seeds and then die--- the only way they can propagate themselves (by proxy) into the future when the rain would come again.

Throughout the desolate landscape, overwhelming all life, is the gray and glaring dirt that amplified the heat and threw it back into space. People are fools to enter the desert without hats, but they also need to cover their lower faces, chins, and necks when entering the vast white brilliance: while ultraviolet light burns skin faster, the low wavelength infrared radiation coming off the ground also damages skin. It is not a casual thing to venture into the deserts of the American Southwest at any time, let alone the height of summer.

The sky is usually a pale blue, with no clouds anywhere. At times a lone white cloud will drift eastward, way off in the distance. Rarer still are the dark clouds that carry the promise of rain; even rarer is that promise fulfilled.

The rain, if it comes at all, comes mostly in April. In some years rain will fall in August, but it usually evaporates before it reaches the ground.

There was a year when the April rain brought flooding to the Avawatz Mountain Range, and a great wall of water swept down Sheep Creek. I had been spending a few days in the cabin at the spring there, enduring the mice that would jump on me at night in the dark (yes, I screamed like a real man every time it happened), listening to the rain hammer the tin roof. It was a good feeling knowing I did not have to sleep in the rain, and that the pile of fire wood I had brought would last the night. I was laying in the best of the three beds when I heard a monstrous roar approaching the cabin from the south. The cabin was located hard up against the north side of a rock cliff, so I was not greatly worried about being washed down the mountain. The roar became deafening, with mighty crashes and thumps as boulders were washed northward.

In the morning I looked out over the creek bed and saw the trunks of salt cedar trees broken and scattered where the day before there had been only sand and rocks. “New” boulders had replaced others. The old creek bed had been filled in, and a new water course cut into the sand and rock. It was as if a giant bulldozer had careened drunkenly from one side of the valley floor to the other on its way northward, shoving a mountain of debris in its way.

The days crawled by, and piled up into weeks, and then two months passed. My days were spent laying on my back 22 hours a day, reading; sleeping; making trips outside the cave only to drink the warm water from my solar still; use my toilet area; and listen to the news. I ate very little. I moved very little, abandoning my planned hikes because the summer heat had turned fatal and I could not carry enough water on my back to go any distance. I found my mind ceased to engage in thinking any more than what was essential to do these simple tasks: I barely thought at all, and when I had a problem that needed addressing I found my thoughts muddled, confused, and lethargic. I stewed in stupidity, like an automation, where my mind was absent while my body took care of the daily chores such as preparing coffee in the morning, cleaning the solar still now and then, washing the grit and grime off my face. I had no mental stimulation, and even the books I read did not stay in my mind longer than a few hours after I had read them.

The writer and journalist Douglas Preston rode across the American Southwest with his friend, artist Walter Nelson, on horseback and followed the most likely route the invasion force lead by Coronado took. In his book ***Cities of Gold*** Doug mentioned that he found his mind shutting down, little by little each day, as his body endured the tedious and torturous travel over a terrain that can, and has, killed even the strongest and hardiest of men and women. Without social interfacing with others of his species except Walter (whom he found unbearable and unendurable at times), and without mental stimulation to keep his mind active, his brain shut down to the essentials of horse, saddle, reins, thirst, sun, wind, and trail. The miles passed slowly, stretching far ahead in the distance, as they made their way at a pace at times slower than one mile per hour. He did not use the word, but he described the dehumanizing effect of survival in the dry wasteland being reduced down to the very basics.

I spent two months in the same reduced, dehumanized state. My leg muscles grew weak, as I barely walked. My arm muscles did no work harder than lifting a pot of hot water every morning. I had been crossing off each day on my wall calendar, but many days would pass and I would forget, and I lost tract of the passing of the days. This sluggish dimwitted lassitude persisted for over 60 days.

It was within this stupor that I awoke one morning craving canned peaches. I had a stack of them in the cave, but the effort involved in using my P-38 can opener to get at the peaches was far more than I wanted to perform. This morning that effort felt worth it. I sat up on the plastic sheet, brushed the night's vermin off me and the surrounding area, and struggled on my knees to a can of peaches. The P-38 rested on an ammo can, and I picked it up, set the can of peaches on my left thigh, and started to work with the can opener around the lip of the can. It was a slow, laborious process, but eventually the lid was punctured enough for me to pry upward with my left hand.

In grabbing the jagged razor sharp edge of the lid, I sliced open the palm of my left hand so deeply it felt like I had chopped the hand off just below the four fingers. A thick stream of blood poured out, and I lifted the hand to watch as the bright red fluid dripped on to my lap. With my right thumb and index finger I pinched hard against the gash, trying to close the wound, thinking maybe I could plug the wound with a rag and bind my closed fist with tape. When I removed the pinch, the wound opened like a yawning mouth and gushed blood, and I knew a bandage would not be enough.

I did, however, have the sewing kit that I had purchased at the Army surplus store. Included in that kit was a bow-shaped needle designed for sewing together tight surfaces such as skin. Could I sew together the wound of my own hand? I would have to go deep into the meat, not just the skin, since the skin would not be strong enough to hold the thread.

Liberally splattering blood, I fished out the sewing kit,

unwound the green thread from the little cardboard tube, and shook out the needles that were stored inside the cardboard tube. Spewing blood, I held the bow needle in my left hand as I threaded it with my right hand.

Taking the needle in my right hand, I set it on the right edge of the wound, at the top, held my breath, and pushed the needle inward and to the left. The agony was worse than I had expected, and I yanked the needle out. Sweat was streaming off my face as I pinched the wound shut again, pressing my left hand hard against my left thigh, trying to “soak up” the pain. When the pain decreased a bit, I picked up the needle again, found the same hole, and quickly shoved all the way under the wound and upward on the other side. I pulled the needle through, jerked the needle off the end of the thread, and tied a crude knot using my right hand and two fingers from my left hand.

My hand felt like it was being incinerated. It looked like a horse had stepped on it: puffed up, swollen, purple under the little finger and its two neighbors, with dark purple climbing towards the wrist. I assumed the color change was a bad sign, but I had no idea. The flow of blood had decreased, yet I needed at least one more crude suture.

Sweat, tears, and snot streamed down my face. I was only dimly aware that I was crying. I had dropped the needle somewhere on the plastic sheet, and it took several minutes to find--- and every second I was losing blood. I found the needle, wiped it on my shirt to “clean,” and got more green thread off its spool. My left hand hurt too much to hold the needle, so I stuck the needle in my shirt and used my right hand to pass the thread through its eye. Then, once again, I placed the point to the right edge of the wound, held my breath, and shoved the needle down, across, and upward. I then pulled the needle through, pulled the thread out of the needle, and tied a tight knot.

I used my belt knife to cut off a piece of my shirt. I put the cloth in my palm and then made a fist. I then bound my fist with black plastic electrician’s tape. Placing my left arm on my lap, I pressed down on it with my right arm and rocked back and forth on the cave floor for hours, crying and whimpering, consumed with pain. I fell asleep sitting hunched over my arms, waking often, feeling very sorry for myself, and then sleeping again.

In the morning my entire arm was on fire. I "walked" on my knees to my back pack and fished out the bottle of Ibuprofen, and I consumed two grams. I then laid down on my plastic sheet, squashing blood, peaches, and peach juice under me, and stared at the ceiling as the drug turned the inside of my stomach into a roiling churning hell. I laid my left arm across my body, fist down at my knee, and I waited to die. Death would be a huge relief.

And then I got angry. I wanted some peaches: was that too much to ask for? I sat up, fumbled for another can of peaches, and wedged it between my knees. The P-38 is not easy to wield with one hand, but I carefully worked the perforator around the can's lip and then set the opener back on an ammo can. Then, instead of using a hand to pry up the lid, I used a fork--- proving I may be slow to learn, but I get there eventually.

Since the peaches cost me so much in blood, sweat, and pain, I probably only imagined enjoying them as much as I did. I ate the peaches, then added water to the "juice" (a vile, sickly sweet sludge), and drank it. I felt better emotionally, but my stomach was rebelling. When had I last eaten anything of nutritional value? I had been drinking coffee in the morning, some times followed by a few spoonfuls of re-hydrated dehydrated refried beans, at other times only by some raisins.

I got to my feet, swaying a bit from weakness, and I rummaged around in my food supplies. I found a box of "macaroni and cheese," which has powdered cheddar cheese in it, and noticed that someone had chewed a hole in a corner. No doubt some of the macaroni had been carried away by a rat, but the cheese pouch was intact. I set water to boil, and added some powdered milk to a jar of water and gave it a vigorous shake. The powdered milk was "fat free" and tasted like shit, but the alternative was canned milk in containers that have twice as much as I ever have need for at one time.

"Macaroni and cheese" on the whole is a vile food, with no nutrition to speak of, but it was a source of fat and mighty good with salt. After stuffing the whole pot of bright fluorescent orange "food" down my neck, I mixed a batch of pancake batter and started that frying on the stove, using corn oil. I fetched another can of peaches, opened it without decapitating myself, and when the pancakes were done I put sliced peaches on top of the cakes and ate everything. Once again I added water to the "juice" and drank it. I found out just how much I depended upon my left hand when doing these chores with just the right hand.

Since I was feeling so good (yet also in screaming agony due to my hand injury) I figured a visit to the solar still, to collect water, and my toilet area, to deposit uric acid, was a good idea. I collected my empty water bottles and started eastward, first to the spring, then to the toilet area, then to the rock wall that marked the end of the arroyo. My left arm throbbed painfully, and I was afraid to look at my hand. I came to the rock wall, and I looked for a way to climb to the top.

As I looked over the area, it appeared to me that the rock wall was actually a mostly buried fault line that ran generally north to south. I walked up the left (northward) fork of the arroyo, which was at a slight incline, and gained about ten feet in elevation. I found a way to the top of the wall and climbed an additional 30 feet or so, though when I reached there I was utterly exhausted.

My joints ached in my pelvis and knees. My entire body ached. I was out of breath and panting in the heat. I had not noticed just how badly out of shape my body was from two months of almost no activity: my muscles were atrophied so badly that when I reached the top of the wall I had to sit down, or I would fall down.

Looking eastward, most of Valjean Valley stretched out in front of me. Part of the northern end of the valley was blocked by the mountain range I was sitting on. Far to the south, hidden behind the Salt Hills, was the town of Baker. The Kingston Mountain Range stretched left to right, blocking my view of the distance Provenance Mountain Range (in fact Earth's curvature was enough to do that). I thought it would be a great place to bring my hand-powered radio receiver, binoculars, and a blanket and spend a few nights up there.

Looking south, it appeared that the rock formation I was sitting on might have been the westward fault edge that separated the Valjean Valley land mass from the Avawatz Mountains. That valley was sinking, on a time scale of centuries, while the rock wall I was sitting on and the mountain behind me was rising. Titanic forces were contending against each other under my ass, on a grand scale, but slowly. Still, the urge to scratch my ass of imaginary itches was overwhelming.

I climbed down the north end of the wall, went south a few minutes, and then westward up the arroyo I was living in. That arroyo climbs when going west, and I found the gradual incline to be difficult: after just a few steps I had to pause to rest. A distance that would normally take me about fifteen minutes took me almost one hour, and when I finally reached my solar still I fell on my knees in the sand and sucked up all of the water produced that day.

That evening, before the light of the day fled, I removed the black tape from my left hand and pried open the fingers to look at my palm. Golly, it was frightening: if I saw the wound on anyone else I would have shot the person as an act of mercy. The piece of shirt was stuck hard against the bloody wound, and I had to soak my hand in warm water to get it off. I gently pulled the bloody cloth away from the wound, and saw that the bleeding had almost completely stopped. The entire hand was swollen, purple, and alien-looking. The crude sutures were holding, but the flesh was bloated and putting a strain on the thread.

I cut another piece of cloth off of my shirt, pressed it against the wound, and ran a piece of black tape across my palm. I added a second strip running between the little finger and its neighbor, over to the base of the thumb, and then up the back side to the little finger. Then I made a fist, and bound the fist together. For dinner I consumed another two grams of Ibuprofen--- a mere 1,800 milligrams more than recommended.

For the next few days I ate all my stomach could hold, and I exercised throughout the nights by walking in a circle around the spring area, changing clockwise to counterclockwise after a few dozen circuits. It was not safe to walk the northern edge of the spring in the dim moonlight, since a ledge of rock ran the length close to the brush and trees that thrived in the wet sand, but stepping up and down the ledge was good for my legs. As I walked, I swung my arms around a bit, flexing my hands up to my shoulders to work the muscles. The pain in my left arm eventually receded until it stayed in my hand and wrist.

I felt ashamed at myself for growing so weak that I could not walk far if an emergency had occurred. Cutting my hand was bad enough, but it would not have prevented me from walking the 2.2 miles to my car, nor prevent me from driving to the emergency medical team in Baker. My weak legs and arms, however, could have left me trapped in the cave since the walk to the car might have taken me an entire day--- longer than I could carry water enough to be safe.

Every night I checked my hand, and the swelling slowly decreased. I noticed that the wound was healing, but the line on my palm that looped from below the little finger to between the index and middle finger no longer lined up on each side of the cut. I wondered what that means in palmistry--- the fake "science" of reading one's fate in the lines of one's hands. Many years ago I read a few books by the confidence man "Cheiro" who had claimed to have defrauded kings, prime ministers, presidents, and theater actors. If I recalled correctly, my newly broken "Heart Line" meant I was now even more unlucky in love. Maybe I should have fixed my love life by rearranging the usual lines in my palm while it was still ripped open: I'll remember to do that next time.

Slowly my strength returned, and my nightly walks were replaced with morning hikes in the direction of my car. I was hoping to find an easier route to my hidden vehicle, but The Maze was so broken, complex, and twisted that any route that looked like a reasonable way through ended in cliffs too steep to climb, or wandered in the undesired direction. The task was hampered by my weak legs, and even short distances left me exhausted and out of breath.

From my explorations in trying to find an easier route, I discovered that, somehow, my first route was also not only the best, but the only way to come and go over the terrain that was reasonably safe and did not require a mighty effort to cross.

I had been at the cave for four months, plus a week: was it time for me to leave? I had spent the time span that I planned, and I was suffering physically and mentally. I was tired of being filthy. I was eating just enough to keep from starving to death, even though I had food at hand. I was weak from lack of exercise, and walking was painful. I was weary of sucking stale warm water from a tube and then spitting the bugs out. I wanted to go dancing, and bowling, and sailing, and hanging out at the Dana Point Harbor Liar's Club in the morning after fetching a box of doughnuts from the store on the top of the Headlands.

On the plus side, I was "free." I had clean air, no neighbors, no "drive by shootings," no enraged irate angry infantile assholes trying to run me off the highway as they went to and from their city-side slave plantations ("office buildings"). I was surrounded by a stark, barren, alien beauty that was indifferent to the fact that it was trying its best to kill me--- put that on the "plus side" list. Also on the plus list visits by: wild burros; Thompson Long-eared Bats; a green-colored Mojave Iguana that followed behind me as I checked the solar still; Merriam's Kangaroo Rats (hundreds, and hundreds); Gambel's Quails.

I would include the Tarantula in my list of frequent visitors, but this is a "plus side" list, and these freaky monsters always spooked the bloody shit out of me every time I saw one, slept with one, ate with one, defecated with one, or almost wore one when shaking out my pants. The woman at the Mojave Preserve visitor's center, under the "world's tallest thermometer," told me tarantulas are only harmful if I'm an insect, but she must have lied: I mean, just look at the horrifying things!

The question was: "Am I done here? If I meant to accomplish anything by living alone four months in the desert, have I done so?" I would have to ponder that question for a day or two.

FOOLS FLOOD IN TO SANDY VALLEY AND WASTE ITS WATER

***"I would rather sit on a pumpkin, and have it all to myself, than be crowded on a velvet cushion."* -- Henry David Thoreau**

As the sun was setting behind me, I walked eastward down the arroyo and to the "great rock wall" that marked the end of the arroyo. With me was my back pack (as always) and my human-powered radio receiver, binoculars, blanket, and drinking water. I walked past my solar still, walked past my green iguana friend, and eventually came to the rock wall and turned left (northward), up the side arroyo, and then climbed the steep slope to my right until I was on top of the wall.

The Kingston Mountain Range was aglow with a dull orange flame, as the setting sun cast light upon its west-facing surfaces. Deep black slashes marked where the hills were cut diagonally, creating narrow and steep canyons that tended to run from north at the top to south at the bottom. I sat down and made myself more or less comfortable, dropping my back pack by my side. I fished out my binoculars and looked through it to the east, working the sight southward until I picked out Turquoise Mountain that was poking up behind the lower Kingston ridge.

Kingston Wash slashed through the mountain range as if cut with a knife. There's good water at Coyote Hole Spring in there, next to an ancient corral, where the steady drop of water falls into a small concrete basin tucked deep inside willow brush. The only time I visited the spring was many years ago, approached on foot from the west. At the spring I found two assholes sitting on the hood of a Jeep with a shotgun, trying to blast the ravens who came for water out of the sky: I was liberal when I told them what ruffian scoundrels they were--- and they looked at me like I was the raving lunatic, not them.

Tucked away behind the Kingston Range, to the south a bit, is Shadow Valley and Shadow Mountain, though I could not pick out the peak from the haze and the decreasing light. There is a ruined cabin hidden in that valley, hard to get to and mostly unknown, where perhaps some day I will squat on and repair.

Closer to me, embedded in the valley like a superfluous nipple, the Silurian Hills showed as a pale gray bump, dwarfed by the Kingston Range. There is a dry well at Silurian Lake, walled by timbers, that is a popular nesting place for birds. At Silurian Hills there is a cabin that is laying in ruin, with trash scattered around. The sign at the cabin reads “Please youse don't abuse this cabin.”

Far to the south lay the Salt Hills, Salt Spring Hills, and the town of Baker, but they were blocked from my view by the southeastern edge of the Avawatz.

Looking northward a bit, loathsome Sandy Valley was hidden behind Kingston Peak, even though it should be hidden in Hell. My favorite stomping ground was over that way, up at Tecopa Pass, but in recent years the place has become a tourist attraction, and some days there are as many as two cars that visit the area. Twenty-five years ago I had spent more than a week up there and not seen another human being: in fact, I often pitched my tent on the road and was left unmolested by cars or people, though wild burros some times passed me. There is even talk by the Bureau of Land Destruction of putting picnic tables up there! (If and when that happens, I shall remove them. Fuck those people, in the eye, with a pointed stick.) The Hell of Sandy Valley is just an evil symptom of that growing popularity, as city people flood into the Mojave Desert looking for places to destroy, shit on, leave their trash, and shoot at defenseless animals and plants.

Around year 1983 I passed through Sandy Valley, after exploring the old Kingstone (not “Kingston”) town site, Leander “Cub” Lee’s homestead and his fresh water well, and the Snow White Mine. Sandy Valley was sparsely populated, with tar-paper shacks made of plywood burned from the sun, sheltered under rusty sheets of tin. In these shacks, poor elderly people managed to live, without electricity and without water. Nobody bothered them, and they bothered nobody: they just went about their business, living on land that might have cost them at most $100 for five acres.

Since year 1983, and my first pass through the valley, City People With Money have been steadily moving in. These people would not think themselves wealthy, but compared to the people living there the newcomers were fabulously wealthy. The CPWM’s bought land, drilled wells, demanded electricity service, installed sewage tanks, mandated CC&Rs (Covenants, Conditions, and Restrictions) to "improve the neighborhood" (that is, evict the poor people living there), planted water-hungry trees and water-gulping grass lawns. A few of the poor fled to Goodsprings; a few of the poor fled to Sloan (the very anus of the Mojave Desert); most just remained silent and endured the efforts of their new neighbors to destroy them and their way of life.

In year 1996 I passed through Sandy Valley again, and the change was shocking. I drove my pickup slowly down the dirt wash that had been recently designated "Mojave Street" looking at the new houses. Even though they may have been less than five years old, most of them looked like World War Two era military base housing: slumping, weather beaten, cracked stucco, broken swamp coolers hanging out of broken windows. I headed north up "Osage Street" and at the end I saw a crazy person working on what passed for his "front lawn."

Crazy Person was pushing a gasoline powered lawn mower over his dead, brown, dirt-covered Kentucky Bluegrass. I guess since the name of his street came from the American Indians in Kentucky, he thought his "lawn" should too. As he pretended to mow his "grass" (that is: dirt), a cloud of dust and sand and gravel engulfed him and followed him around as he worked. On the other side of his "lawn" he had a garden hose issuing a slow dribble of water out of a "sprinkler," perhaps being run by an electric water pump somewhere inside a well near or on the property.

I had to stop and stare at him. I just could not believe what I was seeing. A man, apparently human, and more likely than not gifted with a brain at birth, was trying to grow grass in a region that could only support cactus, creosote, salt brush, and rabbit brush. Two tiny, very dead, trees had been planted on the "lawn," their slim trunks split open from the dry wind, homicidal sun, and lack of water. The valley is full of sand--- therefore the name "Sandy Valley." To get grass to grow on the valley floor would take a massive amount of water, applied every night: the moisture passes through the sand so quickly that the grass has to suck as hard and fast as it can at the water while it rushes past them.

I stared at him, wondering if maybe he wasn't really human. He noticed me watching him, and he stared back. By golly, he looked mostly human, even though a stupid one. I continued driving, astonished and dismayed at the dozens of new houses that had "front lawns" also--- though most owners were not foolish enough to try growing grass and trees.

Up on my rock, with my binoculars, I looked more to the north and tried to pick out Ibex Pass. Perhaps I could only imagine seeing the pass, since the angle was too acute, but I thought I found it: a notch on the ridge-line, like a saddle. If a car were to head southward through the gap at night I would maybe be able to see its headlights with the binoculars. Over the pass lay Tecopa Hot Springs, and my once-favorite place to bathe: Hepatitis Spring.

HE PROBABLY WOULDN'T HAVE TOLD ME HE LOVES ME

"A commitment to sexual equality with men is a commitment to becoming the rich instead of the poor, the rapist instead of the raped, the murderer instead of the murdered." -- Andrea Dworkin

"Hepatitis Spring" is the name given to one bathing pool near Tecopa Hot Springs. The pool is walled in concrete, and a plastic tube delivers warm water from a sandy hill, gravity fed, into the tank. There is no shade, and the sparse grass at the site makes a living from evaporation when the warm water meets the cooling night sky and condenses. The cottonwood trees located about 120 feet from the bathing pool shows where the overflow water drains into a depression in the sandy Earth before it sinks too far to provide moisture enough for anything else to live. The pool is a rectangle, about seven feet wide and eleven feet long, and about four feet deep. It is, or I should write "was," maintained by volunteers: cleaned and disinfected and scrubbed with chlorine every seven or eight days.

The United States of America's Department of the Interior has been ordering people to cease bathing in the pool, citing "health care" reasons. I suspect the actual reason is venal: the Bureau of Land Destruction made plans for fencing in the larger two bathing pools in town and having a private company charge people five dollars each time they wanted a bath, turning a volunteer donation-run operation belonging to The People of The United States of America into a profit-making business: still owned by The People of The United States of America, but no longer free and with none of the profit going to the people who own the place.

And that is exactly what happened. Now only tourists can afford to bathe at the publicly owned bath house; the people who live there can no longer afford it, so they turned to visiting Hepatitis Spring (and other, more secret, springs in the area) and leaving their $5 each at home where it belongs.

The use of Hepatitis Spring grew in popularity when the once-free facility fenced poor people out. Throughout the day one or two people every two or three hours (more or less) would show up at

Hepatitis Spring to spend ten or fifteen minutes. Usually they came in pairs, took off all of their clothing, entered the pool, drank a beer or two, got out of the pool, dressed, and went on their way. Come sunset, the pool became more popular: pairs of people showed up perhaps every hour or so, spent half an hour, and gave friendly welcomes to other people that showed up if they did. It was not unknown for sex to happen there, in the water, under the light of the stars and moon.

When the pool was occupied, it was a courtesy for a person showing up to ask if she or he may enter the pool, or if she or he should come back later. Nobody had cause to bitch and gripe if the answer was "No: please come back later." In most cases that I know of (personally) the answer was almost always "Yes" when the person asked politely, in a friendly and gracious voice, and said she or he was willing to return later.

Hepatitis Spring had been my favorite place to get a quick bath, every two or three days, for several years. I would drive slowly past the house where the dirt road started, so that I would not send up a cloud of dust to smother anyone living there, and slowly drive to the pool. If someone was there I would wait for them to leave. I would then spend five or ten minutes scrubbing my filthy, flabby, stark white cheese-fed body in the warm water, some times also washing my shirt (never my pants, which would have turned the water dark brown), then be on my way to whatever desert mayhem I had planned for the day. My preferred bathing time was in the dark, around midnight.

I ceased going to Hepatitis Spring after I had my one and only bad experience there. It was well past midnight, and nobody else was there. I thought to stay for at least an hour, or leave earlier if someone else showed up. My clothing was draped on a horizontal stick that at times provided support for a wind break (that is, a "blowing sand break"), and I was singing loudly to the night as I merrily splashed in the water, taunting the nocturnal desert night beasties to come and get some water if they didn't mind the skill of the singer.

The cottonwood trees in the near distance lit up with the light of an approaching automobile, and when I looked left I saw a car approaching. It was a disappointing sight, since I had hoped to stay longer and I did not want to leave.

The car stopped at the cottonwood trees, next to my vehicle, and eventually a man came to the pool. He said “Howdy,” carefully and with deliberation set his bath towel down on the ground, and started to take his clothes off, without a polite question asking if I minded his company. I was dismayed. I crammed myself into a corner of the pool, and he got into the pool and into the opposite corner. Golly, he sure did look pleased and delighted to see me.

He was loud; he was obnoxious; he was without any sense of how to behave around people he didn’t know. Right away he started talking about sex. Or what for him passed for “sex:” whore-mongering in all of the countries he claimed to have visited. (That isn’t sex: that’s masturbating with a temporary business partner.) My attempts to change the subject of conversation were met with complete disregard, as if I had not spoken. Then he asked me about my sexual experiences.

The realization came slowly: I was bathing naked, in the dark, far from help, in a pool with a very rude Shit Chute Shagger; a Poop Pipe Pirate; Rodger Rectum Reamer, Rear Admiral of the Brown Fleet; Hershey Highway Henry; Captain Colon Ramjet The Third.

Women everywhere in the world experience this same “conversation,” in the same or similar circumstances, nearly every day. I was completely inexperienced with encountering the behavior. Shit, it wasn’t until I was around thirty years old that I learned homosexuals existed. In the past when a stranger (usually a much older man) seemed extra friendly, I just assumed he was lonely.

I said I had to leave. Placing my hands in front of my crotch, I stood up and walked to the steps and out of the water. He said he also had to leave, and he climbed out also. We had the pool between us, and I managed to get my pants and get dressed while he was still climbing out.

Then he bent over, picked up his bath towel, and revealed the jar of Vaseline he had hidden under it. “Oh my,” he said. “How did that get there?” he asked with a giggle. He turned and gave me a big smile.

I grabbed my boots, leaving the socks and shirt behind, and sprinted barefoot to my car. I retrieved my Old Timer Deer Slayer belt knife from the passenger seat of my pickup, drew its razor sharp blade from its leather scabbard, and then turned to look to see if I had been followed--- I was not. I fired up my vehicle, barefoot, and drove out of there: I have never been back, these twenty-something years later. The beauty and attraction of the pool ended for me then and there.

Yeah, I realize I'm old-fashioned: I do not have sex with people I do not know, and certainly not when they are rude, overly-familiar, discourteous, crude, and/or male. What the bloody ***Hell*** could he have been thinking? Fuck him! No wait....

THE NIGHT OF THE LONG NIGHT

"I like too many things and get all confused and hung-up running from one falling star to another till I drop. This is the night, what it does to you. I had nothing to offer anybody except my own confusion." -- Jack Kerouac

Sitting on my rock wall, gazing over the scourged, blistered expanse of desert valley and the rough, bare mountain ranges with my binoculars, darkness descended upon me like a thick blanket. The pyrexic air seemed to quiver around me. I imagined a great sigh of relief silently rising up around me from the very ground, at the temporary respite from the torrid battering the sun had been gushing down upon the desolate landscape. The Kingston Mountain Range, which was stretched out before me as if an altar at my knees, turned from crimson to orange to copper, and was then lost to shadow and darkness.

Far off in the distance, slightly to my right and seemingly a thousand miles away, the tiny, bright aircraft beacon on top of Turquoise Mountain was barely visible through the binoculars.

There was much for me to think about.

I thought about Mike, who labored at his turquoise mine up there, among the cracks and crevasses of the waterless, parched, dusty west-facing hills. What a shitty, dreary, but noble task that must have been: to wrench the most patrician and sacred of minerals from the Earth, with no reasonable hope of anyone paying for his exertions. I thought about the twenty dollars I gave to him for a simple, "nothing-special" piece of turquoise a few months ago: a chunk of rock that may have taken him many hours to locate and extract. A decent human being would have given him more.

I thought about Mike dying a few weeks after I bought that piece of turquoise from him, of a cancer he had only just recently learned he had. That $20 should have been $40 or $60 instead: not for his benefit--- a man irrevocably doomed needs no paper money. I should have paid $60 for my benefit: a guilt appeasement from one slightly less doomed person to a more immediately doomed person. The extra $40 wouldn't have helped him, but shit: it wouldn't have hurt me. Walk into the light, Mike, and here's another couple of twenties for cab fare if the hike is too far, or for a beer if there's a pub up there: god knows you needed a cold one down here in this desert.

I thought of Cochise, who worked with Ed some times in another turquoise mine in the same area. I was told by a stranger in Baker that Cochise had died in one of the worse possible ways I can think of: on a bunk inside a shelter for homeless people. When the men sleeping around him discovered he was dead, they robbed his body of anything and everything of value, including the turquoise jewelry he had made.

It's the way of the world here on Earth: the living feed off the dead and dying. Among the well-fed, that obscene act would be unthinkable; among the hungry, the act was prudent. Maybe that should be a new social metric we can adopt: if the thought of robbing a dead man is repulsive to you, then you're not doing badly economically. I hope I never become so desolate in mind and body that my pragmatism leaves the range of human behavior and enters that of the other, more reasonable, mammals.

Among my thoughts were the cabins and towns that once dotted the East Mojave Desert, but have long since fallen down, crumbled and rotten, and were blown away with the sand and the Russian thistle and the ubiquitous beer cans that cover the desert floor. People came to the desert, they struggled, they toiled, they bled, they cried, they laughed a bit, and then they died--- and what they moiled at, and for, turned to dust with them. Nothing built by humans last long in the world, except our trash, yet billions of people seem to believe that what they do with their lives has some kind of importance, some significance. Arrogant, deluded bastards.

Less than 100 years after ancient and mighty Nineveh fell to the Babylonians (and their allies), the descendants of the Assyrian Empire's victims, when stumbling over and living within the vast city's ruins, had no idea what culture had built the city; the names of Sennacherib and Ashurbanipal were unknown, and Assyria was not even a bad memory. Sennacherib bragged, in various stelae, how he had destroyed vast cities (and captured Jerusalem), and used the grass-stuffed skins of the kings of those cities as decorations in his throne room. Where's that bitch Sennacherib now?

Less than 100 years after the ancient and populous *Mogollon* (and perhaps Late *Hohokam*) culture fell during a brutal and extended drought, the *Tohono O'odham* and *Akimel O'otham* had no idea who had built the mighty cities that lay in ruin throughout what is now the American Southwest; when Spanish invaders asked the current residents who had built the cities, none could answer except with "*pi 'añi mac*" ("how can I know?").

I seem to detect a pattern here....

When Avalon faded into the mist, Camelot fell; humanity knows in its collective psyche that civilizations cannot last, given human behavior.

The insanity of working hard to create wealth for one's employer: who came up with that absurd idea? Not the people creating the wealth they seldom benefit from. If I left my cave and went back to work in some vast corporate machine somewhere, how would I benefit? It would mean I get to eat longer and die later---- but why?

If I left my desert Fortress of Solitude, who would hire me to work for them? My social skills were that of an unwashed, sarcastic, smirking, immature troglodyte. The ugly fact is that there was no employer anywhere in the world who would hire me to do anything.

Why not stay where I was? I had enough money to last at least another year, and likely two years. Why the bloody fuck go back to the abomination, the horror, the sewer that passes for "modern civilization?" I could not think of any valid reason for not staying where I was.

If I stayed in the desert through the winter, I would need a plan. I would need to eat better: I must buy food high in fat; I must eat food with actual vitamins in it, and not the dehydrated pseudo foods I had been living on (which when re-hydrated was as appealing to eat as window pane sealant). I would need to bathe more, exercise more, and take an interest in my health again. I would need more clothing, a few more blankets, fire wood, kerosene, more supplies.

As the night grew cool, I pulled my blanket around me, pinning its two leading corners against my knees with my elbows, and rested my binoculars against my eyes with my uninjured hand and peered into the darkness, looking for--- I had no idea. A spark of light maybe, out there among the Kingston Mountains, or down there on the Valjean Valley floor.

Maybe I was looking for the spirits of the women and men who had struggled across the area over the centuries, eking out a tenuous, brief existence: Southern Paiute families living on the meager protein of insects and lizards, huddled near muddy seeps hidden far from the foot trails traveled by Ute slavers from the north. They also hid from the Holy Men of Gods (elderly Mormon males) looking for little Indian girls to "marry" and turn them "into a white and delightsome race" as Brigham "Bring 'em" Young wrote. Or, later, hiding from American Army soldiers who found their existence inconvenient. Or the ghosts of the Timbisha (Shoshone) over there at Tecopa Pass, where the water was good and a sparse crop of melons, "tobacco root" (*Valeriana edulis),* maize, beans, and squash each summer was enough, just barely, to keep a dozen or so people alive.

A vast army of people had passed through the area I was looking down upon, a handful at a time and spanning a few millennia. It is conceivable that at times some of them were happy. Their lives must have been harsh, routine, and oppressive: now and then I envy them and their lack of The Monstrous Automobile, asphalt highways, poisonous air, and teeming swarming fetid crowds of humanity.

I put down my binoculars and blinked the strain out of my eyes. The question before me: "Do I leave this place and rejoin the horrible human world, or do I stay here?" A slight lightening in the east hinted at a rising moon. I fished into my back pack and found a bottle of water and drank.

As I set down the water bottle, a tiny yet blinding spark of light drifted down from the sky, illuminating a circle on the rock a few feet in front of me. The pinpoint of light was brilliant white, with an infinitesimally small core of sky blue at its center: an incandescent mote of dust, casting a circle of light about three feet in diameter. My knees, and the edge of my blanket that covered them, were lit up as if they were in bright sunlight, while the rest of my body and the rock around me was left in inky darkness.

The point of light struck the rock in front of me; where it struck, a fountain of bright blue streaks jumped up off the rock and scattered in the form of an inverted cone a few inches from the point of impact. The light went out and I was surrounded by darkness again, blinking at the suddenness of the phenomena.

What the fuck did I just see? Did Tinker Bell fall from the sky and die in front of me? If so, was it suicide? The Mojave people believe that if a person thinks about someone who has died, or speaks that person's name, part of that person returns to haunt the thinker or speaker: maybe the spirit of some ancient, long-dead Timbisha chief floated down to me in a brilliant spiritual shroud, and tried to communicate to me. If so, I cannot imagine what we would have to say to each other: each of our lives would seem alien and inhuman to the other.

Of course, it was a incredibly tiny, and long-lived, micro meteorite.

A crescent moon lifted itself above the eastern horizon, over there where Shadow Mountain lurked dark and sinister even in daylight. The western ridge line that marked the boundary of Owl Canyon caught the silvery light, casting the canyon behind it into ebony relief. The top of the Avawatz Mountain Range glowed in syncopation with the rising of the moon.

I laid on my left side, tucking my back pack under my cheek, pulled my blanket up to my chin, and stared into the charcoal gray darkness to the east. Some where in there I fell asleep, and Primary Dream Number One fell upon me like a street mugger.

In my dream I was on foot, walking through a massive city. The city spanned a huge continent, and the seemingly infinite number of streets ran in perfect, laser-drawn lines that met at right angles to other streets, and every street was a cacophony, a riot, of cars racing at high speed through a blinding and endless series of traffic lights, stop signs, empty pedestrian crossings, roadside billboards, and gutters heaped with filth of every imaginable kind. The air was the color of burnt orange, through which a bloody red sun glared banefully down on me from the wounded, ruined, suppurating, bleeding sky. The immeasurable number of cars, with their imperishable stream of noxious fumes, came upon me from all quarters, passed me, and vanished in the distance as the very curve of the Earth blocked them from my vision.

My legs ached, my pelvis ached, my back ached from the labor of walking without rest for many days; fear, dread, and anxiety clutched at my chest as I walked, augmenting the agony of breathing the vile putrid air. My head turned at every street intersection as I looked for a way out of the city.

No matter how long I walked, no matter in which direction I walked, the omnipresent, monstrous city spread from horizon to horizon. There was no escape, no relief, no hope of reaching the edge of the city and stepping past it and into clean air, into quiet, into beauty. My anxiety turned to panic, and I started to run. The panic turned to terror and I started to sprint. But I had no idea which direction to run, no idea where I was going. I began screaming as I ran...

... and I woke up with a yelp. The tiny crescent moon was above me, and my clothing was damp from sweat. My heart was racing, and a cold gritty patina of sweat covered my face. I sucked in cool air to calm myself. The dream was so frequent a visitor to me at night that there were times when I wondered if it was more a memory than a dream, or perhaps a prophesy. I thought that if I had a dollar for every time I woke up screaming, I could afford a better grade of tequila.

I scraped my face dry against my back pack, rolled over on to my right side to face the towering Avawatz, and slept again.

Primary Dream Number Two followed. In this dream I was in a corporate office building that had a few floors: perhaps five, maybe six. The building was square at its base, with each side measuring about five miles long. I was on one of the middle floors, trying to find a door that would let me leave the building. I found hundreds of stairways, some going up, some going down, and many hundreds of hallways. The outer walls were of glass, and at times I could see outside, and at times the inner walls blocked my view of the outside. I searched endlessly for the correct doors, the correct hallways, the correct stairways, in the correct combination, to leave the building. All the while, people dressed in expensive suits hurried about their business and paid to me no attention at all. Relentlessly, methodically, tediously, I tried every possible way to get out of the building but I could not. Eventually I stopped walking, sat on the lower steps of a random staircase, and went to sleep...

... and when I awoke, the crescent moon was just setting above Avawatz Peak, in my face. I sat up, rubbed my face with a fist, and worked the stiffness out of my now-chilled body. I drank more water, shook out my blanket, and wrapped the blanket around me again.

From far off in the distance, in a direction I could not detect, the tiny jingle of bells was heard. It was like sleigh bells, or perhaps a few cow bells, from very far away. It was the same sound I had heard a few months earlier. The sound seemed to approach me, then fade away, then approach again. Even as I was hearing the bells, I told myself I was imagining it. There was nothing out there that would be wearing bells, surely. Tinker Bell was dead, apparently, and cows were outlawed from the area a few years ago. Do cows really wear bells? I had no idea: I programmed computers for a living, not "punched" cows. Crack whores working the Southern Baptist conventions have a better life than ranch hands. Young white men hooked on methamphetamine selling blow jobs in Salt Lake City to Latter-day Saint elders for $3 per "head" (less for bishops I'm told; by bishops I mean) have a higher standard of living than ranch hands. John Denver lied to us. The only life worse than being a cowboy is being an Indian--- American Indian or India Indian. My mother's side of the family are American Indians, but with jobs. (The editor will scalp me for that joke. And that one.)

I strained my eyes and ears looking for the source of the sound, but eventually the sound faded away into the murky gray night and did not return.

There are canyons that grumble when the wind blows from a particular direction. Some people describe the sound as like hearing large earth-moving machines working in the distance: a low rumble that some people can hear, but when they mention it to people standing next to them, those people cannot hear it. Maybe the sound I was hearing came from some complex desert geology, with perfectly reasonable and well-known forces acting upon it. Not being superstitious, I did not worry about it.

The moon fell below the ridge line behind me, and the Kingston Mountain Range was once again swallowed in darkness except for a small chuck of it over there on the left a bit: Kingston Peak. I wondered what I would be seeing if I were on that peak looking back at me: probably a dark cookie-cutter outline of the Avawatz, in front of a milky gray sky.

To the east, as the horizon was showing the slightest hint of lightening from the rising sun, Betelgeuse and Rigel reminded me that winter was coming: did I really want to stay a winter in a cave?

The truth was that it was not a matter of what I wanted but a matter of what I could bear--- the horror of living among humanity was vastly stronger than any argument I could think of to once again join the ravening, alien horde and what passed as "society." I was either too crazy to fit in with society, or society was too crazy to fit in with me. Either way, we had to avoid each other: we couldn't both live in the same universe without one of us destroying the other.

Living in a cave through winter would be difficult due to the cold; the winter nights some times got below freezing, and my cave was shallow--- no deep tunnel to hide within.

I knew of a place where there is a mine adit almost 100 meters deep into the side of a hill. There is a spring near by, but the water was all below the ground; past that spring another mile was an excellent source of fresh water. I could live at that mine for the winter, but there were two major problems with doing so. The first problem was that people visited the mine adit, though rarely, and I did not want anyone to know where I was living. The second problem was that there was no place in that area where I could hide my automobile effectively.

The decision was made: I would stay where I was for at least another few months, and if the cold got too much to bear I could leave.

This called for another trip in to town to buy supplies. As the sun was jumping over Shadow Mountain, I got to my feet, flung my back pack over a shoulder, and went back to my cave. I had a hell of a lot of work to do that day.

PHONE COPS, MAN! I'M PROBABLY WIRED FOR SOUND RIGHT NOW!

"I envy paranoids: they actually feel people are paying attention to them." -- Susan Sontag

Back at camp, I shook the bugs and rat shit out of my bedding and packed it into the plastic sheet (using one hand: not easy), gathered up my emergency traveling gear, and put everything else inside the cave in case rain fell. I drank as much distilled water as I could fit in my gut, then strapped four liters of water to my hips and headed to my vehicle. I stepped over the large green iguana camped at the solar still by the spring, told her or him that I would be back in a day or two, and made the tedious hike to my hidden vehicle.

The long walk to my pickup was slow and painful. My injured hand throbbed, and I had consumed far too much water to be hiking comfortably. But I reminded myself that I needed to drink as much water as I could, when I could, to avoid dehydration: it snuck up on me once or twice in the past few months, and I did not want to be a fool and let it happen again. I told myself I must drink every drop the solar still produced, even if I felt I didn't need to.

My hand oozed a colorful mixture of rusty red and fluorescent green fluids, overwhelming the ability of the toilet-paper-and-electrician-tape bandage to soak up the festering, suppurating, stinking, poisonous, pestilential slime welling up from my wound. My wrist and lower arm was a pale "burnt green" color, like a... like a.... well, like my iguana friend back at the spring.

I made a mental note to get some alcohol to wash my hand wound.

My pickup started immediately, without any problems: if it had not, I would need to hike all the way back to my cave and return with the spare battery which I was using for light at night---a major struggle since it weighed 47 pounds (21.3 kilograms). On a decent road I could "push start" my pickup, but it was parked on plywood sheets under which was loose sand, and the dirt road itself was far away.

The immediate task was daunting: I must move the vehicle

over the sand to the dirt road, five or six feet at a time, moving plywood sheets under the wheels, with one hand.

I put a plywood board behind each of the four wheels. I then reversed the vehicle four feet, and put the gearbox in neutral, set the hand brake, got out of the vehicle, moved four other plywood boards behind the wheels, got back in the vehicle, and backed up another four feet. At times I did not back up far enough, so I had to get in and back up a few inches farther, then get out and move the plywood. At other times I backed up too far, setting the wheels on the sand, and I was filled with anxiety until I managed to get plywood under them. In this way, foot by tedious foot, I moved the pickup backwards off the loose sand and onto the road. It was amazing how much work it was using one hand instead of two.

The day was brutally hot, and as the sun punished me mercilessly while I labored, I consumed an amazing amount of water: more than three liters in just under one hour. The water I kept inside the vehicle for the radiator had coolant in it, and was not fit to drink. I was reminded once again about the First Law of Desert Travel: never travel a distance farther than the amount of drinking water you have can support. If my vehicle stopped working before I made it to the highway, my risk of dying would increase by a few hundred percent: the thought made me laugh, since I could easily see the highway (and therefore rescue) through binoculars. I could die of hyperthermia, loss of electrolytes in my body, snake bite, or from a dozen other hazards a mere 200 feet from the highway and only the buzzards and ravens would see me, until the coyotes and rats joined them.

I vowed to be kinder to my vehicle than I had been: it was keeping me alive. With that happy thought in mind, I slowly and carefully drove eastward off the mountain and to the highway.

In the lovely, beautiful town of Baker I rushed to the burrito store and I filled all of my water containers at the water spigot outside: that is, of course, the Second Law of Desert Travel--- never pass up a source of water, and fill your containers immediately and to the brim.

The burrito store had a pay telephone outside near its door, in an open-to-the-sky vestibule and in the way of people attempting to enter or leave the bean slinging business. It seemed like a good time for me to "check in" with a few people and see how the real world was doing since I had been away for several months. I rummaged through my pickup's glove box and fished out about a dozen quarters, and walked to the telephone.

The dial tone was present, which surprised me: pay phones in America are common, but working ones are not. The vast majority of the species get vandalized within a few hours of being placed. They last about as long as do sacrificial victims at an Aztec temple; like staked goats at a tiger's watering hole; like a pretty little girl whose parents just joined the Church of Jesus Christ of Latter-day Saints. The phone buzzed in my ear.

I used my thumb to hammer in a ten-digit number, and presently an artificial voice demanded that I cough up seventy-five cents for the first three minutes. I inserted a quarter and heard in the ear piece a dull "ding!" noise as the payment registered.

The quarter continued on its gravity-induced journey through the mechanical guts of the telephone, and clattered into the coin return cup. I paused in wonder at the event.

"Please deposit fifty cents for the next three minutes," the voice said.

I retrieved the quarter from the cup and inserted it into the slot again. Another dull "Ding!" sounded in the ear piece, and again the telephone regurgitated the quarter with a clatter. I wondered at it again.

"Please deposit twenty-five cents for the next three minutes," the voice said.

Same quarter went in; same quarter came out. Again a "Ding!" Then a voice followed, telling me, "Thank you."

"Why, you are certainly welcome!" I said. I retrieved the magic quarter and examined it with amazement as the ring tone sounded in the ear piece.

"Yellow! Captain Ron speaking," a new voice said.

"Hi, Ron. It's me, David Rice. How'z yeah been?"

"Well I'll be damned!" Ron said.

"Probably," I agreed. Where ever there were loose women, or tight women and a supply of alcohol, there Ron would go no matter how hot the climate.

"Where the Hell you been? There's people looking for you."

I immediately thought about who might be looking for me. San Bernardino County Sheriff; Federal Bureau of Investigation;

Scientology salespeople; debt collectors; my pals in the white suits from the mental health care facility whom I had promised in writing to go and finger paint with but never did. I could think of no one I wanted to have find me, and I could think of a dozen people, organizations, institutions, agencies, lawyers, wistful maidens, and outraged husbands that might be looking for me.

"Shit!" I said. "Don't tell anyone where I am! *Fuck!* **DON'T TELL ANYONE!**" I yelled into the mouth piece, in a panic.

"Well, where **HAVE** you been? Johann has been looking for you. And I might have a boat job for you."

"I've been hanging out in the desert, up in the hills, suffering from hyperthermia and malnutrition. I spent a few days exploring the second-most toxic spot in the United States, up there near Clark Mountain at Mountain Pass; had a nice picnic lunch up there. You know, doing healthy fun stuff." His chuckle made me think maybe he didn't believe me, and I wished I had thought of a clever lie instead.

Ron started to tell me about the possible boat job, which I did not want, when the artificial voice demanded more quarters: I fed in the same quarter a half-dozen times or so to keep it happy. I wouldn't want to upset the phone company, by golly.

I told Ron that I would call some of the people he told me to, "if I have enough coins," I added, and then I asked him about his teaching job. If there was anything that might compel me to come down off the mountain and join society again, it was spending one evening a week in a class room full of young woman who didn't need my help to tie a bowline but asked for it anyhow. The Celestial Navigation class had started already, and anyhow the odds that the love of my life would (#1) be in the class and (#2) be half my age, was greater than the odds of Shania Twain accidentally calling me on this amazing (free) telephone and telling me she's lonely and ask me to come visit her.

"I sold my Urban Shopping Cart," Ron said. This was his old, but in great condition, all-wheel-drive vehicle. I asked him how much he sold it for, and when he told me I lamented, into his ear, that I would have bought it. In my mind I pictured myself driving over sand to the spot where I hid my Toyota, without the need to drive on plywood to keep from getting stuck.

After I made a few verbal promises to keep in touch and to call some people, which I would never swear to and would never put in writing because I had no intention of doing so, I wished Captain Ron well and hung up.

Fishing into my wallet I hauled out a faded, well-creased piece of paper with a telephone number on it that I had only called eight times in the past thirteen years for obvious reasons. My brother answered like a professional employee and not a human being:

"Good after noon. This is Fredric Rice, at [Corporate Division Name], part of [Corporate Name], in [Corporate Division's Tertiary Location]. How may I help you?"

"Good after noon, Corporate America. This is what's left of your brother calling you."

"How do I know you are who you say you are?" My brother asked. "Tell me something that only the two of us know."

"I am cursed by having an extraordinary high intelligence, which I seldom use," I told my brother. "Often when my brain tells me to do something, I do the opposite." There was an extended silence. "Human civilization ended when the first unjust law was passed." There was more silence. "It is the nature of apples to fall out of trees. It is the nature of fools to sit under apple trees. Satan is an honorable profession: if no one stood up and accused, few wrongs would be righted. We need more smart people for the same reason we need smart people. When I see a beautiful sexy woman I think of hot buttered popcorn. The correct response to tyranny is sedition. I think humanity should go extinct for the sake of everyone else. When police officers are the problem, more crime is the solution. Disloyalty to government and 'authority' is a sign of superior intelligence. When I die I shall die a whole man, with the bark still on me," I told the silence.

"Jesus. A torrent of sexist Hippie Commie Zen Buddhist shit. It must be you."

"Further more, am I who I think I am? Can I be other than I am?"

"You saw one season of **Kung Fu** on television twenty years ago and you're still staggering around the American Southwest sounding like Sawaki. Jesus!" My brother seemed to be mixing at least three religions together at me. My brother asked me how life was going, out there in the desolate uninhabitable Forbidden Zone known as "Southern California."

"While I was communing with a bayonet cactus I met the Buddha," I informed my brother.

"Jesus!"

"No, The Buddha. Knowing it is a student's prerogative to ask questions of a teacher, the Buddha paused and awaited any question I may have."

"Cheeses H. Jhrist!"

"No, the Buddha. But," I continued, "it is impolite for a student to speak first to a much-venerated teacher. So there we stood, each trying to 'out-Buddhism' each other. Whoever broke the silence would be less Dao than the other."

"If this doesn't end soon, I shall, I believe, scream," my brother said with a weary tone.

"Forty days and forty nights passed while we stood there silently waiting for the other to speak," I explained.

"Gosh, how very Jewish," my brother said.

"No, Buddhist," I replied. "As I was near death from lack of food and water, I picked up a big rock and painfully walked the few step required to stand next to him. I spoke, telling the Buddha, 'I'm sorry,' and struck his head a mortal blow. Death was immediate."

My brother remained silent for a few seconds. "Okay, so what's the moral of the idiotic story," my brother asked. "You killed the Buddha and took his place like you people are supposed to?"

"No," I said. "I killed him because I was starving and I needed to go eat. If one seeks Enlightenment, the first step is to accept the world as it is before moving on to how the world should be."

"That's just Zen bullshit."

"Yes," I agreed. "That is Zen."

Telephone receiver jammed hard against my ear and left shoulder, working the same quarter through the telephone every three minutes precisely, we brought each other up to date on personal news. I explained to my brother that yes, thank you, I was doing well. I noted that I had encountered no bears in the Avawatz Mountains, only Chicago Bruin fans, but my brother didn't get the joke because the only hockey stick he's seen is Dr. Michael E. Mann's.

I finally got to the point.

"I have decided to stay where I am for the winter," I said, knowing my brother would object because he loves me.

"What? You're not flying south for the winter like a fucking Mallard? You do know it gets at least twenty degrees below cold up there in the mountains, right?"

A lengthy argument followed. I argued in favor of madness; my brother argued on the side of sanity. As is almost always the case in human history, sanity lost the argument. My brother and I made arrangements when to meet now and then so that he could check in on me. This is what brothers do.

It was time for lunch.

AND ME WITHOUT MY TIN FOIL HAT

***"A pretty girl can do no wrong."* -- Edward Abbey**

I entered the burrito store and was punched in the face with cool air. It felt strange to suddenly go from 108 degrees Fahrenheit (42.2 Celsius) to 66F (19C) in the time span of two heartbeats. The sweat on my face seemed to harden and then ice over in a patina of alkaline, calcium carbonate, and feldspar dust, bonded to my face with the greasy sweat my body produced from processing dehydrated refried beans and saltine crackers. I worked my jaw to alleviate the numbing chill from my cheeks. The smell of fried bovine and chicken flesh assaulted by sinus cavities.

The place was crowded with road travelers who had paused in their journeys to and from no where of any importance to eat food just as dull and tedious and flavorless and vapid as their lives were. I envied them and their Real Life lives, jobs, loves, companions, incomes, and endless worries.

I looked around again, slower, as I stood at the door next to the propaganda rack of sales literature, examining the women. Golly, many looked very nice.

Like the painfully attractive one over there standing in line at the counter, wearing very short shorts. The bright yellow shorts gleefully hugged her dimpled ass which had a college volleyball team's logo on it (the shorts, not her butt, as far as I know). Her legs were shaped as if sculptured by a heterosexual Michelangelo: sun-kissed a tawny brown, they started at ground level from two pink sock-free tennis shoes and rose in slim strong clean fresh curving lines up to a spectacular and well-muscled butt. The shorts left very little that needed imagination to fill in. I didn't know if she was pretty: my gaze didn't get up that high.

Good GODS I want to love that woman! I thought. *Oh, man! I want to love her, and love her, and* ***LOVE HER!*** *Wow! Just, just, wow!* I thought some more, as I stared at her legs while trying to look like I wasn't. I got in line a few people behind her.

A dozen faces had turned my way and were glaring anger and outrage at me. Another dozen faces were turned away, studiously avoiding looking at me, except for their children who were staring at me.

It suddenly occurred to me that some how, while I was in the mountains, humanity had gained the ability to read my mind. That thought flashed through my puzzled head, and was replaced with a possible alternative: did I say that out loud? Like the other times?

I thought hard, as the person at the counter stepped away, the angry faces continued to glare at me, and the queue I was in took a collective step forward. Thinking over the past fifteen seconds or so: I did indeed seem to recall someone speaking out loud and the words did indeed sound like the ones I had thought I had only thought. But I couldn't be sure: maybe I was just convincing myself that I must have spoken out loud. My memory of the past few dozen seconds did not tell me I had spoken, but my ears kind of.... *felt* like they had heard what I had thought.

What was the more frightening explanation: people can read my mind, or I don't know I'm talking when I'm talking? My brother wasn't here to take a punch in the face for me, but then, no one appeared to be stepping towards me to deliver an outraged punch. I pretended no one was staring at me, and put on my face my sanest-looking expression.

The queue progressed and I bought some burritos and a soft drink. I was handed a paper cup for the drink, and I moved away from the counter and over to the soft drink fountain.

Lusting after women in fast food places was getting to be a problem. Every time I smelled grease frying, I got an erection.

At the soda fountain there was a man of about 35 years in age who was wearing a camouflage shirt, camouflage pants, camouflage belt, and camouflage baseball cap. It was crappy clothing, like the cheap stuff one can buy for a few dollars at K-Mart for their children to sleep in. I stared at him. He stared at me because I was staring at him.

"I can still see you," I said, just trying to help. He blushed and turned his face away, maybe a bit afraid of the crazy person talking at him.

I filled my cup with ice, and added a wee bit of cola. A few minutes later my burritos were ready for me to pick up: I did so, then I walked outside to eat. I didn't want to hang around people who could hear what I was thinking.

LORD OF THE BEANS

"The preachers and lecturers deal with men of straw, as they are men of straw themselves. Why, a free-spoken man, of sound lungs, cannot draw a long breath without causing your rotten institutions to come toppling down by the vacuum he makes. Your church is a baby-house made of blocks, and so of the state." --

Henry David Thoreau

The heat punched me in the face like an irate father. Hell, I was used to that, so I pressed on to my pickup, sack of burritos in my good hand, and looked inside to see if anyone had stolen anything, such as my back pack. All was well, so I walked over to the large battered trash bin, to squat in its shade and eat.

Next to the trash bin was a very tiny car, in roughly the shape of an armadillo. Its front end hovered a few inches above the pavement, and its ass end did the same. The car's body was like half a wheel of cheese: a semi-circle disk with a door on the left and right surfaces, and a wind shield sloping sharply like a fish bowl in front. The whole thing crouched low to the ground like an abused and battered dog. I felt sorry for it.

I also felt sorry for the massive, quivering, gelatinous obese man who was standing next to the car. I stopped feeling sorry for him when all 0.141 metric tonne of him saw me and started walking my way, his eye sockets embedded deeply in a sea of fat. The sound of labored panting and gurgling got closer, and my viscera rose throat-ward and threatened to strangle me as the heat-shrouded apparition came thitherward.

Warily, I got to my feet and stepped away from the trash bin so that my escape route was less hindered. I stepped a few feet to the left, and The Walking Flesh changed its vector to intercept me; I stepped a few feet to the right, and The Heaving Mound once again changed its vector. I stood my ground and let it come at me. A rill of fear wended through me as it got closer. I wish I had a CO2 fire extinguisher to fight it with, like Steve McQueen in the movie THE BLOB.

With my injured hand I patted the left front pocket of my

pants, and I felt the tactical defensive ball point pen within. I had foolishly left my tactical defensive belt knife in the glove box of my car, though at the moment I wished I had a tactical defensive pistol. Or perhaps a tactical defensive harpoon. Even a tactical defensive stick would have been welcome.

The leviathan spoke with a gurgle:

“Good morning! Have you praised the lord today?”

I knew the answer to that question immediately.

“Well no, I have not. I live here in the United States: we don’t have lords here. We don’t ‘do’ feudalism here. Perhaps you’re thinking of the United Kingdom.”

The two deep pits where the eyes presumably were closed briefly, then opened again: a double blink, I assumed.

“No,” he burbled. “I mean the lord god, almighty. Your *father in Heaven.*”

“Well thank you, but my name is not ‘All Mighty,’ and dude, my father ain’t up there and I’ll wager never will be. You must never have met him.”

The dual eye pits on his face closed and opened again. He tried a different approach, though for the life of me I could not guess why he was annoying me; nor could I guess why I was not walking away. Perhaps he wanted my burritos; perhaps I wanted to see how long he could keep standing hatless under the harsh, torturous, unrelenting sun as the temperature was well above 100 Fahrenheit.

“What brings you to Baker?” he asked.

There was a time when it surprised me at how rude some complete strangers are. It would never occur to me to walk up to someone I don’t know and speak to the stranger, unless that person appeared to need help, or if I needed help. More to the point, I would never walk up to a stranger and start asking personal questions such as why she or he was standing in Baker talking to a rude person.

“I’m working a turquoise claim in the hills over there,” I lied, gesturing to the north. I thought about lecturing him on how to be polite to strangers (that is: he should ignore them), but lecturing adults about being polite when they need the lecture is not polite. A fucking conundrum. Americans ceased being polite in the late 1500s. Shit, I’ve even encountered strangers who insisted I shake their hand (which I find overly repugnant), as if it was normal to just seize some stranger for a few seconds. And don't even get me started on the strangers who insisted they had the right to hug me.

"Ah," he said, finding a new route to brainwash me with. "Hills created during the GREAT FLOOD OF NOAH." The way he spoke, the words must have been all upper case letters in his head thing. Shit, I had that answer rehearsed also.

"I've no idea who or what that is. Do you mean the GREAT FLOOD OF UTNAPISHTIM?" I could speak in all upper case too.

"Who which?" he asked. "No! No! Um, no..." he blubbered and gurgled, trying to keep up, and he interrupted me before I could tell him the Real True Story and convince him to start worshiping Enki and the other Sumerian gods (but I vowed to get it in there some how, later). "The flood! The only one. Well, not the only one. I mean the only ONE! The Great One!"

"That's what I said," I said. "The Sumerian god Enki rescued humanity and all other forms of life on Earth by warning Utnapishtim. Eventually Babylonia incorporated the Sumerian story in to its cosmology. During the captivity of the elites of ancient Israel, the Hebrews incorporated the Babylonian version in to their cosmology, and gave us Noah." I was not only educating him: I was punishing him for his rudeness by inducing painful dissonance in his head.

He closed one eye pit as he pondered what I said, and left the other open to keep a wary watch on me. Both eye pits opened again and the rubbery lips parted in a happy smile as he turned to look to my right, and so did I.

Coming towards us was what I still think was a woman. Her 0.163 of a metric tonne was situated above two large feet clad in massive tennis shoes. Above the shoes about ten inches, her cylinder-shaped upper body started and continued for about four feet until there was a head. Two massive arms held several cardboard trays stacked on top of each other, and each tray appeared burdened with paper-wrapped burritos, hamburgers, deep fried potatoes, and other American health food. I greeted her and she returned the greeting with a smile.

The man fished into a tray and retrieved a burrito and unwrapped it. Then, giving me a stare to make sure I was watching (I was trying not to, but couldn't help myself) he forced his chin bone deep into his chest fat, stared intently at the burrito in his palm, and started to yell at it.

"DEAR LORD THANK YOU FOR NOURISHMENT AND ALL THE OTHER GIFTS YOU HAVE GRACED US WITH TODAY! WE ARE SO GRATEFUL OF...."

"Your lord is a burrito?" I asked. "Dude, you're talking to a burrito." I was trying to be helpful again.

"... YOUR DISPENSATION IN LOVING YOUR SINFUL CHILDREN IN THIS TIME OF GREAT INEQUITY! WE ALSO THANK YOU FOR...."

"And if you want the burrito to answer, maybe you need to shout at it a little louder because beans and cheese ain't got any ears," I suggested.

"... SENDING THIS NEEDFUL CHILD..." he looked from his lord of beans, cheese, tortilla, and hot sauce and glanced at me, then turned his head back to address the burrito again. "... TO ME TO HELP SET HIM ON THE PATH BACK TO YOUR LOVE AND GRACES! I HUMBLY ASK...."

"Does your lord need any salt? I got some packets of salt. Maybe you could do what I do, and stuff your lord with French fries." His companion, if I could read what passed for her face correctly, looked confused.

(Religion is the fashionable alternative to thinking. I learned early in life that it is fun to tease people: "early" as in before conception. I once made a hamburger for someone who had Obsessive Compulsive Disorder using two bun bottoms for him and the two tops for me, just to see what would happen; I hid the kitchen knives first. One early morning I told a co-worker with OCD, "I never tell the truth," then let him stew in that infinitely regressive unparsable statement the rest of the day.)

I tuned him out so that I no longer heard what he was saying. We stood there, me besmirching my lunch and he beseeching his. When I finished eating I interrupted him and said, "I beg your pardon, but I'm still hungry. I'm going to go buy another lord or two. Thank you, and drive safely!"

I walked away, fearing I would be followed, and I went inside the burrito store to hide from them. I didn't want any more food, so I just sat at a table next to a window and I watched them (which is not polite), waiting for them to drive away. They stood in the sun eating, after placing the cardboard trays of food on the top of their odd vehicle.

Eventually their meal was finished, and they put their trash in the trash bin, and then they engineered themselves into their tiny car.

It was very much an engineering feat. The man went to the passenger side and opened the tiny door, and with his feet still on the pavement he stuffed his head and upper body into the tiny space inside the car. The car lurched sideways as it took his weight, but only dropped about two inches: the vehicle had no shock absorbers.

He then shoved hard against his feet to force as much of his lower body in to the car as he could, and then pivoted his mass leftward on his massive left ass cheek and drew his left leg inside. The car shook violently. The right leg then followed the left twin.

Once he was in, the maybe woman performed similar maneuvers, but in a mirror image. It was like watching two giant squid ooze themselves into one tiny mustard jar.

I was glad I ate first before seeing that.

IS THERE A DOCTOR IN THE CLOSET?

***"Tampon commercial, detergent commercial, maxi pad commercial, Windex commercial - you'd think all women do is clean and bleed."* -- Gillian Flynn**

I am a human male. That means I would rather die after a prolonged period of a little pain, than live after a brief period of great pain. Women do the opposite: that's how we can tell the sexes apart when our pants are still on. I did not want to clean my hand wound, nor even look at it, but the time had come to do so: I had access to hot water at the Mojave Preserve Visitor's Center (in the bathroom outside, where the water heater had miraculously not been stolen nor vandalized yet: maybe some day I'll steal it), and a store that sold alcohol.

The "general store" was over next to The Mad Greek, so I drove to the intersection, waited for the stupid shits at the stop sign to figure out if they wanted to turn left, turn right, or continue straight (it's amazing how many people rush at great speed to go where they are going and yet they have no idea where they're going), and parked in front.

The denatured alcohol was right next to the kitchen matches, which I thought was excellent arsonist-friendly planning. I was shocked at the price, but I figured the loss of my hand would be more expensive.

There were several tourists in the store buying ice cream, so I yelled at the prison convict (freshly released from the county's work farm) behind the counter a question: "Hey, where are the fucking condoms?" As compared to the not fucking ones. The store clerk avoided eye contact. I walked over to the ice cream freezer to get a few snacks, and the crowd of tourists parted, avoiding eye contact. Funny how people look away when I enter a room. I fished out as many ice cream bars as would fit in my one good hand, after tucking the alcohol under my left arm pit.

At the cash register I ponied up the treasury notes, and then I stepped aside and ate the ice cream while in the store: if I had stepped outside with it, the fierce sun would have consumed the snack faster than I could.

Dreading the next task, I got in my vehicle, waited for the fresh crowd of bewildered tourists to figure out how the stop signs at the intersection work, and drove to the Visitor's Center. I parked in the back, next to the hamburger joint.

The bathroom door was locked. Well golly, I had a universal key that opens all kinds of doors: I went to my pickup, rummaged around inside the tool box, and came up with a screw driver. After a few probing motions of the screw driver between the door jam and the door knob's locking mechanism, the door opened. Since it only took a few seconds, why the hell did they even bother with a lock? Why even have the door? I left the door standing open, and went inside the bathroom.

The hot water heater sat, tall and fat, in the corner in front of me to the left; the toilet was in the right corner, with about 18 inches of space between it and the water heater. Visitors who wished to pinch off a loaf had to place their feet to either side of the tank. The sink was to my right, next to the door. The entire space measured about four feet square. I put the bottle of alcohol in the sink, since there was no place else to put it except on the floor, and I opened the hot water valve.

The disgusting "bandage" on my left hand was revolting to look at, and in retrospect I suppose for the sake of being polite I should have covered the hand with a bag or tee-shirt or something so that people didn't have to look at it. I'm very "big" on being polite to people.

I put my hand under the stream of hot water, moving the fingers around a bit, and washed away the dried blood and other unguessed-of fluids. Slowly, while under the water, I tugged at the tape and slipped it off as a single unit towards my fingers. I did this without looking, under the assumption it would hurt less if I didn't look. The pain was bearable, so I looked at my hand. The pain increased by six orders of magnitude, so I looked away again.

One of the "sutures" had pulled out of the tasty meat I had shoved the needle through, ripping open one side of the wound. On the plus side, the other "suture" held, and the wound was mostly closed. A small section was still gaping open, oozing blood a bit, but it hurt worse than it looked. The bad-looking part was the green hand and blue lower arm.

I turned off the water and braced myself for the hard part: the alcohol. Do I swab gently with alcohol, or pour alcohol into the wound and force it around in there? The man in me said to do the former; the woman in me said to do that latter.

Getting the cap off with one hand wasn't easy. Why the fuck did anyone think it necessary to put a "child proof cap" on a bottle of rubbing alcohol? Any child that tasted it would puke her guts out at the first sip.

Cap finally off the bottle, I placed my hand palm-up on the edge of the sink, took a breath and held it, clenching my teeth, and poured.

The pain was not anywhere near as bad as I had anticipated: it was worse. Of its own volition, my hand flung itself away from the sink as it screamed. I heard it scream: really, it did. I forced it back on to the edge of the sink, poured on more alcohol, and then set the bottle down inside the sink. With my other hand I pressed the alcohol into the wound, forcing alcohol into the little nooks and crannies.

Blood gushed upward, and my entire body exploded with sweat from the pain. My every pore oozed pain. My vision was dulled and clouded from pain. Fumbling with the cap again, I closed the bottle of alcohol, turned the hot water back on, and thrust my hand under the stream and left it there until the hot water tank emptied of warm water and the stream ran cool. I turned the water off.

Turning towards the flimsy wall behind me, I kicked it in the usual "if I kick something hard enough and often enough, the pain will decrease" human behavior. I kicked the water heater. I kicked the door jams. I raised my right leg and stomped the floor a few dozen times, to "soak up the pain," as sweat dripped from my face.

After many minutes of this silly behavior, I stopped kicking things, and realized I couldn't see. Fear that I had been blinded washed through me, and I felt a flush of dread pass through my body. Then I realized I had my eyes closed in a tight grimace, and I relaxed my face enough to open my eyes.

Sobbing with pain, I sat on the concrete floor, put my back against the water heater, clutched my hand to my chest, and rocked back and forth like I had done in my cave after cutting myself, and I waited for the pain to diminish.

Looking through the open door, I saw human beings coming

and going about their business, chiefly to and from the hamburger joint to my right. If anyone saw me sitting on the bathroom floor, they didn't feel it worth the effort to expend the tiny bit of human compassion necessary to walk over and see if I needed help.

My sweaty hair dried. My damp clothing dried. The blood in my hand dried. The sun passed overhead and went westward. Eventually I got to my knees, then to my feet, and with one hand I cleaned the sink using cool water and paper towels, washing away any trace of blood.

Staggering out of the bathroom and into the sun, with a paper towel in my left hand and the bottle of alcohol in my right hand, I made my way to my pickup and got the roll of duct tape from the tool box. I folded the toilet paper into a square, pressed it to the palm of my left hand, and clumsily secured the paper to my wounded hand. I then made a fist, and put more tape over the fingers to keep the hand closed.

My entire arm was on fire.

GHOSTS IN THE SALOON; THAT COLORFUL DESERT CHARACTER, YEAR 1925

"This calls for a very special blend of psychology and extreme violence."
— Ben Elton

Trailing drops of bright red blood, which turned a crispy brown when they hit the sizzling concrete under my boots, I went around to the driver's side of my vehicle with my arm against my chest, and opened the door. I shook the loose blood off my fist, scattering it liberally in many directions, and startled a white family walking towards their car from the hamburger store.

They were ***white***. By "white" I mean the blinding white of freshly fallen snow in harsh sun light. Sickly white. Whiter than egg shells. Whiter than a sheet of paper. Not albino white: they were Highlander never-in-the-sun live-in-a-crofter's-shack-by-the-loch white. Their sturdy milk-white haggis-fed bodies squatted firmly on their sturdy milk-white legs. Dark brown hair sat over milk-white faces. To look at them was to hear bagpipes. The only color other than dark hair were the blotches of sun burn on arms and noses. Wide-eyed, they paused in their journey to their car and stared at me while I bled from my green hand.

Perhaps they had just finished eating bloody meat, and were inured of the sight of blood in the parking lot, but I still felt guilty. I gave them my "best smile" and waved with my good hand, and levered myself into my car. Maybe they would be lucky and not see the bloody spots I left on their car. Hell of a way to treat tourists.

One handed, steering with my knees, I made a loop out of the parking lot, turned left on the main street, turned left at the stop sign, and headed eastward on Kelbaker Road. I had important things to do.

Wyatt Earp moved in to the East Mojave after his time in Alaska with his wife Josephine Sarah Marcus ("Josie")--- possibly after he felt the law was no longer seeking him for the deaths of four men who were suspected of murdering his brother Morgan (surely, it's a brother's duty to avenge a sibling's death). Serial Killer Wyatt and Spouse had a summer residence at Vidal, California, and some people think Wyatt owned and operated an illegal saloon in the

Macedonia mining district. I had visited the site of the saloon many years ago, but a few months ago I heard a rumor that some stupid shit had dug under the ruin looking for treasure, completely destroying what had been left of the adobe structure: I wished to see if the rumor was true.

At Kelso Depot I turned left at the stop sign. There is talk about the depot being restored as a tourist attraction, which horrifies me because the last thing the desert needs is more tourists. Best to just burn the depot down than have tourists buying plastic tortoise souvenirs and shitting in the plastic toilets ("Comfort Stations" they call them) the Bureau of Land Management loves to litter the landscape with. In any and every public land in the United States, it's a contest between the tourists and the BLM to see who can vandalize the land the worse: usually the BLM wins, since they have the bulldozers and bigger budgets, and they plan for years on how best to destroy and make ugly that which is clean and beautiful and lovely.

After a few miles on Cima Road I panic braked and took a sharp, high-speed right turn into deep sand, gunned the engine in the hope the pickup wouldn't get stuck, and shot through a narrow concrete underpass, the Union Pacific railway just inches above the top of the car. Back on firm dirt again, I slowed the vehicle and read the worn, broken sign:

= MACEDONIA =

The actual site of the saloon is a secret (if indeed the ruin is what's left of Earp's saloon: it might not be), in the hope that looters would not come and destroy the ruin, but the secret is widely known to anyone who takes sufficient interest to learn the location. Located on one of the many dozens of small hills, the saloon would have been easily seen by miners new to the mining district, and conveniently located near the most profitable mineral deposits and whore cribs.

The compact dirt road into the mining district passes a ruined house to the right, southward, where the roof had fallen in decades ago and left shelter enough only for small desert beasts where once there was shelter for human beasts. The trash is typical of desert houses of the late 1940s and early 1950s: a swamp cooler's turbine drum sits in the dirt next to what had once been its housing, with the water pump missing--- long ago someone salvaged spare parts to fix a swamp cooler elsewhere. The trash dump lays within an arroyo that is choked with creosote brush, rabbit brush, broken glass, tar-covered plywood, and rusted tin cans. The walls of the house all lean in the same direction, eastward, and some day the prevailing westerly wind will finish the job and knock the structure over for good--- if a human doesn't burn the place down for "fun" first some day.

Farther up the hill is a concrete shelter large enough for a few people to sleep in, if they do not mind crawling on their knees to enter. The road can be seen from the opening of this shelter, and now and then when a homeless person (or a few) lives in the shelter, she or he can see cars arriving from several miles away and she or he can gather up bedding and hide in the hills until the car and occupants leave.

Long ago, in Wyatt Earp's day, there was fresh water at the site. When I first visited the area many years ago the spring had decreased to a tiny trickle, little more than a damp spot among the pale green brush that "riots" in a side arroyo to the east of the area where the major mine shafts lay in wait for fools and their dogs to fall to their deaths in. On this my latest visit, even the dampness is gone: the desert water sites have been drying up at an alarming rate for the past two decades, and a great many historical water sources are gone.

I got out of my car, flexing my left arm to relieve some of the throbbing pain, and headed towards a particular hill where the remains of what is thought to be Earp's saloon squat.

The ruin had not been disturbed; the rumor was not true.

The rough adobe half-wall still stood unmolested by any recent abuse, and still held back the many decades of silt that had worked its way down hill to come to a rest against the old unfired clay bricks. The stump of an ancient cottonwood tree that had once provided some shade for the building was also not disturbed. Of the roof nothing is left: it had long ago been hauled away and used for some other structure, or perhaps burned as fire wood. Yet there is evidence that someone cared enough about the roof to make it water tight: if one digs around in the dirt one will find rusty nails with lead-covered heads that had been hammered flat over the nail holes to help keep the water out.

I stood next to the wall and looked around me, making a full circle. The area was ravaged by wind and sun, with pale gray dirt and the occasional desert bush spaced well apart from each other, amid a rocky and sun-tortured series of low hills, all of which squat on the side of a larger incline that climbs eastward into the mighty Providence Mountains. To the south the high mountain ridge was still populated by Bighorn Sheep, watering at Summit Spring and Tough Nut Spring; father south was once the town of Providence tucked in there in a wide valley, up against the hills.

As the land rises in elevation to the east and a bit north of east, hidden from my view, there stands what is left of a pine tree forest tucked into a small canyon. The pine trees had been cut down and turned to charcoal for iron smelting many decades ago, and only a few young survivors are left.

A few miles from where I stood, at a place called "Banning's Well" (also "Government Holes"), Matt Burts and J. W. Robinson stood face to face in a small cabin, about four feet apart, and blasted away at each other with single action .44 caliber revolvers. Both blew chunks of blood, bone, and flesh out of the other, and both died. The horror of the event is beyond my imagination, and perhaps most modern American's imagination to comprehend--- an act of violence only survivors of the wars and invasions can adequately conceptualize. Even inner city warfare, where killers execute their unarmed victims from speeding cars, does not match such homicidal brutality, such manly well-matched violence. Living and working at these mines took a heartier, more sturdy American than what we have today.

By our modern standards, Wyatt Earp was a homicidal sociopath serial killer. In his era, he was a man of peace. I find that thought horrifying. 129 years ago and 220 miles to the east, Captain Thomas Byrne single-handedly saved the lives of about 1,000 Hualapai men, women, and children at Camp Beale's Springs ***TWICE***, and yet almost no one has heard about him; Wyatt Earp killed a man or two near the OK corral, and every school child in America knows his name. Why?

Was the site I was standing on really a saloon? If so, was it owned by or run by Wyatt Earp at any time? Local tales say it is, but only the ghosts know. The shades of Matt Burts, Bob Hollimon ("Robin Hood of the Mojave"), J. W. Robinson would know, but they are silent forever.

-0-

Twice I have mentioned Matt Burts, J. W. Robinson, and Bob Hollimon. I would be remiss in not mentioning their story. The East Mojave desert saw some amazing women and men pass though the area who performed feats of bravery and horror; their stories are known to few people, and perhaps that is a good thing: it is good for people to come into the world, live for a brief time, and then fade away--- to make room for the people that follow. Dust belongs to the Earth though it had become flesh for an instant. However it is also good to learn from history, though humanity usually fails in that task; here I have included the story. Please note the following is my conclusions, which may or may not be correct.

Matthew "Matt" Burts was a train robber; that is, he was a member of a gang of violent thugs who robbed people and baggage on trains. His grave marker (Needles Riverview Cemetery, block 20 section 8 grave 5) reads "MATT BURTS | 1870 - 1925 | FAMOUS GUNMAN | A PLACE, A TIME, A SPIRIT THAT NEVER WAS BEFORE, NOR EVER WILL BE AGAIN." It is an odd epitaph considering his occupation (officially listed as "cow puncher", unofficially listed as "lunatic with a hand gun who robs trains"). Burts was born in Hamilton, Texas; and he was also born in Tennessee, according to prison documents--- I have not been able to find the official birth notice, so either location could be correct, or both are incorrect.

On September 9, 1899 at Cochise, Arizona, four men (Burt Alvord, Bill Downing, Matt Burts, and Billy Stiles) robbed an express car on the Southern Pacific Express train, using dynamite to open the iron safe. Evading a sheriff's posse, the robbers fled into the Chiricahua Mountains. At least two of the robbers later robbed a train at Fairbanks, Arizona, on February 15, 1900, and one of the robbers who had surrendered (Billy Stiles) "fingered" Matt Burts as one of the Cochise train robbers.

-0-

"San Francisco ***Call***, Volume 87, Number 31, 31 December 1900

"BATTLE WITH CONVICTS. Sheriff's Deputies Have Desperate Encounter at Yuma.

"PHOENIX, Ariz., Dec. 30. - Matt Burts, sentenced to the penitentiary for train robbery, made a desperate attempt to escape at Yuma on Friday. He had just been brought from Tombstone and was at a lunch counter guarded by deputies. He was handcuffed with Sid Page, a murderer. Seizing an opportunity Burts attacked Deputy Richey, and pulling Page along he tried to secure Richey's gun and a hard fight ensued. Deputy White mixed in the scuffle and Burts grabbed his gun and was about to use it when another guard grasped his arm. The convicts were then quickly overpowered."

-0-

It was, perhaps, a good thing for Matt Burts to have not escaped the Yuma Territorial Prison. The few prisoners who had escaped the prison in the past had been hunted down and captured by Yuma Indians (for which the Territory paid the Yumas a modest fee), and returned them to the prison mostly or completely dead---depending on how much trouble the escapee gave the Yumas. Burts received a shorter prison sentence after he named some of his accomplices.

After serving his prison term, Matt Burts came to the Lanfair Valley to start and own a small cattle company, and to file on a homestead of his own. Known as a desperado who was good with a gun, Burts was not welcome in the valley but he was tolerated.

J. W. Robinson was your typical hired gun, who also made the best whiskey in the area of Eastern Lanfair Valley (east of the Providence Mountain Range, west of Pah-Ute Hill) during Prohibition years, and in direct competition with Whiskey Pete to the west (near present day State Line: the border between California and Nevada and near where the casino "Whiskey Pete's" is located). Robinson was also a cattle man, and presented himself as educated and refined and a "gentleman."

Robinson had been hired by the Rock Springs Land and Cattle Company to "keep open" the water sources in the valley, as well as in the Providence mountains, as well as points west of the Providence mountains. The Rock Springs cattle company, known as "the OX" (later: the 88) held land extending in to Southern Nevada as well as the northern edge of San Bernardino County, and the number of water sources to "keep open" were many.

By "keep open," the job was to make sure that homesteaders, farmers, and other ranchers did not "file on" (claim) water sources that the Rock Spring Land and Cattle Company considered theirs. Anyone found locating near a source of water, or fencing in a source of water, would be driven away by J.W. Robinson and his ilk. Even worse than the cattle homesteaders had brought into the valley, they also brought in sheep to the region where they must have known they and their sheep were not welcomed.

The homesteaders, however, flooded into Lanfair Valley and at least two small towns were built. Hart Town was located at 35°17′20″N 115°6′12″W and Lanfair Town was located at 35°07′36″N 115°11′00″W. A few fresh water wells were dug by wealthy homesteaders, but most relied on surface water that The Old OX considered theirs. One well is still producing water by wind power, and the area has been named "Maruba" after the book written by Maud Morrow Sharp.

Into this incendiary mix came "a native from Texas," **Robert "Bob" Henry Hollimon**. Where Robinson was typical as a gun man, Hollimon was in some ways atypical: he had a social conscience that induced him to feed some of the more hard-pressed homesteaders in the valley to keep them from "being starved out." Hollimon was known as "the Robin Hood of The East Mojave," among many less polite names.

Hollimon had come into Lanfair Valley in year 1918 with about 300 head of cattle, which he had driven from Arizona and was driving to the California coast where he hoped to find grass and water to file on for his quarter-section homestead. The story is that Hollimon rode out to scout the land ahead of him, and he came upon a group of ranch hands who worked for the Rock Spring Land and Cattle Company. Hollimon rode up to the morning breakfast fire and he politely asked for a cup of coffee; he was roughly and impolitely told to "go punch sand." Hollimon then offered to buy a bit of beef; he was told even more forcefully to keep riding and make sure his 300 head of cattle followed him out of the valley.

Hollimon was not the type of person to go away when told to. It was Hollimon who had named "The Hole In The Wall" camp site in the Mojave Preserve, and it is thought that Hollimon had been a member of one of the gangs who had a hide-out at "The Hole In The Wall" in the Big Horn Mountains of Johnson County, Wyoming. Filled with ire and spite, Bob Hollimon decided he had pushed his cattle far enough, and he filed on a homestead in the Lanfair Valley near Black Canyon Road. His well, named "Holliman Well" on the topographic maps, was still producing water in year 2008.

(Ausmus, Bob. 1989. *East Mojave Diary.* Tales of the Mojave Road #16.)

Hollimon was considered a cattle thief, and in May of year 1925 he was accused of stealing a steer by Rock Spring Cattle Company employee Tom Stewart. The accusation might have been true, as the established cattle ranchers in the area had persecuted Hollimon with frivolous law suits to such an extent Hollimon had to sell all he owned, including his cattle, to pay for his legal defenses. Hollimon may very well have thought he was entitled to take a occasional Rock Springs OX (later: 88) steer now and then.

Hollimon was known as a superior hunter with a rifle as well as having an "uncanny" skill with two pistols: one in each fist, drawn with a blur of motion from his twin holsters.

Just how tough was Bob Hollimon? According to the Los Angeles Herald, Number 63, 14 January 1920, two hired guns ("revolver experts") named Pat and Roy Woods (father and son) had a "conversation" with Bob Hollimon at Government Holes on July 2, 1919, at which time Roy Woods, sitting on a horse, reached for his rifle. Hollimon drew his one and only pistol on him at the time and shot Roy Woods' horse to death. Undeterred, the Woods persisted in their folly; Hollimon sent another bullet through Roy's hat "just above the eye." Being slow learners, the Woods attacked in earnest. Fortunately for the Woods, Bob Hollimon's pistol jammed and he was forced to flee. Hollimon later stated under oath that his gun had been tampered with, implying the assault had been a premeditated assassination attempt (*San Bernardino Sun*, Volume 45, Number 133, 10 July 1919).

The image of Roy Woods shows. . . Roy Rodgers. Well, actually it shows Roy Woods dressed up like Roy Rodgers, complete with jaunty neck kerchief with a fancy knot and ten gallon hat. The hat band is a length of hemp rope, and a carefully applied dent had been pressed into the side of the hat. Woods' eyes in the image are narrow, as he squinted into the sun; closed, thin lips were in a slight smile over a small nose. In every way, he looked unremarkable.

On November 8th., 1925, Robinson was in the tiny cabin at Government Holes (Phineas Banning's Well) built by the Rock Springs Land and Cattle Company, and he may have been there to keep homesteaders from collecting fresh water. The well had been fenced to keep cattle, sheep, and people out, and Robinson was thought to have been "guarding" the well. Matt Burts and a woman friend of his, along with her son, drove up to the well in a Model "A" Ford and Burts yelled out to the cabin asking if he and his friend may draw water. A yell from the cabin said that they may do so.

Inexplicably, and with no known motivation, Matt Burts walked to the cabin, opened the door, stepped inside, and closed the door behind him.

As soon as the door closed, Robinson let loose with his Frontier Colt at Burts. Burts was mortally wounded, but he managed to draw his hand gun and blast chunks of bone and flesh and guts out of Robinson before he died; both men emptied their guns (five cartridges each) from less than ten feet away, in under 60 seconds. Robinson lived long enough to raise himself on one elbow and loudly curse Burts.

San Bernardino Deputy Sheriff Jack Brown, under Sheriff Walter A. Shay, was the first law enforcement officer to observe the site of the shooting. In one of his reports is mentioned the fact that Robinson had three pistol wounds (shattered arm, gut, and spine) and also, mysteriously, one rifle wound; in all other reports the rifle wound is not mentioned.

If Robinson had been shot by a rifle before Matt Burts walked into the cabin, who had shot him? Well, several weeks before the "gun fight" there had been a rumor passing through the Lanfair valley that Robinson had been paid $1,500 bounty to "finally deal with Bob Hollimon and Matt Burts:" a staggering amount of money at the time. Perhaps Robert "Bob" Henry Hollimon, who was not a man to wait for danger to come to him, had managed to shoot Robinson earlier in the day, and when Burts walked into the cabin, Robinson thought Burts was there to finish the job--- which, of course, he did.

My mind can not imagine what the horror must have been like. The sudden and extreme violence as each man paused to thumb back the hammers on their guns before pulling the triggers; the dread of each not knowing how badly they had been wounded; the desire, I imagine, of each man wishing he could stop the violence and flee. Deputy Sheriff Brown reported that the dead bodies were three feet apart when he walked into the 10 feet square cabin; the ravening fear, anguish, and regret must have lasted mere seconds before Death came and took them both.

Later, Bob Hollimon gave up cattle and turned to mining. His spouse (married in Las Vegas, Nevada, December 8, 1925), Mrs. Marie Frances Hollimon, was granted a divorce from Bob Hollimon on October 3rd, 1927, two years after (she told Superior Judge Charles L. Allison) he had shot her in the leg "without cause." Alas, poor Bob must have been under a great deal of stress at the time. The San Bernardino County *Sun* newspaper liked to call Bob Hollimon "that colorful desert character."

The story is told by Al Mosher about the time when Bob Hollimon invited to dinner one family of his homestead friends, of whom he had many. At Hollimon's dinner party was a young man who wore a gun belt, with pistol, to the table: shocking behavior and not to be tolerated. The young man, feeling larger than he actually was, may have been upset at his gun-brandishing being ignored, so he drew his pistol, scooped up some butter with the end of the barrel, and said, "I'm a lone wolf and it's my night to howl!" Bob Hollimon stood up quickly, went into the room next to the dining area, and retrieved his gun belt; he then invited the young man to step outside to see how much louder the young man could howl. The young man apologized for his bad manners (of course; I would have) and left. Hollimon was around 70 years old at the time.

County Clerk Harry L. Allison, District Attorney George A. Johnson, and Sheriff Shay witnessed Bob Hollimon quickly draw and fire two pistols at a time with "lightning speed" and deadly accuracy. The demonstration occurred in the basement of the courthouse during the noon break at one of the "cattle theft" trials Bob Hollimon was subjected to. Hollimon earned his nickname "the two-gun man." Hollimon lived his life as a man with the bark still on him.

There is a drawing of Old man Hollimon in Ausmus' book. The drawing shows a mean, narrow-eyed man with thin hair and a proud, stubborn, never-back-up twist in his lips. Hollimon is said to have been buried in a San Bernardino grave, Mountain View Cemetery, on February 11, 1953, but the cemetery has no record of him there. I have in my possession a copy of the year 1940 census of the area, which shows a "ROBERT R. HOLLIMON" born in Kansas, living at Kelso Depot. Kelso Depot is located a dozen miles south from "Hollimon Well:" perhaps this is the same man, as his age is given as 73 years, and he affirmed that he had been living at Kelso since April First, 1935. The fields for "Occupation" and "Industry" are filled with straight lines: blank.

Now, in modern times, the entire region is observed to be in ecological ruin; cattle have destroyed Lanfair Valley and all points northward and westward. The town of Lanfair consists of one large house, several smaller buildings, and an "early warning" aircraft radar dish. As for the town of Hart (near "Hole In The Wall Camp Ground"), strip mining at Hart Consolidated Gold Mine has removed all signs of the town.

Bob Hollimon's cabin was allowed to burn to ashes because the fire that swept through Cedar Canyon and Black's Canyon was "natural" (started by lightning). The labor of his hands have passed away, but the memory remains in the minds of a fortunate few.

-0-

Thinking about Bob Hollimon, Matt Burts, and J. W. Robinson, it once again strikes me at just how little control some humans appear to have over their own lives; their futures were determined for them by their pasts, by their very DNA, as if dictated by the Fates. These three men were archetypes that fed upon each other to magnify their assigned roles in the world, on a level that Homer would have recognized and cherished.

Hollimon with his two guns, unfailing moral certitude, and unbending code of what is honorable and what is to be despised--- he would have loathed and detested me and my soft life; my lack of respect for what he would have considered sacred; my immaturity; my struggle to accept evil, and shades of evil, that I cannot successfully change or oppose.

The major differences between Hollimon and Robinson, from my perspective as an observer distanced in time, were actually quite simple: to Hollimon, "right" equaled "might;" for Robinson, "might" equaled "right." Both extremes are not reflected in reality: the real world falls in the middle, and that is where Matt Burts lived. Burts was a bandit who matured and tried to leave behind his past, walking the middle road; the gods, in the form of J. W. Robinson, would not allow Burts to change his fated violent end.

The bitch of it all--- the spooky, frightening thing--- is that I suspect this is true of all human beings.

Thus filled once again with ennui, I made my way back to my

vehicle, fried my ass on the blistering hot driver's seat, and drove northwest back to the railway.

PARDON ME, IS THIS THE BUS TO POTATO SALAD?

***"A man who has never gone to school may steal a freight car; but if he has a university education, he may steal the whole railroad."* -- Theodore Roosevelt**

At the railway, I waited for a slow freight train to make its ponderous way northward. The dirt road I was driving on passes under the rails, with mere inches to spare above the cab's roof of my pickup truck, but I stopped anyhow to watch the train go by. It was passing at a speed slow enough for a person to jump on.

Now that was a fine idea, I thought. (Or maybe I said it out loud: I never knew these days.) What would happen to me if I just got out of my vehicle, grabbed a gallon of water and my back pack, and got on the train? Where would I end up, other than in jail for trespassing? Did it even matter where I went, as long as I ***went***? I've seldom concerned myself in the past with where I was going: it was the moving that was the attraction.

The urge to jump on the train was overwhelming. The train beckoned to me like a siren; like an enticing and beautiful sea nymph; like Inanna leaning naked and seductive, glossy black pubic hair trust forward, waiting for me to stop and talk to her. It was like Shania Twain standing there wearing a tiny bathrobe and a smile, wondering why I wasn't already climbing on her, and was I man enough? Shania Train.

But then the train passed, the urge left me, and I put my weary Toyota in gear and drove under the tracks, then turned left.

Highway 40 heading west brought me to Barstow. The sun was setting, making driving westward a blind task, with much swerving and guessing on my part, but eventually I made it to the best part of town (the run-down, disreputable side) and to the grocery store.

I needed maybe 90 days worth of food, mostly canned, mostly dried, that would not spoil. The lack of refrigeration meant many food items would not last more than a few days. Thanks to modern canning technology, I had much to choose from. I would also need to visit the crazy guy at the Army surplus store for more ammunitions cans to store food in: a trip I was looking forward to, since I like paranoids with hand guns. (It's the paranoids with atomic bombs and world-wide delivery systems I'm shy of.)

I bought ten boxes of pancake mix that required only adding water to make; I bought three bottles of corn oil to fry it all in. Butter would not last, so I bought ten small jars of jam to spread on the pancakes. In the "drink mix" aisle I loaded up my shopping cart with artificial flavorings to add to my drinking water, since the taste of distilled bug-shat-in bee-drowned-in desert water was growing tedious. I bought ten pounds of granulated sugar to add to the vile drink mixes, and twenty pounds of dehydrated milk.

In the canned fruit section, I emptied the shelves of pineapple and apricot and peaches. I got the "packed in syrup" kind so that I could use the fruit sugar in my morning coffee, or add it to water with drink mixes.

After paying for the food and hauling it to my pickup, I went back into the store for a second load. The "cooking" section yielded four plastic jars of dehydrated minced onions, powdered garlic, several cans of tree nuts, and salt. I got ten boxes of dry cereal, two jars of instant coffee, and four cans of "black bread." (I had no idea there was such a thing.)

Canned pasta sauce is almost as good as the sauce in glass jars, but could be man-handled without breaking. I got thirty cans of red sauce--- all that were on the shelf. I also got six one-pound bags of spaghetti noodles.

Toilet paper! I needed toilet paper. For the past two weeks I had been wiping my sorry ass with a wet cloth and then rinsing the Hell out of it because I used the same cloth to bathe with. Back home, my cave, I had a large plastic bag full of used toilet paper that I planned on using to start camp fires with, and the rats love the stuff: I got thirty-six rolls of toilet paper, which the rats could have after I was done wiping my stained ass with it.

I bought a real can opener; a can opener that would not turn the lid of cans into lethal Kung Fu / Ninja death disks with 37 razor-sharp points.

I bought four one-pound bags of sunflower seeds.

For some unfathomable reason, against all sanity, I also bought three pounds of lasagna noodles; I had neither pot large enough to boil them in, casserole dish to assemble the lasagna in, or oven to bake it in. But my mysterious need to buy the noodles was too overwhelming to ignore.

After three trips in and out of the store, with several hundred pounds of food, I was ready to face the Army Paranoid Guy.

I FEEL SO MUCH SAFER NOW

***"If I have to beat you up to keep you safe, that's just what I'll do. It's this kind of regard for others that makes me believe I'd be a good politician."* -- Jarod Kintz**

As I was putting the shopping cart into its "docking bay" cage, a police car rolled into the parking lot, headed towards me (I pretended to not notice), and stopped next to me, blocking the route to my vehicle. An obese short stark-white man-thing in a police uniform, 70 inches tall and 90 inches across, got out of the police car and confronted me. It was like being approached by a giant dinner roll; a huge hamburger bun with legs, made out of bleached white flour and pig fat.

"Sir, we have a complaint that someone in the store was acting strangely." He then waited for me to reply. After maybe fifteen seconds while he stared blankly at me, and after he started looking enraged, I said "I didn't see anything. Why, I haven't even seen the musical 'Cats.'"

"Someone matching your description was seen dancing and singing in the store, disturbing people," he said.

That could indeed have been me, since I often have no idea what my body is doing when my brain is doing something else, but I would never admit that to anyone let alone a police officer.

"Nope. I didn't see or hear anyone doing that." I suggested maybe he got the store location wrong, and maybe it was some place else. He clearly did not believe me, and he demanded that I produce identification. Rather than explain to Hamburger Bun that I was not required to do so, I meekly submitted because #1 he had a hand gun and #2 his radio could summon a half-dozen violent gang members to beat me, put me in jail, tow my car away to a city impound lot, and rob me. He ordered me to stand next to the police car while he used the computer to check me out, as the punishing sun hammered my hat against my head. While he waited for the results from the computer query, he sneered at me and asked, "How much have you been drinking this evening?

I was touched by his concern for my health and hydration. The question took considerable thought, though. If one counted the entire day, the total was slightly less than one gallon of distilled water. If the time span in question was merely "this evening," then only about one third of a gallon or a bit less.

"About a quarter of a gallon, I guess," I said. "I try to drink every drop my still produces," I said, trying to anticipate his next question. Again it looked like he didn't believe me.

Apparently no local law enforcement had been looking for me, since after a few minutes Dough Boy In Blue handed my ID back to me, then cautioned me to not disturb people, and said I may have a good day and leave. I promised I would not contemplate doing so (disturb people, that is), let alone do so, and he watched as I got into my pickup.

I sat in the oven-like heat of the car and fumed with rage and ire. I fantasized my revenge; perhaps a biker gang rolling into the parking lot, engines screaming, to surround the tedious toad-like gnome in uniform, kicking and tormenting him while slowly riding around him as he wailed and cried for his mother. No biker gang showed up to revenge my humiliation, so I fired up the pickup and exited the parking lot, turned left on to the main road, and then a right into the Army Surplus store.

R.E.S.P.E.C.T.

"Raising the flag and singing the anthem are, while somewhat suspicious, not in themselves acts of treason." -- Terry Pratchett

The man with the spinning Oliver North eyes was still sitting behind the hand gun counter when I walked into the Army Surplus store. I did not have any trouble imagining him running around a motel with a butcher's knife in one had, American flag in the other, stabbing people as they showered, wailing "Stop persecuting me!" I smiled at the psycho, and started sorting through munitions cans.

I bought some winter clothing, and a water-proof rubber blanket certified to keep me from freezing to death if the ambient temperature is 20 degrees Fahrenheit or greater.

After making several trips to load ammo cans into my pickup, I sorted through the food containers in the bed of my pickup. I opened all of the pancake mix boxes and placed the plastic bags of mix into two ammo cans. The boxes of powdered milk fit into a third ammo can. Pasta and other plastic-wrapped food items went into the other ten ammo cans, with cans and jars of food left in paper bags. It was a massive pile of gear and bloody awfully expensive.

Also, I wish I had a gun. Maybe if I had a hand gun I could get a little respect. Show the fools around here what time it is. I wanted a gun. I went back into the Army Surplus store.

"I wanna gun," I told Oliver North Eyes. "Where can a Real American buy a gun, a big gun, at short notice?" Eyes spinning yet not quite managing to look directly at me, he suggested I try a gun store. I thanked him and went back into the dreadful sunlight.

Back in my pickup, I made a left turn on the main road and drove a few hundred yards, made a sharp right turn into the El Rancho Deep Fried Pork Products Restaurant and pulled up next to a handful of homeless-looking men. "Howdy guys!" I greeted them, leaning out my window. "I need a gun. A hand gun. Fast. Where can a white man in a hurry go to get a hand gun?" They looked at each other, uneasily, and as a group, with no signal between them that I could detect, they slowly walked away and behind the restaurant. Talk about lack of common courtesy; a lack of respect. If I had a gun they wouldn't treat me so shabbily.

I fitted eye glasses to my face, drove my pickup in a loop, took a right turn on the road, drove past the south bound on-ramp for the highway, took a right on the north-bound ramp, and as the stars came out I headed back to Baker. It had been a tedious, long day.

ON EARTH WE HAVE A WORD....

***"Life is a gamble, at terrible odds. If it were a bet you wouldn't take it."* -- Tom Stoppard**

On the drive north I contemplated dinner. I could stop at the same old burrito store in Baker yet again and order the same "six large bags of French fries please," or I could continue on the highway to State Line and stop at a casino for dinner.

The last place I would want anyone to see me enter is a casino where people go to leave their money in the odd and irrational and observed false belief that handing over their money to the casino will result in the casino handing it back and more with it. I would rather someone see me enter a whore house than a casino. The one and only time I walked into a "house of prostitution," in Pahrump, Nevada, I thought it was a restaurant and I asked the frightening-looking lady at the desk if I may see a menu. As embarrassing as that *faux pas* was --- I am still blushing, in fact --- being seen entering or leaving a casino would be even worse.

At Baker I left the highway, stopped at the STOP sign, turned left, and headed home to my cave.

MY KINGDOM DOUBLES IN SIZE

***"Awkward disturbances will arise; people will not submit to have their throats cut quietly; they will run, they will kick, they will bite."* -- Thomas de Quincey**

It took me three days to unload my supplies from my pickup.

On the first night the moon was nearly opposite the sun, and therefore close to full, and the denuded landscape of ancient, broken, sun-bruised rocks of the mountainside lay in blunted, grayed, muted repose--- as if basking in the cool respite from the sun. Moonlight lay like a thick goo on the ground, and driving up the mountainside was like driving up the side of a cake heavily coated with confectioner's sugar.

In the bright moonlight I stopped at the roadside where I must hike cross country to my cave, and I went through my supplies seeking out all items that heat might render dangerous to consume. These items would go to my cave first, and I would leave the heat-tolerant items in my vehicle and transport them later.

The night was so bright from the full moon that I could read the fine print on the cans of black bread, and I was intrigued enough to hunt for my new can opener and, without suffering bodily injury, I pried the bread from its tin cocoon and took a bite. It tasted a little revolting, but in a sweet and appealing way: nutty with walnuts, fruity from plenty of raisins, sweet with the sulfur bite of black molasses. I wish I had more cans of the horrible stuff.

After unloading the perishable foods, I went through the tedious and time-consuming chore of hiding my vehicle behind its hill. It is a curious thing about working in the desolate wilderness in moonlight: the sounds I made seemed to travel only a few feet before being swallowed up by the preternatural gloom--- as if the moonlight were a thick snow falling. The sense of quietude was likely only my imagination, and my noise may have carried for a mile or more, but the feeling persisted.

After my vehicle was finally in its hiding spot, firmly squatting on its plywood boards, I climbed onto the top of its camper shell and rested, looking westward so that the moon wouldn't blind me. The night was utterly quiet, as desert nights usually are when the small furry "prey" animals are hiding from the large furry blood-splattered monsters seeking them: even the coyotes had paused in their yipping and barking. Townsend's big-eared bats flew silent Figure Eights a dozen inches or so above me, gobbling up the insects that my blood, sweat, and body heat attracted.

The silent night felt magical, as if a glory of unicorns was approaching. Captain Ron wrote in a few of his boating magazine articles about "The God of the Two AM Watch" and maybe that god was present. Unicorns or gods, I felt its benign gaze traveling over the silent, rocky, mountainous desert tableau. I said to the night, "A fart right now would be a form of blasphemy," which caused me to laugh (in the desert I am my own best entertainment), and the spell was broken.

My injured hand was feeling better, with less pain than the day before, and I took this as either the good sign that it was healing, or the bad sign that the nerves had died, and the rest of me would soon follow. With that happy thought, I made myself as comfortable as I could, back pack as a lumpy pillow, and I waited for the eastern sky to lighten.

The night cooled. As the desert cooled, the scents of creosote brush and chamisa filled my nostrils.

Once again I wondered why I was living alone in the desert wilderness. Was I really, as I thought, a lazy gutless coward hiding from society and people because I could no longer deal with the horror of "modern civilization?" Was I an intrepid manly handsome sexy adventurer joining the ranks of people like John Muir; William Willis, John Fremont; Burro Bill and Edna; Father Garces; and Marcos de Niza? Pressed to pick one, my money would be on the "gutless" side. I told myself that I was "doing this" so that I could later write about the experience, but the reality was the thought of going back to work in an airless, sunless, regimented corporate building filled me with dread. Far better to die of heat prostration, snake bite, starvation, and dehydration (all at the same time) than face Corporate America again.

The sky spun westward, dragging stars and moon along with it. The moon tumbled ass over tea kettle down the western slope of Avawatz Peak; Orion in the east faded in the pink rose blush of dawn; shadows turned in slow degree from argent to black as the sun crept over the Hidden Hills.

Dawn: time to drop my heavy emotional load and take up my flesh and bone load.

Burdened heavily with supplies, I reached my solar still and the fresh water spring about 90 minutes later. The green iguana had left toe prints on the damp sand next to the solar still, and I felt a sharp stab of guilt that I hadn't thought to buy her any treats when I was in the store.

What do iguanas eat, anyhow? I had no idea. Probably not pork chops and applesauce. Cactus, maybe, along with the Canterbury Bells and Owl's Clover I step over now and then, and perhaps the watercress choking the spring where the water is the deepest. If I put a slice of pineapple on a rock near where the iguana liked to hang out, would it be eaten? I told myself to remember to offer a guilt-appeasement pineapple slice.

At my cave, I discovered hundreds of tiny pieces of used toilet paper had been scattered liberally by the rats or mice. The bag I had kept it in had been chewed open. I had never been able to figure out who was the host and who was the unwanted visiting guest when it came to the life forms I shared with the cave: my assumption was that I'm the guest and everyone else --- rats, mice, tarantulas, assorted *Solifugae*, stink bugs, bees, beetles, and (my personal favorite horror) Bark Scorpions who loved to share my blanket and body heat at night --- were my hosts and I was the rude guest.

Tediously I picked up the tiny paper pieces while on my knees, trying to keep the place looking neatly and tidy. The pieces I put in a bucket that had a few inches of water in it. I then added the bag of used toilet paper to the bucket, added more water, and tamped down with my fist the sodden mess tightly inside the bottom of the bucket. I then upended the bucket in the brain-boiling sun, smacking the bucket a few times to free the wet lump of toilet paper, and left it to dry. Once dry it would make a hard brick that would act as fire wood.

I set out eastward towards The Wall, passed the spring and my solar still, passed the pineappleless iguana. At The Wall I turned left, walked a bit, turned right, climbed the incline to the top of The Wall, and squatted on the rock that was as searing hot as the top of a wood-burning stove. It seemed to me that The Wall would make an excellent sleeping platform, and a good place to spend the warmer part of the days if I would set up an awning to protect me and the rock from direct sunlight. At my cave the arroyo walls acted like an oven, reflecting the heat back at me; on top of The Wall, now and then a breeze would come and take away some of my body heat.

The rock ledge had many narrow cracks wherein I could tie a line to a small rock, insert the rock into a crack, and have the crack act as a jamb cleat to hold up poles for an awning. With enough twine, my new tarp, and using four sticks, I could make a decent shelter; the awning would gape open widely towards the northeast, and slope closer to the ground to the southwest to keep most of the sun out.

A MINE OF HER OWN

***"You have reached Powell. Please leave a message in which you recognize that life is fleeting and death is forever."* -- Brad Parks**

There are more than 6,300 mines and prospects in San Bernardino County, about 180 of which are located in the Avawatz Mountains. That does not include the many tens of thousands of places where greedy unloved unwashed woman-less men with dynamite wandered the region looking for quartz outcroppings to blast with Dupont's finest 60%, using #6 blasting caps and a Lucifer stick to see under the exposed rock. From the year 1825 to 1944, every gold nugget and every gold vein that could be found had been: with three known exceptions, only dust and a few nuggets are left--- and a bloody hell of a mess was left behind from the plunder.

Some of that mess is still usable for various building projects, for people who lack absolutely anything better. There are also amazing structures made out of oak and pine beams, intricately cut and fitted together, for hoisting and loading ore, that stand thirty feet tall above the mine shafts they serviced; engineers and architects still visit these structures to measure and draw and photograph them.

The Avawatz Mountain Range is littered with ruined and discarded steam engines; water boilers; condensation tanks; wind-powered air and water pumps; steel cables; steel pipes; narrow-gauge rails; copper wires; glass insulators for electrical power lines (purple from the sun); swamp coolers; tin evaporation pans; concrete piling and footings; and piles of sardine cans.

It was a miner in Baker named Old Man Andy who told me about the haunting of Coyote Hole Spring. The ghost is (or perhaps was) that of a hard rock miner turned gunman who robbed the payroll for one of the mines near Avawatz Peak. It was around year 1930. The pay master for the mine drove his fragile automobile down the sandy road that passes to the west of Salt Basin, turned eastward and eventually in to Kingston Wash, and on to Resting Springs, then finally Las Vegas where the payroll waited. The robber saw him pass Kingston Spring, and knowing the pay master's task, thought to ambush the driver on his return trip.

The ambush occurred at Coyote Hole Spring. The car carrying the payroll made its slow, laborious crawl along Kingston Wash, and stopped at Coyote Hole Spring to get water for the radiator, and lunch for the driver. The robber jumped out of the willow brush, pistol in hand, and demanded the money. The driver asked the robber to not shoot, and told the robber he could have the money. The driver reached in to the car to "get the money," grabbed a pistol instead, and shot the robber "dead five times" (as Andy put it) from less than five feet away. After blasting huge chunks of guts, muscle, gristle, and assorted viscera out of the very surprised would-be robber who screeched and wailed in pain, anguish, horror and terror during the brief medical procedure, the driver added water to the car's radiator, ate a can of fish, and continued on his way to pay the men at the mine.

During the following fifteen years, miners and cattlemen who had stopped at Coyote Hole Spring told other people about hearing five gun shots, during which they heard a man screaming. People swore upon their honor when reporting the sounds, and they could not be compelled to go back to the spring. Even future pay masters bypassed Kingston Wash and took the alternate route past Ibex Spring rather than encounter the Ghost of Coyote Hole Spring.

I have visited Coyote Hole Spring, 68 years after the killing, and the ghost appears to have finally fallen silent. I wonder if, up there in Heaven some where, he still believes a few thousand dollars was worth his life, let alone the agony and horror while losing it.

As I sat on my rock wall, gazing eastward over the Valjean Valley and thinking about all of the gold that people had wrested from the rocky desert, it occurred to me I could visit some dry, sandy arroyos and pan for gold dust, and perhaps that would help finance my life here in the desert wilderness. I had a frying pan that would work on panning the "black sand" during the afternoon, and work on frying pancakes in the morning. I liked the idea.

THIS BOOT WAS MADE FOR WALKING

***"He gave the impression of being a man who knew the world was crazy and had decided to become part of the problem, rather than the solution."* -- Warren Murphy**

A few minutes after the sun set, the evening temperature plunged from "too hot to bear" to "too cold to bear." It was as if Someone Up There had slammed closed the doors of Hell and kicked the doors of Niflheim wide open. The transition was so sudden that I imagined seeing Frost Giants flood in to Midgard (Earth) to use the Avawatz as a foot stool. Shivering in the quickly darkening dusk, I carefully picked my way off the rock wall and retreated to my blankets and sleep.

Pulling the edge of my blankets to my chin, I noticed Orion already high in the sky; if I had been able to look eastward, through the rocky hill behind my back, I could have seen Sirius low on the horizon; the winter months would soon arrive.

Chilled, blankets warming slowly, I slept.

I was awakened by a scream. For a second or two my mind flashed back to my thoughts of The Ghost of Coyote Hole Spring the day before, and I thought I might be lucky enough to be haunted. The sound resolved itself to a squeak that ended abruptly, located perhaps ten feet above where I was laying. The chthonic silhouette of a large owl, grasping a now-quiet victim in her fists, blotted out a path through the stars on wings so silently beating that I only heard the wind passing through her feathers.

"Well, that was unpleasant," I told the night, shivering more from dread than the cold. "What? I'm next, is it? A friendly warning, eh? I'd fucking **LOVE** to see the owl large enough to haul my fat ass away!" I immediately wished I hadn't said that, tempting Fate as it did, and I tightened my blankets more firmly around my throat (where a vague terror had taken hold), my eyes wide and staring into the murderous, ominous, ill-omened night. After a few minutes, when the night became "too quiet," I became convinced an owl forty feet tall was about to carry me off to her nest of six-foot-tall babies some where up there in the crags and clefts of Avawatz Peak. I thought about making a run for it to my cave, but the night was cold, my blankets were warm, and I fell back to sleep before choosing between the cold and a beaked, clawed, avian death.

I dreamed that I was living in a cave in the wilderness, and that I wished my brother would come and visit me. In my dream there was a mighty clap of thunder; the sky opened up in a funnel of dark clouds in a starry sky. There was a scream as a body was ejected from the funnel and plunged to Earth. Just before it splattered on the ground, I said, "Hi, Fred." He apparently didn't seem inclined, nor have the time, to waive a greeting at me before his blood and guts made an unsightly stain on the rocky, parched desert floor.

The sun rose once again, driving away the dreams of my many improbable (and impossible) deaths. I rose from my blankets, stomped my feet hard to get the cold out of them; I put on my hat; I pulled on my socks; I shook the dirt off my shirt and put it on; I pulled my pants on, leaving the zipper open briefly to let Little Davie enjoy the morning sun a few seconds longer; I zipped up and then put on one boot.

One boot, which had been placed next to its twin the night before, was missing. Somewhere in Germany, surely, there are legends of trolls that take people's boots at night (probably when snow is falling), but this was the United States of God-damned America, where such troll behavior was not to be tolerated.

There is a hell of a lot of salt in the East Mojave Desert, and more than enough to go around in the Avawatz Mountain Range. But some furry beastie out there wanted salty leather, and had carried off my sweat-stained boot. I wondered how far a skunk could drag a boot; farther than a squirrel, surely? Not as far as a raccoon? I had no idea. I figured the boot was probably far down a coyote's burrow by now, being enjoyed by coyote pups, Mother Coyote saving the tongue for some special *Canis latrans* occasion.

Getting on my hands and knees, I studied the ground where I had placed both boots. The ground was well-trampled by my feet (bare and booted), in a circle at least twenty feet wide, so I crawled in a spiral until I found marks that might possibly be that of a boot being dragged; when I found such a mark, I placed a small pile of rocks next to it.

I continued to crawl, in an ever-widening spiral, for about fifty feet until I came up hard on the east side of the arroyo. I then sat at the opening of my cave and looked at the several dozen piles of rocks I had made.

Among the chaotically spaced rocks, a distinct line of rocks was apparent. I set off, back on my hands and knees, in slow, delayed, rather comical but relentless pursuit.

Northward I crawled, picking up signs of a dragged boot more easily as I strayed away from my lonely habitat. The signs of the ground being disturbed were faint but distinct, and at each mark I placed more piles of rocks. If I lost the trail, I wanted to be able to easily locate the mark I thought was the last, and the small piles of rocks would let me do that.

What ever carried off my boot was in the mood to travel, the bastard. Up the arroyo I crawled, over patches of sand, between boulders, through clumps of dirt and dry brittle brown grass. The sun rose over the east edge of the arroyo, and the gates of Hell were again propped open. Onward I crawled.

The arroyo split in two, and the bandit's trail took the left-hand fork. The sand in this arroyo was packed harder, perhaps with subsurface water that, farther down the drainage I was crawling over, provided the water for me at my spring. The harder sand made tracking the wandering boot more difficult, and every mark took many minutes to find.

The drainage system I was crawling through, tracking a boot that apparently was too heavy for the thief... the brigand... the larcenist to lift off the ground for very long, was fed by many dozens of washes, and during a hard rain the washes funneled rills of water into the main arroyo. That water resurfaced the sand, leaving a series of corrugated trenches that cut through the otherwise flat and smooth sand. The ground was heavily littered with the tracks of birds; hares; snakes; lizards; coyotes; rats; and what I can only imagine was a tortoise, with its four flipper-like swimming-motion foot pads. Picking out the marks of a boot being dragged a bit, lifted a ways, dropped and dragged again, quickly grew tedious, and I considered giving up and hopping one-footed in to town to buy new boots.

At any moment I expected my wandering boot to deviate from the main channel and take a side channel some where. I considered myself lucky the highwayman couldn't pick up the boot and climb out of the arroyo with it, on to the hard pan and rocks--- if that happened, I would never be able to track it.

I *slithered* northeast, up a side wash, crept a few dozen feet, placing little rocks next to boot marks, then dragged my body northward again up yet another side wash.

At a patch of gravel where several washes joined at a wide sandy beach about 80 feet wide, no mark was left that I could detect. I spent more than one hour slowly crawling around and through the gravel before I found a few marks that might have been made from a dragging boot. It took another hour to then select the correct mark and continue The God Damn Quest For The God Damned Traveling Boot, God Damn It.

The sun crossed the meridian, and made its way westward. Onward I crawled, feeling exploited, abused, persecuted, and poorly treated.

When my hands and knees were sufficiently sore, and my back in agony, Fate allowed that the tracks ended at a large clump of rabbit brush, where my well-gnawed boot rested. The laces, up to the eye holes, had been eaten; the insides of the “uppers” had been gobbled up, including the nylon padding; the soft rubber insert, where my heel once toiled as I hiked, had been sampled also and evidently found unpalatable as it was nibbled but left intact.

I removed the lace that remained, slammed the boot against the ground to dislodge anyone that might be inside, and put the meandering boot on my socked foot. With the partial lace, I tied the boot on as best I could.

Standing up was a struggle, accompanied by stabbing pain in my back, but once on my feet I felt human again. I gave my foot a shake or two, with the boot wobbling loosely, and followed my little piles of rocks back to my cave. Tracking the boot had taken me almost seven hours.

That night I slept with my boots on.

GUILT ENGULFS ME

***"If anyone from Texas is reading this, nice to know you have Internet access in your tree."* -- Greg Laden**

I felt guilty, as I lay on my tarp, under blankets, staring up at the stars, boots on. I thought about the immense toil and time it took me to find my purloined boot; whoever had taken it must have worked just as hard to drag it away, but with a vastly different mindset than mine. She or he must have been overwhelmed with happiness at finding a leather boot to eat, and my taking it away must have been a great and sad disappointment to... whoever. The more I thought about it, the worse I felt. I had deprived some small furry (presumably) desert wilderness denizen her or his legitimate right to salvage and eat anything that might be discovered. Perhaps there were babies to be fed, called from their den to gather around the boot and chew on it, like a human family at a fat Christmas goose.

It rankled my mind with shame. I flung my blankets away, grabbed my flashlight, and stumbled to my cave in the dark.

Inside the cave I opened the ammo can that held saltine crackers, and fished out a package; a stack of ten crackers, each perforated in to quarters for easy breaking, wrapped tightly in waxed paper. I sealed the can, and opened the can that held Graham crackers. After taking out a package of these sweet crackers, I rummaged through my sliced bread can and found a half dozen stale pieces.

Into the cold and dark I groped and blundered, using the flashlight to find my trail of rocks and sand piles, wending yet again the torturous route northward up the arroyo, then northwest, then west, then north again, covering the same ground on my feet that I had covered on my knees the day before.

At the rabbit brush where my boot had been, I opened up the packages of crackers and carefully laid them on the ground. I placed the stale bread on top of the crackers.

"I'm sorry," I said loud enough to be heard by anyone in the neighborhood. I explained, to the night, at considerable length why I needed the boot; eventually I started to feel silly. I apologized again, then rushed back to my bed.

WINTER

***"If there's someone who is watching / Who sees but will not act / Someone who's protecting us / B' can defend but not attack. / Like a shield, invisible / Like a patron in the fight / Perhaps he was chained, with his hands behind his back."* -- Melina Lindskog Lindvall**

Cold fell upon the East Mojave desert like a mugger upon a trust fund baby asleep in a crack house. Winter came with gleeful hostility, suddenly, with single-minded malignity. The day time temperatures plunged from the low 100s way down to the mid 60s, and night time temperatures hovered around 45 degrees. This is not cold to 99% of humanity, but for Southern California daisies such as myself it was brutal.

The desert of the USA Southwest triples its human population in the winter as foreigners from The Far East (New York, Maine, Missouri) flee the snow and ice and rush westward to places like Tecopa, Kingman, Quartzite, and Winter Haven. Life in these winter hobo camps is NLAWKI (Not Life As We Know It), but a simulacrum of life. Imagine all of the world's soap opera TV shows combined, then magnified six times: people in their 80s, and 90s fornicating with each other, stabbing and shooting each other, getting in drunken brawls, and mysteriously vanishing as likely murder victims... and the survivors cannot wait to do it all again next winter.

Unwary visitors, such as myself, who might happen to walk among a winter hobo camp and politely inquire "How do you do?" will be expected to sit (or stand in one spot) and listen for hours as the stranger one was being polite to answered the query in tedious, painful, embarrassing detail. I have discovered that if anyone wants to hear the most sordid, the most criminal, the most depraved accounts of what humanity can inflict upon each other with joyful malice, one need merely visit a winter camper park, find an elderly lady with blue hair, and say "Good morning" to her—- the rest will follow as naturally and as closely as a dog follows a sausage wagon. Often I have been amazed at how some people can hold a grudge into the late 1990s over a humiliating slight they experienced (from a total stranger they never saw again) when trains and river boats were still powered by steam. If you have ever wondered why SkyNET decided to destroy humanity in the movie *Terminator*, just visit a winter camper park in the desert. You would ***Push The Fucking Button***, too.

My solar water still ceased producing enough clean water for my needs as the sun headed southward. No amount of fiddling with the plastic sheet, nor placing rocks along the northern edges to act as heat reflectors, was enough to produce more than a few ounces every hour. With limited fuel available, I kept and drank any water that I happened to cook with-- water used to boil pasta I left in my two quart pot, lid on, to cool and then transfered to plastic bottles in my back pack to drink while hiking. In times when I was thirsty and lacked the luxury of heating water first, I used my 0.25 inch copper tube to suck water out of the sand, with the end hovering just below the surface to help keep the dead bees and rabbit turds from fouling the opening.

The air itself grew dryer, and the back of my hands turned dry and split open. Old defensive knife wounds on my hands and arms, collected from an early life of being honest instead of being polite, opened and gaped with the color and texture of beef jerky.

On the plus side, my green left hand slowly faded back to sunburned brown, the pain easing at times to brief moments when I forgot the injury. When reading, or walking, or sitting on the rocky wall to the east and gazing into the distant haze, I worked my left fingers constantly to get the stiffness out of them.

Winter days in the Mojave Desert (and more so in the high desert such as among the Avawatz Mountain Range) are often uncomfortably hot for people standing in the sun. What little shade there is, when they step into it, awards the overheated person with a sudden and biting chill. Like most things in the desert, there are seldom "happy mediums:" there are only extremes, and temperature is one of them.

As the days grew shorter, and nights grew longer and cooler, I spent the daylight hours laying on my reclining beach chair reading under the shade of a blanket that I had rigged as an awning. When an arm or leg got too cold, I would stick it out into the sunlight for a few seconds. When the light began to fade, I would collect my blankets, back pack, binoculars, and hand-powered radio and hike to Lookout Wall east of the spring. Climbing to the flattest part, I wrapped myself in the blankets, then watched the darkness spread across Valjean Valley, Kingston Range, Turquoise Mountain, and (perhaps) the highest peak of the northern Providence Mountains.

As the weeks passed, this routine was punctuated with extended hikes northward and westward. I explored the few roads that are still traveled among the Avawatz, and I also wandered the many ancient roads that are no longer used. There is an astonishing amount of trash in the Avawatz: abandoned shacks; grave yards with human bones, broken glass, and rusted tin cans; mountains of abandoned mining equipment; miles and miles of pipe; billions and billions of tiny pieces of tar paper; and (inexplicably) an extraordinary number of cracked and splintered plywood toilet seats.

During my extended hikes I would find rocks to sleep on, with a blanket wrapped around me. The sun-warmed rocks would surrender their heat quickly, leaving me to shiver through the long night. The exercise kept me strong, but there was no fun in it.

December came, and with it the terrible winter night wind. Windless days ended in nights of icy gales that howled and wailed over the mountain range, and flailed unsheltered living beings with shards of hail that were ripped from the low dark winter clouds that hung over the desert like a cast iron lid. I fled to my shallow cave, pulled the plywood sheets over the hole, and burrowed in for two months.

It is a terrible thing to experience an extended period of time in a dark place, with a dim light bulb that only worked if there was sufficient sunlight to charge the battery. The blackness entered my mind, and there were days that passed when all I did was sleep; reading became a chore, as my mind could not retain anything I had just read. Holding up a book to read, my hands would turn white and bloodless from the cold. On other days I felt sufficiently motivated to cook a decent meal, open a hole in the plywood wall for fresh air, and even go outside and walk around for a few minutes. On other days, I summoned only enough energy to crack open the plywood to piss and shit through, not caring about the smell, then go back to sleep.

My companion was a small rat who had taken shelter with me in the cave. I started calling her or him Hey Rat on the rare occasions I complained when toilet paper was scattered around or forbidden cracker packages chewed open. Hey Rat received her own drinking tin, kept full of water I didn't bother pasteurizing first; she also was provided with clean toilet paper, as well as the cardboard tubes inside toilet paper rolls, to make a comfortable bed. I soon learned that she coveted my dirty socks, so I gave her one and hung up the other for Santa Claus to fill with walnuts, bits of chocolate, and raisins (which he neglected to do). The plastic lid from a coffee can served as Hey Rat's dinner plate, upon which I placed saltine crackers; sunflower seeds; dried apricot slices; pancake bits; soggy mushrooms from jars of pasta sauce (I hate those things); potato chips; stale, hard, dehydrated, disgusting lumps of shrink-wrapped pineapple. When dinner was late, or when I skipped a day, Hey Rat would scold me and do an annoying little rat dance that was more threatening than cute.

The year ended and a new year came. I endured, spending days and nights in a befuddled lethargy. I had nothing to keep my brain interested and attentive, so it went in to hibernation. I plodded through the days like an automation, no longer wondering or hoping if the cold would end and light would return to my world. I existed; I did not live.

NO DOUBT YOU ARE NOT WONDERING

"When were the good and the brave ever in a majority?" **-- Henry David Thoreau**

What did I do for sex in the desert by myself for 29 months? It is probably well known that Desert Bighorn Sheep, no matter how cute and enticing, are protected species and must remain unmolested (in all ways). I therefore had to make do with whatever was at hand. Considering how much I loathe being touched by humans, it is a wonder I had any kind of "sex life."

I shall tell you two related stories. Don't worry about making me blush; the only time I blush is from having my face slapped.

I had a girlfriend who loved sex. Sex with anyone, everyone, and by herself I mean. She was ready for sex at a moment's notice, and often with no notice at all. If I was busy still rinsing the dinner dishes, she would go into the bedroom and start without me. This jump start was even more noteworthy with the fact that it took me at least ten minutes to catch up to wherever she was in the process. The final fact to note is that she needed less than ten minutes from start to finish. By the time I removed my neck tie and one shoe, sex that evening was over for both of us.

But I did not resent it. In fact, I was pleased: think of all of the hard work I avoided.

In my defense, I really suck at romance. Let me put that another way. I am ***horrible*** at romance. For one example, I had a friend who was unhappy with her breasts and was anxious that I "would not like them." So of course I complemented them at the first opportunity. Well, actually the second opportunity since that's when I had my mouth empty. I wanted to say to her something nice and also entertaining to help ease her anxiety, so I said, "Garsh, sis! Pa wuz right! Ah haint never dun seen tits so fine since th' county fair li'stock show!" A raging torrent of violent motions followed, and I found myself outside wearing boots and clutching my pants to my chest. I though furiously trying to think what went wrong.

That wasn't the worse part: we made up a few days later, and while we were on her bed she just happened to complain that when growing up her younger sister (a slovenly doe-eyed nymph with wet blue eyes and bow-shaped lips) always had to have the same things she had. Yeah, you guessed it. I found myself outside again only this time without my boots.

I try my best to not be hard on women. Let me rephrase that. I try very hard to be kind to people and women. But I have spent a life-time looking for a Mae West to play opposite my W.C. Fields, and there just ain't women like her any more.

- 0 -

During the long winter I had yet another reoccurring dream. In the dream I had died and I was sent to My Eternal Reward. To the shock of everyone who knows me, I apparently had ended up in Paradise. As I stepped through the gate and into The After Life I was greeted by all of the women I have ever thought about while masturbating.

"Good God!" I exclaimed, trying to take in the vast multitude, the legions, of those whom I have lusted for. They spanned the afterlife's geography in every direction and to the horizon.

A bright flash of light, a clap of thunder, and God stood before me.

"You called?" She asked.

"Gosh, I have been a busy little boy, haven't I?"

"Meh!" said God. "I've seen bigger crowds of lust objects. You should have seen the mob of nubile girls that met Mother Teresa."

God beckoned to me to stand closer to Her, so I stepped up and stood by Her side. She placed one dark brown arm across my shoulders and with Her other arm gestured to the huge army of women before us.

"All of these harmless, mostly blameless women you have...." She began.

"How many were blame-worthy? And how do I get their telephone numbers?"

"... women you have debauched in your filthy little ape head while...." God continued.

"And there's Veronica Lake, at the head of the line!" I exclaimed in happy amazement. "And there's Julie Newmar standing next to her!"

"... little ape head while pleasuring yourself with both hands and assorted home repair tools."

"And Barbara Eden is standing behind them!" I was feeling all warm and fuzzy, even though I was dead, thinking about all the fun

I would be having for eternity here in Heaven.

"Heaven?" God asked, reading my mind.

"Yes," I said (continuing to ignore God in death as in life), not suspecting even slightly any other alternative. "And looking over the fine female flesh, gosh, they do tend to shape up all alike, don't they?"

"I sorted them by tit size," God said.

"Ah, thank you," I said, appreciating the extra effort. "So, you mean Sandy Duncan is at the back of the line?" I asked.

"Yes, way over there," She pointed, "next to Pearl Bailey."

A thought occurred to me.

"Where's Jessica Rabbit?" Seemed to me she would be up front, right there next to my good friends Julie and Veronica.

"She's a cartoon, you sick fuck!" God pointed out, echoing what many dozens of mortals have told me. "This is the afterlife."

"Oh. Ah, yeah. A cartoon," I mumbled, thinking back. "I never noticed that before."

"Now then," God said, getting down to Her business with me. "Your eternal punishment will be...."

"Wait!" I yelped in dismay. "'Punishment?'" Surely I had not heard correctly.

"Your eternal punishment will be to live with every one of these women and get to know them as a person; get to know their personalities, likes, hopes, dreams, silly quirks, what makes her smile, economic theories, opinions on music and food and art, biggest regrets, and loftiest goals."

"Oh, my God!" I wailed. "This is Hell!"

I woke up screaming, like every real man would.

JOHN DENVER LIVES IN ME!

***"This whole thing just screams 'I'm a whiny pathetic cunt.'"* -- Santino Castagna**

A day came, around the middle of February, when I shoved my head through the plywood wall and found the day had dawned sunny and clear after a quiet night. The wind had failed to arrive the night before, and golden light lay scattered around the dusty hills and peaks like streams of gold. I shoved a plywood sheet aside, stepped outside, and stood in a winter's worth of half-dried shit as I blinked at the dazzling glare.

A fancy breakfast was in order, to celebrate.

Heating water on my camp stove, I spooned powdered pancake mix into a bowl and added a little powdered potato (for bulk). I spooned powdered coffee into a cup, and added powdered sugar. From the ammo can that held saltine crackers I recovered the canned butter (good to eat if one doesn't look at it). Into an empty olive can I put powdered "orange drink" and sugar and added dirty water. This hot meal, such as it was, motivated me to survey what food supplies I had left.

I had dehydrated refried beans, yellow mustard, and lasagna noodles. It was once again time for a trip to the city for groceries.

Heaping food and water on Hey Rat's plates, I disconnected my tiny light bulb from its car battery. I checked my water bottles in my back pack, and then wrapped my blankets in a plastic sheet. Items I wanted Hey Rat to leave alone I placed on top of other items in the vain and pointless hope she wouldn't be able to get at them.

Shouldering my pack, I picked up the battery with my now-healed left hand and headed towards my automobile. Every two or three minutes I shifted the heavy battery between hands, and as the miles passed I contemplated leaving it behind: if my car did not start, I could always come back for the battery. I discarded the idea: it is amazing how often people set something down in the desert, intending to come back for it, and they never find it again. (An acquaintance of mine once set down a box of Dupont's finest #6 blasting caps, with a fancy fiberglass crimper, to unload his bladder; three days later he gave up looking for it. Some where out there is a jack rabbit wandering lose, armed and dangerous, squeaking "Earth First!")

My tedious scramble through sand, gravel, cactus, alkali flats, shallow arroyos, and creosote brush finally ended at the dirt road west of Old Mormon Spring. As always, I walked the final half mile on what few rocks and spots of gravel I could find, loath to leave boot prints that anyone might wish to follow, and I headed eastward to my hidden automobile.

It is utterly pointless to lock one's automobile when it is hiding in the desert; anyone who cares to loot an automobile need merely pick up a rock and smash a window. Upon reaching my weary-looking Toyota, I retrieved my wallet from my front right pocket, zipped open the "key pouch," and extracted the car's ignition key. I also noted I had two five-dollar bills: two fins my entire net worth.

Squatting inside the automated beast, I inserted the key, stomped on the clutch pedal, and gave a twist. The engine started immediately, feeling good for a change, and I sat there staring at the heavy spare battery I had just hauled through the desert. Better to have the spare if needed, though I already dreaded the return trip carrying the battery back to the cave.

The tedious process of moving the pickup from its hiding place to the dirt road commenced. The sheets of plywood were easier to move when I had the use of both hands, and it did not take more than 30 minutes to find myself driving the miserable rocky road eastward, Hank Snow on the radio telling me he's been everywhere.

At the highway I paused at rest to contemplate where I could go, and what fun could be had, for a sawbuck: ten dollars didn't buy much in the way of entertainment. I made a left turn on to the highway, and headed towards Tecopa.

At the community bath house in Tecopa I parked in front, got out of my pickup, removed from my wallet one five-dollar bill, and "hid" the wallet under the passenger's side floor mat. Unlacing my boots, I set them on the driver's seat, removed my belt and belt knife, and set them on top of my boots. Slamming the door, I walked in to the bath house in my filthy socks. I paused briefly at the "donations" pipe, which had a slit cut into the top where people can drop in Treasury Notes, pesos, used tampons, pocket change, suggestive condoms (the host was a hot babe in her 80s), bottle caps, and what ever else they believe might be useful to the people who volunteer to clean and maintain the place.

I waited my turn at the shower, as old and (to be frank) scary naked men stared at me. A Tecopa Bomber (a horsefly the size of a bread toaster, as loud as an Aggregat-4 rocket) took a bite from my right shoulder, then flew away before I could punch it in the face. A rill of blood oozed from the wound.

A wet naked man, holding his balls in both hands so they wouldn't drag on the rough tile floor, stepped out of the shower and I stepped in—- fully clothed. It wasn't merely Shower Day for me: it was Laundry Day!

Scrubbing vigorously under the hot water, I worked some of the filth out of my hat, my shirt, my canvas jeans, my socks. Gouts of black crud covered my hands as I scrubbed at my face and beard. The hard black patina of desert grime that had covered my face fell away, mostly, and I found I could once again smile and even lift my eyebrows without a struggle. I took off my shirt, turned it inside out, and scrubbed it. I took off my pants, inverted the legs, and scrubbed. The socks, of course, I left on; the gods only know what diseases lurked among the revolting shower floor. For around fifteen minutes, as the queue outside the shower curtain increased in size, I scraped off the filth. Every minute I used more water than I had used in the previous two months.

I stepped out of the shower to face a half-dozen angry naked men who glared hatred and rage at me because I had made them wait. Well, fuck them (not all at once, please) if they can't let a man bathe and do his laundry at his leisure.

Shuffling wetly across the bath house, clutching my sodden clothing to my chest, I walked outside and to my automobile. Gods, it was fucking cold. I tossed my clothing on the engine hood, and sat inside the cab on the passenger's seat where it was warmer in the dim early spring sun. Stretching my left leg to the clutch pedal, I started the engine and set the heater on "Inferno" and aimed the air vents my way. Once the chill left my blood, I opened the door long enough to grab my wet clothing; I held the shirt up to the hot air vents until it was warmer, then put the wet shirt on. My wet pants followed the procedure.

The inside of the pickup turned into a sauna, with a fine mist of water vapor clinging to every surface, the fog on the windows blotting out the view outside. Rivulets of water flowed down the wind screen and collected in pools on the dash board. Using my water-wrinkled fingers, I tried to wipe away the mist that blocked my view of the outside world-- in vain.

It was Car Japs who planned and executed the bombing of the USA's Pacific Fleet at Pearl Harbor; why didn't the same Car Japs plan and execute the obvious need for internal windshield wipers? To be fair, it was Mitsubishi Car Japs who sunk half the battleships at their moorings, not Toyota Car Japs, but don't they plot these things together? Like the Kar Krauts? I mean, just look at the Kriegsmarine's *Bismarck*: I bet it had windshield wipers inside and out as it sunk the battle cruiser HMS *Hood*.

Clammy, damp clothing clinging to my otherwise naked body, I rolled down the driver's side window, put the vehicle in reverse, stuck my head out the window, looked behind, and let out the clutch. The pickup slid backwards a few meters. Clutch pressed in again, gear shift put in forward low, my pickup and I lurched forward as I turned my external head's gaze forward. So far, so good. Left turn; miss the tourist staring at me like I'm the lunatic and not her; careen to the stop sign; stop. Shit, this was easy: who the fuck needs to see when driving? I thundered south.

While I drove with the window down, the internal fog faded; the late morning air grew warm, and the left side of my body dried. It was a fine day as I rolled to the stop sign at Baker, waited for the tourists to make up their fucking minds regarding where they were going, and turned left. Thirty seconds northward, then a right turn in to the taco shop for lunch.

As I climbed out of my curiously internally damp automobile, I noticed a young man at the side entrance to the fast food store. He was sitting on the hard concrete ground, legs sprawled out widely in front of him, clutching his head with both hands in what appeared to be a desperate vice-like grip as he rocked sideways and moaned in agony. He was blocking the door. Trying to not make eye contact (because then I would be required to care, out of basic human compassion which I had no time for or interest in), I estimated the distances involved. Door way; door travel; free play in door hinges; where I could stand to grasp the door handle without stepping on him; the position of the head and knees of the man wailing in agony--- I determined I could not politely open the door without smacking him with it. Still averting my gaze, I went around the corner of the building to the front where there was another door.

A burned out hippie was lurking at that door, sucking on a fag. Too late to avoid it, our eyes locked. His eyes grew wide with surprise. His sallow, haggard, sun-ravaged face broke out in a huge grin.

"Hey! Wow! It's John Denver!" he yelled at me. He flung his cigarette butt in my direction and yelled, "I'm a huge fan of yours!" He was so convinced that I was John Denver, I momentarily wondered if maybe I was; I then shook off the thought. I greeted him verbally, and shook him by the hand as he thrust it at me (mental note: wash my hands before eating).

"I love that boat song you do! Dude! Oh, wow! Sing me that boat song!"

A police car drove into the parking lot.

"Sure!" I said. Why not? And, why the hell not? I cleared my throat, and started.

"To sail on a dream / On a crystal clear ocean / To ride on the crest / Of the wild raging storm!" I did my best to sound like John Denver, as I always hated to disappoint a fan of mine and John's. I got to the yodeling part, and to my surprise he joined in. To my annoyance, the shit head was doing a much better job of it than I was.

A paramedic truck drove into the parking lot.

The song finally, thank god, came to an end and we applauded each other. I dashed towards the door and flung myself in to the building before I would be required to perform an encore.

Inside the building a crowd had formed near the door as curious people watched the agonized young man, now thrashing around on his back against the concrete, scream in agony so intense we could almost feel it through the glass. I thought it was kind of him to draw everyone away from the order desk so that I wouldn't have to wait in line.

"Whudcunah getchyeh?" the cashier "said." He stood about six feet tall, had a head so closely shaved that it looked like a "four o'clock shadow," was the color of a well-stained sidewalk, and appeared to have the intellectual acumen of the average eggplant.

"Well, yes," I said. "Um, thank you." I fished out my last remaining $5 bill. "I would like two bean and cheese burritos and a small fountain drink." That would cost me $4.75 and would leave me with pocket change to live on until I could visit an Automated Teller Machine somewhere.

He took the fiver, punched the shit out of the screen in front of him, and handed to me $15.25

I was amazed.

“Thank you, but you gave me too much in change.” I tried to hand over the $10 and $5 bill.

“Nowzidinna. Yuzg meh fee dullards,” he “said.” He was prepared to argue with me--- me, the man who was trying to keep him from losing his job if the cash tray turned up lopsided.

“I gave to you a five dollar bill. It’s all I walked in with.” Suddenly Perry Mason, I argued my case.

“Izwa zah wenny,” he “said,” getting upset and angry with me. “Zehceng iz keerct! You enema weenie!”

“I gave you a fin, not a dub! You gave back a saw, a fin, and two bits!” Two could play at this unintelligible gibberish game. He glared hatred at me.

Outside, an obese police officer and an emaciated paramedic were wrestling with the young man who was screeching and trying to twist his own head off. The man seemed oblivious to the people trying to help him.

“Okay, thank you,” I said, surrendering. I stuffed the $10 bill in my damp front right pocket. I shoved the $5 back at him. “I’d like two more bean and cheese burritos, please.” With luck, I thought, he will hand to me $16.04 in change. I was willing to milk this cash cow for all he was worth, all day if necessary, until I was heavily burdened with burritos and free money. Sadly, he gave back $1.04 in change. I would have to make a living the hard way.

My order was called; I grabbed the bag; I walked around the counter, went through the kitchen door, and out the building through the employee exit. I walked quickly to my pickup, not wanting to be asked to sing another Denver song.

As I drove out of the parking lot, I asked myself once again, “What the bloody fuck happened to Baker?!”

BARSTOW IS FOR LOVERS; THE PHILOSOPHY OF SELF ANNIHILATION

***"I was accused of being against civilization. I was flattered."* -- Edward Abbey**

I am writing these notes at Barstow after dark, in a notebook that rests upon my knees. My pickup is heavily loaded with many weeks worth of assorted supplies--- canned food; dry goods such as pasta, rice, and crackers; fresh bread to be consumed with fresh butter first, before the desert heat (early spring: 85 degrees Fahrenheit) renders the fatty treat less “treatsome.” It appears that I have managed to get in to town for supplies on a Friday, as the evening traffic heading north has backed up all the way from Riverside to Victorville: many hundreds of thousands of people are flooding in to Las Vegas, Nevada, for reasons I cannot guess at and I suspect I would find incomprehensible if they told me. I am sitting here in a parking lot under a street lamp a few hundred feet from the on-ramp to the highway, and the cars’ red tail lights stretch far off into the distance; there are so many tail lights, so densely packed, that it looks like a river of red light flowing through the moon-lit desert night.

I think, this evening, of the mechanical horrors that humanity has inflicted upon itself and all other life forms on the planet. By far the worse abomination has been, is, and will continue to be The Infernal Combustion Engine--- automobiles.

When people contemplate the worse horror that human beings have created, they talk of the hydrogen bomb, or the cobalt bomb, or the neutron bomb; global thermonuclear holocaust delivered by inter-continental ballistic missiles in an orgy of destruction, a ballet of radioactive death that will render most regions of Earth sterile for tens of thousands of years.

Humanity is predicted, or one should say projected based on past history, to end itself abruptly in a ball of fire out of spite and hatred for their neighbors, their family members, and for themselves. The people who actually push the buttons will not feel those emotions---- they will feel nothing: they will merely obey the orders of the homicidal lunatics out of national loyalty; out of what passes for "patriotism" in their heads.

I do not agree. I think humankind will destroy itself with the automobile; the two billion cars that shuttle ourselves and our material wealth around. Like a cancerous tumor, the ubiquitous stream of cars transport into and out of our ugly, frightening cities our toxic waste throughout the feverish body of society we call "civilization." The internal combustion engine is killing us, individually and wholesale, morally and mentally and emotionally and physically just as surely as any nuclear war would--- just slowly, so that we can tell ourselves there's plenty of time to prevent complete disaster if we want to.

It seems to me we don't want to avert the destruction of our species and others. The ubiquitous automobile has already transformed the world in to a foreign landscape that our great grandparents would not recognize; in the future, our grandchildren will know a completely alien world that is warmer, with higher sea levels, and continents that do not match current maps in sizes nor shapes. The very chemistry of the atmosphere has changed and is changing, far more rapidly than people can adapt to, and even more rapidly than most species can acclimatize to (moving to higher altitude; moving towards Earth's poles).

Look at the USA's rivers, streams, and lakes: the water is not fit to drink, and the fish are all gone. Well, with one exception: the Cornejo river in Colorado still has fish in it--- three, in fact. But two are gay, and the third always has a headache.

Now you will ask me if I will surrender my car. Fuck no! Are you fucking kidding me?! μολὼν λαβέ! **I LOVE MY CAR!** I'm warning you here and now: if you reach for my car keys, I'll reach for my hand gun until you stop reaching. I ain't afraid to use my gun nor my car. I look forward to the end of humanity and what passes for civilization, but I am dismayed at the suffering created during that process. I have no horse in any future human race. It's the people with children and grand children that should care enough to make the future worth living in. How very odd that, as far as I can see, few parents and grandparents care enough about their offspring to leave a world at least as livable as the one they, the older generations, were born in.

Carmagiddon: humanity and all other, blameless, species on the planet choking to death on our internal combustion wastes, and those who do not die from the increased storm surge along the coasts due to rising seas will die with sword in hand fighting over fresh water and arable land. I for one look forward to the end. If you do not agree that humanity is soon to be doomed, just step in to a large grocery store: 600 kinds of candy; 100 kinds of ice cream; 60 kinds of cat food; 30 kinds of “dried meat snacks;" 20 kinds of toilet paper; 7 kinds of "body wash;" 1 poster at the customer service desk asking people to donate food for the hungry children in town.

The future is already stillborn, dead before it arrives.

Humanity has created other horrors of course. The invention of the food vending machine for example: put in a hand full of coins, and a ham and cheese sandwich comes out--- why doesn’t that frighten the bloody shit out of people? It freaks the shit out of me, and I’m not even Jewish. Consider the human invention called the “Chemical air freshener.” Try wrapping your mind around the concept of using a sprayed chemical to “freshen air,” and then argue in defense of humanity being worthy of existing.

When food packages have a longer list of what is *NOT* in them than the list of what is, you know civilization will soon end.

For six dollars one can purchase an entire canned chicken, sans the head, feathers, guts, and toes. Why does that not frighten everyone, not just chickens? This is no way to live.

Anyone caught with a hair drying machine should be executed. No exceptions.

In our defense, we’re just tailless monkeys. We don’t know any better.

-0-

A black-booted male thug in a police car was staring at me from across the road, trying to make eye contact with me. I unfolded a road map and pretended to be lost and confused instead of loitering.

Loitering: the world’s fourth most asinine “crime,” after “criminal substance ingestion,” “vagrancy,” and being mentally ill (number five: being arrested for resisting arrest, and no other reason). Loitering: the crime of sitting or standing idle in one place while breathing quietly to oneself. Loitering is an even better excuse for arresting harmless, helpless, defenseless people than the convenient crime of being black.

-0-

The copper is running my vehicle license plate. I can almost hear his dull, bovine-like torpid thoughts as he sits there waiting and hoping I'm a wanted serial killer or known liberal. Fuck that shit: I'll see if he stalks me...

-0-

I have driven a mile around and through the ugly manswarm, and I have come to rest at a saloon; a bar; an alcohol vending business; a drinking establishment. The building squatted low and toad-like with iron bars across its tiny windows next to a shack that advertised itself as a "Beauty Parlor." (There has never in the history of humanity been even a single person who walked out of a "beauty parlor" looking finer than walking in.) The police car followed me until I stopped at the bar, got out of my vehicle, and walked inside. Officer Friendly continued driving past as I pulled into the bar's parking lot.

Inside the bar some kind of faggy music was playing, now that God (Eddy Arnold) is dead. Men and boys sat around the room and at the bar yelling at each other, trying to be heard over the "music" and the three television sets blaring at the small crowd: one TV over the bar, one TV at each end of the far sides of the room. The smell of fried cheese and beer filled the room as thickly as a sinister fog in a Stephen King novel.

I leaned against the bar and caught the bartender's eyes. He promptly walked over and asked me what I wanted.

"I wanna drink," I said.

He waited patiently for me to elaborate. I waited for my drink. It was a stalemate; no obvious winner, no actual loser.

"Something sweet," I said. "Something where I cannot taste the alcohol. Something fruity, maybe with a paper parasol in it; something popular in latitudes between 16 degrees north and 22 degrees south; maybe something with shredded coconut in it, or a hibiscus flower; something fags drink." I looked around the room, then gestured to the three men sitting at the bar to my left. "Yeah, give me what they're having."

The bartender half smirked and half snarled at the "something fags drink," and said, "How about a Whaga wahda wehaw wadda?" (I didn't catch the actual name.) "It has pineapple in it."

"That sounds good. Gimme one uh them," I said. I looked at the barstool at my right knee, wiped it with the edge of my tee-shirt bottom, and sat.

The three young men to my left were glaring hatred at me for some reason. I avoided eye contact, as a matter of policy. That is, safety. If you don't look at people when you verbally abuse them, it doesn't count. The drink arrived, served with cubed ice in a tall hexagon cylinder and with a plastic drinking straw. I told the bartender to take my money immediately, as I might need to flee the bar at a moment's notice. He took eight of the two hundred dollars I had extracted from the ATM device at the grocery store. Was that too much? I had no idea.

Turning, I accidentally made eye contact with the outraged man closest to my left. It spoke.

"Listen! We don't like that crack about...."

"Go Azul!" I screamed at the television above the bartender's head, raising my right arm and fist as if I were cheering the *Cruz Azul Fútbol Club* instead of avoiding a beating or, worse, apologizing for my behavior. "Woo hoo!" I sucked pineapple and alcohol through the straw, minding my own business. In an instant my glass was empty. I asked for another drink, which promptly arrived and another eight dollars promptly departed. I sucked like a... like a... aw, shit: I was gonna write "like a fag" but that would be impolitic of me. I sucked up my second fruity drink like a $25 whore sucks Southern Baptists during a Republican National Convention "Family Values" conference. There. That's more politically correct.

Four women walked through the door and, as a herd, went straight to the closet wherein was located a toilet. Eventually all four came out again as a group and made their way to the bar while yelling greetings at various men--- all of whom utterly ignored them.

One of the women sat on the stool on my right. She looked to be anywhere from 115 years old to 9 years old, depending on how the dim light caught her haggard tobacco-stained yellow face. I stared at the television, hoping she would ignore me. She turned towards me and spoke.

"Hey, sir! How do I get to the town's cemetery?"

I turned to her and smiled warmly.

"Die!" I said helpfully. My civic duty, my good deed, done for the day, I motioned to the bartender for a third drink and then turned my attention back to the television. Another drink arrived; another eight dollars departed. The noise level increased in distinct intervals, in discrete quantum packets, and suddenly being inside the bar was too great a burden for me to bare.

I stood up; I nearly fell; I stood taller, like a man; I took a step backwards, paused, pivoted my right leg 90 degrees, pivoted my left leg at nearly the same angle, then my right leg again, then my left again, and ventured towards the door. Like a top heavy sailing ship, not in ballast, did I creep towards the door, head sails luffing.

Outside, the night air was cold and the sounds of car traffic washed over me as I inhaled deeply to enjoy the heady smell of automobile exhaust; putrid street gutter garbage; industrial solvents; burning tires (from the chicken and biscuits store upwind); desert creosote; hair spray. Off there in the distance, towards Yermo perhaps, the sound of a horn from a train's power unit floated through the chilly street light glare.

My pickup was parked about 50 feet away, sulking under the sodium yellow glower of the bar's incandescent sign. Getting to my transport seemed too great a task to successfully navigate on foot; Lewis and Clark had Sacagawea to guide them; Álvar Núñez Cabeza de Vaca had the Black Moor slave Estevanico to guide him; I was on my own.

Stepping out with confidence, slowly, I made my way to my car and unlocked the driver's side door. I arrived sooner than I had estimated, and I marveled at how easy it had been. I gingerly sat in the operator's seat, shut the door, and shoved the key in the ignition switch.

A thought then occurred to me. "Maybe I'm not fit to drive," was the thought. My hippie friends drove around drunk, stoned, and otherwise incapacitated pretty much every night--- so how hard could it be? But then my civic conscience took over: is it wrong to drive when one cannot see, nor feel one's fingers, nor know where one's legs are, from alcohol poisoning? I pondered the issue.

What does a person do when she or he wants to go home, but cannot safely drive a car? The answer exploded in my sluggish brain with the blinding light of genius: they take the train! I stomped on the clutch pedal, twisted the ignition key until the engine fired, wrestled the gear shift backwards a dick length, and eased the vehicle in reverse until I had a clear view of the street. Gears in forward, I headed southwestward to the Barstow train yard.

Parking near the old highway heading to Bakersfield, I got out of my car and walked towards the poor white (Mexican) trailer trash standing around looking for free rides northward. Some of the immigrant farm workers looked better dressed and fed than I did, but most looked as shabby as I. Workers looking for catching freight trains can some times avoid the arrival tracks, classification tracks, and departure tracks at the main yard by walking westward towards the Landmark Missionary Baptist cult across the tracks and wait at the bridges if they want to catch out west and then to points north; for northern and eastern travel, bums like me are better off hitch hiking to Daggett and waiting at the right-of-way signals near Highway 40. If a tramp is not careful, she or he will end up in Salt Lake City on the Union Pacific line instead of Gallup on the BNSF line. No one deliberately wants to go to Salt Lake City.

I greeted my new Mexican and Nicaraguan pals in a low, manly voice, inflections close to what I hope would be taken as from someone who is world-weary and worn from hard work and low pay; one of the guys--- no white privileged male here, so sirs.

They stopped talking to each other, and in the dull street lamp light a half-dozen frightening men glared hatred and malice at me. Feigning unconcern, shaking inside with fear, I asked if anyone had a dollar they would give to me. "I would like a dollar," I said. "I would love a dollar." I elaborated, addressing my audience while their looks of dislike turned to incredulity. "If I had a dollar, I would be happy for many minutes. There is no happiness in life, unless one has a dollar." I actually had more than $160 stuffed in my pants' left front pocket, but the tequila in my brain wanted another $1.

A brief conference, in Spanish, followed; I was not privy to the conversation. A man with the gravel of age in his voice spoke in carefully articulated English.

"If you will go away, I will give to you one dollar." He extracted a bill from one of his pockets, and held it out so that I would have to step among them to pluck it from his hand: a test of bravery, I surmised, or a test of fatal foolishness. Without hesitating, I stepped forward and took the dollar.

"Thank you, my new friend," I said. Saying nothing else, I walked back to my pickup.

Light headed with alcohol, I started my automobile and

headed westward to Old Highway 58 and then eastward; some where there is a spur road that joins Interstate 15. In no shape to drive, I made it to Meadow Grove Road where I parked, closed my eyes, and slept.

YEAR 1866

***"The one thing we can be sure of, after we [USA citizens] have mourned the latest massacre, is that there will be another. You wake up at three in the morning, check the news, and there it is."* -- Adam Gopnik**

Morning came with a belch of truck exhaust, the scream of a truck engine, and the cancerous coughing of truck air brakes. Some how, for no reason I could think of, I had managed to open the driver's side door while I slept, and I was teetering half inside and half outside my vehicle. I appeared to be intact, with no obvious signs of having been robbed or ravaged while I slumped in the car seat in my drunken stupor. I had vague memories of asking some migrant tramp workers for money, but it was all hazy in my head. The inside of my mouth felt like I had licked a sea gull clean after it had been a victim of an oil spill. The full, staggering, monstrous, horrific weight of the morning desert sun assaulted my face, as my pickup was facing due east. The tar-like sludge someone had replaced my brain with as I slept was slow to grasp the fact that I had been sleeping in my automobile while it was parked on a dirt road three or four feet from a paved highway; it was a wonder to me that I had not been struck and killed (or worse) while I slept.

Crawling out of the car door, I stood up and put my back to the sun. I unzipped Little Davie and unloaded my bladder. I imagined all of the pineapple juice I had consumed the night before leaving my body while the alcohol stayed to become better acquainted with my liver.

"See? This is why I don't drink alcohol!" I told the morning.

I was about ten miles south of Fort Irwin, on an old dirt road that had once passed through most of the Avawatz Mountain Range. The dirt road went to Bitter Spring, and to the grave yard at the summit near Avawatz Pass; Cave Spring; Denning Spring; and points of interest to the north and the northeast--- for example the ghost towns of Goldstone (west) and Silver Spring (east).

In year 1925 Adrian Egbert set up shop at Cave Spring, where he sold canned food and gasoline; before that time, the cave had been used as a hotel for the few miners who could afford to stay there. 1925 was the year that Matt Burts (train robber) and J. W.

Robinson (whiskey maker) encountered each other at Government Hole and sent each other to Cow Puncher Heaven via .44 Colts while standing ten feet apart (an amusing story, actually). It was the year that Bob Hollimon was forced to get a little bit rough with the Rock Springs Land and Cattle Company (OX brand, later the 88). It was around year 1925 that Old John Lamoigne found, located, and some times filed upon over twenty gold prospects, a few of which developed into paying mines. It was a busy time for the Avawatz.

Old John Lamoigne had been one common visitor to Bitter Spring as well as Cave Spring at the time, and he had a mansion built for him near Bitter Spring (now Fort Irwin) which included a fresh water well and a wind-powered water pump. "Old John" had found so much gold that, he complained, he was always tripping over it as it lay in sacks on the floor of his old pine slab cabin. The story is that Old John decided to waste his wealth on one massive building that had "all the fixings" inside. After the mansion was built, gilded, appointed, furnished, and carpeted, he used a few dozen sticks of dynamite to see how high he could blast the edifice. Old John then packed his mule and walked northwest back into Death Valley, where he and his mule died of thirst and exposure. To this day, some people are still looking for caches of gold Old John Lamoigne might have hidden. Considering the size of the desolate wilderness involved, that hunt seems very foolish to me.

There I slumped, up against my pickup, wishing I could drive that old road and get back to Old Mormon Spring via that route. My pickup would never make it: there are too many sand pits where the road had been. Still, I would like to try the road, if only Fort Irwin had not been in the way. I had to settle for taking the modern highway northward.

Climbing into my automobile and trying to blink the blinding sun from my eyes, I put my pickup in gear and headed east to Highway 15; at Manix Road, I made a right turn and headed south to Camp Cady, where I parked.

-0-

After Major James H. Carleton decapitated a few random Paiutes and hung their heads at Bitter Spring, he established Camp Cady on the Mojave River upon orders of General N.S. Clarke in the spring of year 1860. Camp Cady is about 18 miles northeast of Barstow, and one can take the old Manix Trail Road to visit the site.

(The shores of Manix Lake can still be seen today, about 21,000 years after it went dry.) It was at Camp Cady where the United States Army got its ass kicked by Paiute forces on July 29th, year 1866, after a battle that was so ignoble, so inexplicably pointless and unnecessary, that some military historians may find it embarrassing to mention. Dennis G. Casebier did the research and shared the story in his pamphlet "The Battle at Camp Cady" for us to marvel at now.

Brevet Major (Second Lieutenant) James Richmond Hardenbergh had been left in command of the camp while the man he replaced, First Lieutenant John Edmond Yard, left the camp and returned to the California coast at Drum Barracks (Wilmington). Hardenbergh was 25 years old when he relieved Yard of command at Camp Cady; the image of him shows a young man with eyes placed too closely to each other, a receding hair line, a slight body, and I estimate his height to be around five feet two inches tall. In the image his arms are tightly crossed on his chest, and Hardenbergh is giving what I suspect he believed to be a "military bearing" expression on his rather weak face.

Brevet Major Hardenbergh was unusual in some respects for a graduate of the Peekskill Military Academy (New York): he was barely literate, wrote poorly and at times illegibly, and had difficulty writing coherent sentences. His vocabulary and communication skills appear to have been roughly those of a modern and average junior high school student. His inability to correctly spell the names of the men under his command may have been due to ignorance or disinterest. His official report of the incident, dated August First 1866, left out almost all of the most important details, and focused on how he and his men could have done nothing to avoid the defeat; he marveled that he was still alive to write the report.

A Mormon named Crow lived at Forks Of The Road (near Daggett and / or Newberry Springs) with his family. He knew enough of the Numic language to insult passing Paiutes, which in mid-July of 1866 he did from the porch of his house. Mister Crow's abusive language was ignored by the Paiutes he had yelled at, so in a fit of rage he grabbed his rifle and shot at them. The Paiutes fled. Fearing later retaliation, Crow packed up his family and took them to Cottonwood Station (near Victorville), then went to Camp Cady and asked for military protection from the Paiutes whom he insisted, falsely, were hostile.

Brevet Major Hardenbergh took Crow at his word, and assumed the Paiutes had become hostile. Few experienced military officers would have believed it, since the Southern Paiutes had been greatly reduced by slavery (by the Utes and notably *Wah kara* ("Yellow Man") in the 1840s and 1850s), and starvation. Even Mark Twain, ten years earlier, had noted this fact in some of his newspaper articles.

On July 29th., Hardenbergh noticed a group of about 36 "Paiutes" gathering near Camp Cady, and he decided they were planning to attack the camp. In reality it is likely that the "Paiutes" had no interest at all in attacking the camp, and were *en route* northward and going to Mojave Indian territory; it is also possible that the "Paiutes" were actually River Indians--- maybe Mojave, though facial tattoos were not mentioned in any official report of the event. The odd behavior of white people (and that included black "buffalo soldiers") would have made Camp Cady a bit of a tourist attraction for the Indians who traveled along the old trade route between the coast of California and the Colorado River. Hardenbergh ordered seven enlisted men (one corporal, five privates, one sergeant) to follow him and attack the group. The late morning temperature was over 100 degrees that day, according to later reports.

An armed conflict with eight men against an estimate thirty-six would not be a good decision even when the eight had rifles and the thirty-six had primitive weapons; some of the Indians had bows and arrows; few if any of them would have carried war clubs, some would have had "trade knifes" (tin or iron knives cheaply formed by stamping out the shape of a knife dozens at a time with a steam-powered press, then fitted with a wood handle). But any rock or stick would serve as weapons, and these were readily available along the Mojave River. The order to attack them therefore was not only irrational, but suicidal. The two officers were mounted on horses, and before the attack the officers dismounted and joined the enlisted men on foot for the fight.

The Indians of course defended themselves with a counter attack, killing two privates and the corporal out-right, and causing the survivors to panic and flee "every man for himself" back to Camp Cady. Two soldiers threw down their rifles and ran, one hiding in brush and the other grabbing one of the two horses and riding in a hurry back to Camp Cady.

One private, named "Frank White," (real name: Azamond Stilphen) had three arrows stuck in him as he fled, and he ran far enough to bring Camp Cady within his sight before he fell to the ground under a cottonwood tree with the Indians in hot pursuit. Unable to fight, unable to run, Private White gave up and waited for death as one Indian walked up to him to deliver the fatal blow. Inexplicably, Private White took off the bandanna from around his neck and offered it to the Indian who was about to kill him; the Indian accepted the tribute and left White alive. Private White survived, and returned to camp and to medical care there.

The image of Private Frank White, dated a year before the battle and taken when he was living in Maine, shows a young man with deep-set eyes, large ears, round jaw and cheeks, and a face free from expression. He looks intelligent and educated; he was 21 years old during the battle. He had fought in the American Civil War on the side of the Union, 1st Battalion, Maine Light Artillery.

Bvt. Mjr. Hardenbergh, commander Camp Cady, fled along with his surviving men, but he retained his rifle and he put up a decent fight as he made his way back to the camp. He had tried to retrieve his horse, which he had earlier tied to a tree, but he found the horse had three fatal wounds from arrows. Hardenbergh suffered one arrow wound in an ankle as he successfully made it to camp.

At the military hearing, which Hardenbergh insisted upon, Hardenbergh was "relieved of all blame" for the deaths of three men and the wounding of two others (Private White and himself). Hardenbergh was later sent to Camp El Dorado, Arizona Territory, where he served with equal "distinction."

Now, back at present time, I sat in my sweltering automobile looking out over the Mojave River and the site where Camp Cady had been. One of those old cottonwood trees may have been the one under which Private White fell to the ground while he awaited death, and was spared by an act of grace on the part of the "bloody red savage." I got out of my pickup, stretched the kinks out of my back, and looked up at the sky, Heavenward.

"Hey! Hardenbergh! Yo, Hardenbergh up there!" I screamed. Thinking again, I looked downward at the ground, Hellward.

“Hardenbergh, you homicidal piece of shit!” I yelled. “Fuck you! In the eye! With a stick!” I got back in my car and headed to my home in the Avawatz Mountain Range.

WHEN ALL IS LOST

***"When the machine has taken the soul from the man / It's time to leave something behind."* — Sean Rowe**

Many years ago Edna and Bill, of "Burro Bill" fame, once crossed the distance from Barstow to Baker (65 miles, with burros) in 22 hours and they celebrated that amazing speed with an ice cream cone at Ralph Jacobus "Dad" Fairbanks' gas station. My speed would have crossed the distance in one hour, if I had not constantly pulled off the highway to let people pass, and that was certainly fast enough for me--- but not the rest of humanity around me.

What has humanity lost by this rush through the beautiful East Mojave Desert? Not its soul: humanity lost that, what little it ever had, when the first plow broke the first cultivated field. There is no beauty in the lives of city dwellers; in fact, I wonder if there is any life in the lives of city dwellers. The Grand Canyon Masturbater (Edward Abbey) once wrote that when all hope has been lost, there is no more reason to worry about anything. Anyone talking to city people, or passing through a city, will agree all has been lost.

More than one billion people trample the earth and never see, feel, taste, hear, and smell it: alienated, estranged, divorced from the soil that nurtured and gave birth to them.

When nature became a tourist attraction, all hope for humanity was lost.

I pulled off the highway at Midway, parked at the dog poop area, once again unzipped my crotch, and Little Davie hurriedly fell out. Slacking some mysterious netherworld muscles and tightening others, my bladder emptied on to my booted feet. Fuck the "comfort stations" (toilets) a few hundred feet away; pissing and shitting wherever one happened to be is what had once made humanity noble and upright in character, and the invention of toilets ended all that. Stand up and piss like a man, damn you; do not squat like some four-legged beast. Pissing on one's moccasins was good enough for the Chiricahua Apaches, so it for damn well sure is good enough for me. Never mind the giggling tourists. Just drop your shorts and yell "Geronimo!"

A few years ago in early winter I had stopped at the highway rest stop near the Cima Road exit to acquire some high nutrition food (candy) from the vending machine there. A casino's bus, full of Japanese tourists, had also paused there. I sat in my pickup a few seconds and watched the Japanese men and women take photographs of themselves with tumble weeds. I got out of my vehicle and waved at the happy crowd; the happy crowd in turn asked me to take some pictures of them holding tumble weeds "like in Tombstone." When I told them I wanted to visit Japan and get photographs of Godzilla, I just got happy smiles.

Refreshed and relieved, I drove to Baker. Stop sign; bewildered tourists; urge to yell at people to turn left or right or continue straight but just make up their fucking minds; finally northward to the turn-off towards Old Mormon Spring.

Gods, it felt great to return home again.

THE RAIN CAME

"Men den vackraste stunden i livet var den när du kom..."
-- Lars Winnerbäck

Unloading my supplies from the vehicle and shuttling it all back to my cave was a tedious, weary chore. Most of the packaging I left behind in the pickup, and the pile of trash sold with my food was an astonishing sight. Spend $500 on packaged foods and you will get about $250 worth of food, $250 worth of cardboard, plastic, tin, aluminum, ink, and dyes. Well done, Corporate America!

On the first trip I returned my spare car battery to the cave; about 47 pounds of lead. I paused often to feel sorry for myself. Finally at the cave, I stepped over the sheets of plywood and piles of human turds that I had left strewn on the ground outside, set the battery down next to my sleeping area, and looked around. All seemed to be in order, except for many tiny pieces of paper piled in a corner for what appeared to be a new rat's nest. Hey Rat, my roommate, had either been very busy ripping up a few of my books, or had family and friends over for company.

Investigating, I found one of the paper bags that held paperback books had been chewed open at the bottom, then split open along one side. A copy of John Grisham's ***THE CHAMBER*** was laying open, many pages half missing. I picked up the book and pulled out a few dozen sheets and set them next to the new nest.

"Here. Feed," I said. Finally someone who liked the book.

Hauling the canned food from my pickup to the cave took six trips; hauling the perishables took two trips; hauling plastic jugs full of fruit juice, and boxes of assorted food stuff, took six trips. The task summed to about 66 miles, 15 trips one way (counting the battery), and three days. When the grocery store cashier had asked me, "Would you like help with that?" I wish I had said "Yes" and then kidnapped her as my personal pack horse. I'll remember that for next time.

The slice of pineapple I had left near the spring on the first day of my return was gone on day three; or, rather, the pineapple had been well masticated and most of it eaten, with the dregs mixed in the sand. Ripping the cover off ***THE CHAMBER*** and opening another can of pineapple, I went to the spring and, using the book cover as a dinner plate, I set more pineapple out for my iguana friend. Eating the rest, I reassembled my solar still; with the warmer days, and the sun returning north, I anticipated clean water again.

Fresh chicken eggs, fried in butter, was attempted on the fourth morning of my return. The stove was doing a fine job of it for several minutes before the leak caught fire and spewed a jet of flaming gasoline at me. I stepped back and watched the fire grow larger, as the stove howled in pain. I waited for it to settle down. I stepped back again; I stepped back again; I stepped back again.

The stove did not settle down. Instead, it increased its combustion in an orgy, nay, a ballet of death as the fuel tank, now super heated, increased its internal pressure. Soon it was wailing and screaming in its death throes; the green paint blistered and was blackened; the red paint on the fuel tank took longer to blacken and blister, apparently made of sterner stuff. The "**How To Turn Off**" label on the stove's lid, no longer useful, blackened, peeled away, and fell into my excessively fried eggs. About twenty minutes later the flames decreased, the stove's pain-wracked bellowing wail faded away, and I could once again see my breakfast. It looked... "done" is the word.

Quickly, before the heat and the last of the dying flames were gone, I grabbed two more eggs and cracked them over the hot frying pan in a region I judged to be the least occupied with charcoal. The little perforations in the stove's bottom housing, which acted as legs for the stove, were still filled with a bit of gasoline, and the tiny flames slowly cooked the eggs as the flames died. A bit of salt, a dash of pepper, and then the soup spoon to shovel the gourmet meal down my throat. Carbon for breakfast, I found, is not unjustly unappreciated.

The stove was old, purchased well-used at the Orange County Fair Ground's swap meet when I was a teenager. After almost thirty years of service, I figured the stove had earned its final rest in a place of honor among my cherished and few possessions inside the cave; a trash dump was too insulting, too ignoble for my stove. It had been a good friend.

-O-

The same day I had purchased the stove, I had also purchased a 1957 Olympia Deluxe typewriter, with case, from the writer "Ed

Story." I was nineteen years old at the time, and he had a narrow space at the swap meet where he sold everything he had just to keep from starving to death. The case had a handle made of leather, riveted to the upper section, and under the handle there was a blue strip of plastic with white letters that read "ED STORY" made from one of the popular label makers sold back then.

"Ed Story" wanted $40 for the typewriter: a massive sum for me (year 1979), as I was a drill press operator working in a machine shop for little pay. I handed over the $40 and I asked him if he had given up writing; he said he had just purchased an electric "IBM Selectric" which was The Cat's Meow back then. I thanked him, picked up the gasoline stove I had set down, and then picked up the typewriter.

A look of ineffable sadness fell upon "Ed Story's" face, and his cheeks went white and lifeless as his eyes filled with tears. I paused and looked a question at him. He forced a smile on his face and bid me, "Enjoy the typewriter." I felt like I had just purchased a child's beloved dog or pony; I felt like a little shit. But then, I also felt happy at having such a fine typewriter.

Ed, if you are up there in Writer Heaven listening: thank you again for the typewriter. I have kept your name where it was on the case in repentance for your tears.

-0-

A large grapefruit juice can makes an adequate hobo stove; I used a can perforator (the kind that punches triangles into tin cans) to punch a dozen holes at one end of the can, on the outer surface near the lid. I then used a can opener to remove the lid on that end. Finally, I punched out an opening on the other end in the outer surface and then carefully cut open a rectangle with my belt knife. Fuel would go in the rectangular end, and my sauce pan would sit under the flames on the wide-open end. With the opening at the bottom of the stove facing a breeze, there is enough heat and flame to cook a meal.

The problem was fuel, of course. A hobo stove needs twigs and trash to burn, and I had left most of my trash at my pickup. No matter: the entire desert was scattered with dead brush, which I need only dig up. I would just have to be careful and select plants that were actually dead and not dormant; if a plant resists being lifted out of the dirt, there is a good chance it is still alive and should be left alone. It is not at all obvious, with many desert plants, to determine if their tiny little hearts are still beating in there somewhere.

After forming my hobo stove, I looked up to see dark clouds moving into Valjean Valley from the southwest. Rainfall is as rare in the Mojave Desert as an honest politician in the Senate. I knew to not even entertain the tiniest of hope that water would fall from the sky any time soon.

But gosh, I would love to have rain. I wondered if there was a weather forecast I could listen to. Radio reception where I lived down in the arroyo was very poor, but on top of my look-out station to the east I could get several radio stations. I fit my backpack to my left shoulder; made sure I had binoculars; picked up my radio and started cranking the dynamo handle to charge the battery; collected one blanket under my left arm to rig as an awning; and made my way east.

Passing my solar water still, I paused to watch my iguana friend discover and enjoy the fresh pineapple I had left. As far as I could recall, she had never actually looked up and made eye contact with me before; this time she did, with a look of what I could only imagine and describe as open, wide-eyed astonishment at her good fortune. In the past when I have visited the spring and saw her there, she some times walked behind me a few dozen feet before turning back; most times she stood frozen in place, moving so little that I could not even see her breathing. This time, I watched as she seized a chunk of pineapple, masticated it into a fine pulp, paused a bit, and then swallowed. I did not want to give too much food to her and then have her dependent on me, but it is amazing how hard it is to not feed someone who was so obviously grateful.

Continuing eastward I once again came to The Wall, turned left (northward), took a few steps eastward to the base of the incline to the top of the wall, and then climbed southward a few dozen yards. I sat, after taking off my backpack, and arranged my blanket to block some of the sunlight; one corner draped over my backpack, another corner draped over me. Cranking the radio's dynamo a few more minutes, I gazed eastward at Valjean Valley and the Kingston Mountain Range.

Like a herd of buffalo, small puffs of black clouds came drifting slowly into the region. Meeting the updraft caused by the

Kingston mountains, the Cloud Children seemed to pause a bit as if confused about where to go, then lifted in altitude another 800 feet or so. Caught in a thermal-powered back eddy, the clouds drifted in the direction they had just come. At the higher altitude the little clouds bunched up as if gathered by unseen cowboys, blotting out the sky until large sections of Valjean valley and the eastern mountains were in shadow. More clouds, at lower altitude, drifted in.

Tuning my radio to the FM band, I found a radio station with a repeater at Mountain Pass. Laying on my back, pulling the edge of my shade blanket down to just above my eyebrows, I watched the valley grow darker.

Over the radio, the disk jockey way over there in Laughlin, Nevada, was asking people to call in for music requests. It was a Country / Western music station, so I yelled out, “Play some Led Zeppelin!” Instead someone asked for Clint Black’s song “Where Are You Now?” A fine song for anyone who has not been living alone and lonely in the desolate wilderness for the past eleven months.

I thought about some of the women I had known. Where the hell did they all go? Why did they all leave me here in this desert, on this mountain range, laying here alone on this rock? As the day grew darker with the sky being slowly blotted out with dark clouds, I thought about Kathryn. She used to ride around with me in the evening as we went grocery shopping, or visited some social event, or traveled to and from the Harlequin Playhouse while we were dressed up in thousand-dollar outfits. She once told me that she would be happy and content if all she ever did the rest of her life was to ride with me in my pickup, going towards or away from some destination--- it didn’t matter which, or where. Where the bloody hell was she now?

Women are, on the whole, smart and intelligent beings; too smart to squander their limited time here on the planet with the likes of me. The women I knew all went and found men to share their lives with, recognizing me as the boy I was, am, and always will be. If a male human wants a woman in his life, he needs to become an adult--- something I could never do. There is no secret regarding how to be a Real Man in the modern world: it’s the same way it’s always been--- meet all of your responsibilities without complaining. Far too often I have fallen short in that regard; too many times I didn't even try, taking the easier routes through life.

The "request hour" ended, mercifully, with trite and odious musical pablum being asked for and served up. If they had started to play Paul Stookey's "The Wedding Song," I vowed, I would slice open my wrists, then my throat. Mercifully for both of us, the DJ started to play the entire "The Song Remembers When" CD from Trisha Yearwood.

Slowly, imperceptibly, out there in the valley the lower cloud layer rose upward and the upper layer descended; the cloud layers met, and an inner turmoil in the sky, matching the fermenting emotional unrest within me, induced tiny veils of dark rain to fall. The falling rain came in discrete packets, leisurely, in no hurry to reach the ground and the thirsty desert denizens below. Like water from a garden hose with a sprinkler head on the end, bits of the blackened sky shed long curtains of black water Earthward over there near Ibex Pass; then over there on Tecopa Pass; then a little on Kingston Peak. A bit of rain here and there; not too much in any one spot.

The music continued as the afternoon progressed into evening, and the pockets of rain continued to bless tiny sections of the desert. Crackling blasts from lightning somewhere visited my radio, overwhelming for brief moments the radio station; lightning too distant or hidden from me to see what direction from which it came. Some of the day's heat slowly leached away, and I yanked at my blanket and wrapped it around me. I slept, head on my backpack.

I awoke to the sound of hissing near me. Looking up, in the evening gloom I saw rain falling a few hundred feet from me. Where the rain fell was a maelstrom of sand and bits of grass, plant leaves, and twigs jumping a few centimeters into the air; it looked like the ground was boiling, churning, heaving from some force under the Earth.

"Hey," I said in a low, soothing, and what I hoped was an enticing voice. "Come over here, gorgeous wet stuff." The rain, sweeping southeastward, ignored me and soon passed me by. The hissing faded as the evening grew, matured, aged into darkness. I pulled my blanket tighter around my arms and neck. The scant rain, which had avoided me in a manner I could only think of as disdainfully, did not return that night nor for another six months.

My radio had fallen silent, exhausted. I cranked the handle a few minutes, and the music returned: a great return on my caloric investment. No moon light filtered through the cloudy sky, and the thought of returning to my sleeping place in front of my cave was an unpleasant thought--- many dozens of hazards lay in wait for me in the dark. No matter: the late spring nights were not oppressively chilly, and the rock I was laying on could be endured.

HE KILLED... AND KILLED... AND KILLED.

***"Sir, do we get to win this time?"* -- David Morrell**

Some time in late spring my roommate, Hey Rat, went away and did not return. Iguana toe prints showed up in the sand near the spring every few days, but I did not often see her; most of the bits of fruit I left out for the green beast were eaten by blow flies and the sun.

The months progressed as they tend to do; late spring passed in to summer, with its intolerable heat and glare and hardships. The monsoon weather came, promising rain, and even sent water towards the ground but the moisture never got there--- vast sheets of rain at times blocked the distances at high altitude, but evaporated before touching the Earth. My solar water still produced more water than I could drink and store, and it made me flinch when I had no better use for it than to bathe with it a bucket at a time. I endured the heat by exercising and completing chores in the morning before the sun rose above the horizon, then read while reclining on my chair in my cave.

My chores consisted of eating as much high-fat food as I could in the morning without doing serious injury to myself (as Miss Piggy said, "never eat more than you can lift"). The rest of the day I would then worry only about drinking enough water. Some of this breakfast fat came in the form of "powdered buttermilk" which, when mixed with the stale warm water from my solar still, tasted horrid. The drink never managed to be well mixed no matter how vigorously I shook the lidded jar I mixed it in. Oily sludge formed at the top of the drink, reflecting rainbow colors when the sunlight bounced off of the surface slime. I found that if I avoided actually looking at the mixture, with eyes averted and taking in the distant haze around the rising sun, I could gulp it down without gagging on it.

Morning drink done, I then stuffed my hobo stove with bits of grass leaves, brittle roots and twigs from dead brush, used toilet paper, paper labels from canned food, and splintered pieces of timber that I had high-graded from mines I visited during my hikes. While the frying pan warmed on the hobo stove I mixed pancake mix and water in a tin can, then set it next to the stove to "rise" and to wait for the frying pan to get hot. This required a fairly large amount of desert flotsam as fuel which I collected, ranging far and wide, before sunset every day. With the frying pan hot, I added a few drops of olive oil and then poured the pancake mix into the pan, scooping it from the tin can with a spoon. Then, furiously stuffing the stove with bits of fuel, I waited a few minutes and then flipped the pancake over. After the lone, large, fat cake was cooked I dumped canned fruit on top: peaches, apricots, pineapple. I then ate the mess, using the spoon I used to mix the batter with.

On days when I had fuel remaining for the stove after the pancake was cooked I heated water for instant coffee. I discovered that it takes a large pile of twigs to get a pot of water boiling; most mornings when I bothered with coffee I drank it tepid.

I then washed the tin cup, and inverted the dirty frying pan so that insects had a harder time crawling over the sticky dregs.

Breakfast done, and while the sun was still only an hour or less above the eastern horizon, I picked up my blankets and gave them a hearty shake to dislodge any companions that might have joined me in bed the night before. The two pillows also got a beating. I then shook out my plastic sheet and wrapped the blankets and pillows tightly, then moved the package into the cave and out of the sun.

A morning visit to The Shit Zone followed. I found that poop dried brittle and dusty in less than a day, and there was no smell that I detected. Dessicated poop was strewn over a large area to the east of my spring, and at times I wondered if it would make good fuel for my hobo stove.

With the sun well up over the eastern horizon, I went into my cave, reclined on my chair, and read much of the day. Now and then I would get to my feet and walk in a tight circle, still reading, to keep my muscle tone.

In this way, day after day, I endured the harsh summer. At night, of course, things were different; freed from the tyranny of the sun, I was happy to roam at night when there was a bit of moon light. I often spent nights on my rocky look-out wall to the east, with my radio for company. On nights with brilliant moon light I was able to wander farther, climbing the near-by hills and looking for automobile headlights to the north, east, and south.

Infrequently there would be a car many miles away on the highway, and I wondered at the tiny speck of humanity way down there on the valley floor.

One fine afternoon I remembered that I had purchased a parachute flare from the Army surplus store. Fishing it out of the cave and moving to the cave opening for better light, I saw that the lump of thick cardboard that housed the flare had been submerged in wax, including the black sulfur ignition material. Using a finger, I dug into the wax until a tiny remnant of fuse was exposed.

Gosh: a very tiny fuse, only a few millimeters in length, attached to a phosphorous incendiary device that could easily maim and cripple me if I mishandled it. Did I dare try to light it? The question was not if I would (crazy not to, by golly), but how to do it "safely." I set a few twigs on fire to see if they would act like a fuse, but they would not stay lit nor would the flame travel down the twigs far enough or hot enough for my purpose. I then thought of dunking a twig into olive oil then shaking off the excess oil: that worked--- I had a working fuse.

Waiting for the sun to set, to get the full effect of the flare and my every penny's worth, I set the flare on top of my frying pan on the ground, dipped a twig into olive oil, gave the twig a shake, and pressed the twig into the wax and up against the tiny fuse inside. It looked like a successful launch was ready, and I felt as giddy as I assume NASA staff do when they are about to send a probe to Mars.

The sun set; the night got dark; I grabbed the box of kitchen matches.

Setting the end of the twig on fire, I quickly stepped away and averted my eyes into the inky night. Minutes passed. More minutes passed. I dared a look at the flare, and I saw a tiny glow some where deep within: a fire still smoldered. I looked away. More time passed, and I looked at it again.

At my glance the flare ignited, brighter than the noon-day sun. Brighter than the movie clips one sees of the Bimini Atoll atomic bomb tests. Brighter than a super, super, super nova. The stab of light was as intense as a spear thrust into my eyes; worse yet was the high pitched howl the flare made as it ***Did Its Duty*** and lit up the entire east-facing side of the Avawatz Mountain Range.

Parachute flares exist for only one reason: to attract attention. Oops. Why didn't that occur to me before?

Blinking furiously, I looked westward and I saw towering above me Avawatz Peak bathed in a spooky yellow glow. Shadows for the first time in millions of years were cast from below by the man-made sun instead of from above by the usual, boring, quiet one. 200 miles away, I imagined, a totally blind person, born without eyes and who has never known even the concept of light, wondered what the hell was going on up there in the mountains.

If a blind person can see it, I reasoned, the Army at Fort Irwin could and did see it.

Thinking furiously, I wondered how to put the blessed thing out. With my eyes closed and my face averted I tried to kick sand over the flare, but in reply the flare just disdainfully flung the sand off of itself. Grabbing the jug I used to hold dirty water that I had washed dishes with, eyes still closed and face averted, I made a wild guess where to pour the water and perhaps thereby extinguish the hissing, spitting flame; I managed to hit the flare squarely with about a liter of water.

The flare barked at me, seemed to shutter a bit, then kept on burning undaunted.

Fearing an immediate visit from the Pentagon, and looking up in the sky for the helicopters I was sure were on their way to investigate, I grabbed my back pack and fled the brilliant flood of light. Eastward I ran, ground perfectly visible in the light of the flare, and when I reached my look-out wall I turned right, southward, and fled into the narrow maze system. I would worry about the Army tracking my boot prints later; now, I just had to get away before they came and got me.

Looking back, I saw the arroyo I lived in was filled with a preternatural yellow glow. Every few seconds a flash of red would be thrown out, then the steady yellow would return. I turned back towards the maze and ran.

The flare stayed ignited for about three minutes. When the flare died, the Avawatz was once again plunged into blackness. I crept farther away into the maze, listening for air craft, tanks, infantry, unmanned drones--- what ever the military might have sent to investigate. When hiking any farther in the dark became too risky, I sat at the bottom of the arroyo I found myself in and waited for the troops to arrive.

The next morning, after no soldiers showed up, I walked back to my cave.

-0-

Fall came, and with it came cooler days and chilly nights. With winter soon to arrive, I wanted to get in as much hiking as possible before I once again shut myself into the cave and endured the cold. I spent more time far away from my cave, exploring westward and far beyond the Avawatz and into the eastern section of Death Valley. I found that six liters of water could last me five or six days, and at times I visited seeps and springs as far west as Goldstone, and as far north as Saratoga Spring.

With the bite of winter in the air, one cold morning found me many miles southwest of my cave, my back pack still full with six liters of drinking water from a seep I had found the day before---water painstakingly gathered through my copper tube and taking many hours, drop by drop. With some surprise I realized that I was at Granite Pass. The road I was following was well graded in some places. In some sections there was even long stretches of ancient asphalt pavement, though broken up into pieces the size of dinner plates and smaller. This had once been the road that had connected Barstow with the Avawatz mining district. If I was correct in my guess of where I was, Fort Irwin would lurk south of me about seven miles.

At Granite Pass I climbed over the two hills that the road passed between and I discovered on one eastern hill a tin box with hand-written notes inside on ancient note paper. About twenty people had written on the note paper their names and the dates they visited the tin box; the most recent was three years before I was there. I used the pencil in the box to add my name and the date I guessed it to be.

That night I set up my sleeping area on the sandy alluvial fan located a few hundred feet north of the pass. My method of sleeping in the cold nights was to dig a trench in the sand within which I could fit my body, place my backpack at one end of the trench, lay in the trench with my head on the back pack, and cover myself with a blanket. My head I covered with a black tee-shirt. As I slept, the moon set and the night became very dark.

Around two o'clock in the morning, judging by how high Orion was in the eastern sky, I heard the sound of many boots walking down the road and heading southward. I lifted the tee-shirt off my face and peered into the dark. I could barely make out a group of people, strung out with a few feet between each one, clattering down the road and towards Fort Irwin. The amount of noise they were making by their boots stomping the ground was astonishing, and for a brief moment I thought about complaining to them. Instead, I got a bright idea.

Why don't I follow them? Maybe see what they were up to? I liked the idea.

Quietly I sat up, rolled up my blanket and strapped it to my back back. Looking toward the inconsiderate intruders it looked like a small United States Army squad had just passed me. Were they out on patrol? Were they lost? What were they doing on my side of the mountain, where they were unwelcome?

When the Army guys were just dim shapes in the dark, well down the road about 200 feet, I slowly stood up, put my back pack to my shoulders, draped my black tee shirt over my face, and stepped onto the road and started southward. Unlike my prey, I was careful where I put my boots and I made very little sound.

South we marched, me trailing behind in the gray gloom, taking care to breathe quietly while I wondered just how close I could get to them undetected. In my mind I was Bob Hollimon, a pistol the size of a hog's hind leg strapped to each hip, ready to apply The Final Solution to my 88 Brand employee problem; I was hunting cow punchers from the Rock Springs Land and Cattle Company.

But no; suddenly I was Rambo, in Vietnam, looking for American prisoners of war. I wondered if I could "take out" the trailing guy ahead of me, silently, without being noticed. I had a belt knife, by golly, on my hip: an Old Timer Deerslayer--- not as manly, long, wide, and phallic as Rambo's but surely good enough. Very quietly, in a whisper, I said to myself "He killed. And killed. And killed."

But no; suddenly I was David Morrell, writing about Rambo in Vietnam. In my mind I was high above the Army guys and me, watching us pass in the night, typewriter on my knees as my (that is, his) iconic creation reached out a massive arm and grabbed the trailing soldier by the face while his other hand applied the knife. "He killed. And killed. And killed," I typed on the typewriter in my head.

But no; suddenly I realized, back in the cold dark real world, that what I was doing might actually be dangerous. Not to my Army pals--- to me. That thought was no where near as funny as the other few previous thoughts. I shuddered to a halt and let the squad continue on southward without me.

AS IF FROM A DREAM

***"Don't be afraid / You have so many choices / Hold your head up high / And say 'Good-bye.'"* - - Donna Lewis**

Winter came, and I suffered in body and mind. The thought came to me daily that it was time for me to leave this place, go back to Dana Point, or anywhere, and once again join society and humanity and the modern world. But the thought of doing so had its terrors as well as its charms. The noise of humanity, the smell, the absurd and sudden and pointless violence in every town, on every street--- it was emotionally easier and safer for me to stay where I was; I grew to hate being cold, but facing humanity again was worse.

It wasn't all misery, shivering in my cave under my "below zero" blanket that at times failed to live up to its certified rating; the cold found every opening in the blanket that I could never manage to get completely to cover me. But the cold kept me awake, and my mind did double duty while my body shivered.

During the winter I invented a cartoon strip which I drew, wrote and performed only in my head. The title of the cartoon strip was "Wonder Cock and Thunder Thighs." These two main characters were disembodied crotches, one male human and one female human, with no legs and no upper bodies. They levitated three or four feet above the ground, and they traveled through the air with a soft humming, wooshing sound. Wonder Cock and Thunder Thighs had many exciting adventures as they traveled to exotic places in the world, meeting new people and solving mysteries and puzzles. I would tell you how they manipulated objects in the world, as they did not have hands, but you would not thank me for forever burning the image into your head. Suffice it to note, I hope, that even Doctor Sigmund Freud would flinch.

The spring day came when I needed to return to Barstow for more food and other supplies. All I had left to eat were the boxes of lasagna noodles I still inexplicably kept buying, a box of crackers, and a tub of dehydrated refried beans that had become progressively disgusting to eat. I secured my blankets and pillows, wrapped tightly in my plastic sheet, tugged my backpack to my shoulders, and set off towards my pickup in the dim morning light.

Extracting my hidden vehicle was the usual tedious chore, which I was getting tired of. The slow, torturous drive down the mountain was interrupted by a stream of vehicles going the other way, full of happy desert tourists who insisted that I stop and talk with them about road conditions; weather; spiritual "vibrations" emanating from the moon; and if it was "safe" to visit Fort Irwin "from the back side." I told the tourists that the fort would love to have company show up from the northeast. I made no mention of the barbed wire; look-out towers; booby traps; suicide bomber barrier counter-measures; light anti-tank gun turrets; and DANGER KEEP OUT warning signs they must ignore along the way. They thanked me. I was happy to oblige. If they survived the adventure, maybe they could visit the Army's gift shop afterward.

Barstow: the city I loved to hate; the city that fed me and kept me alive. Now there's gratitude for you. I pulled into the grocery store's massive parking lot, pushed my fingers through my matted and filthy beard, removed my belt knife from my hip and put it in the glove box, and egressed my vehicle. I stumbled on broken, worn-out boots to the front door of the store.

Before the doors of the store opened, I caught sight of my reflection in the glass. I was horrified. My long, filthy, white hair streamed out from under my hat as if trying desperately to escape; my black beard, with patches of white on the sides, made me look like an Old Testament prophet; my eyes were hollowed out, as if I had just returned from the battlefield after seeing and experiencing a terrible slaughter. I was scary looking. I looked like the frightening men one sees in a Mad Max movie, only without the union job. I looked like the serial killer John Joseph Joubert IV but not as handsome; maybe as he looked three weeks after being executed, and rolled in mud a few days, then dipped in pig fat, then lightly powdered with desert *playa* dust. My hat was filthy with dried sweat; my corduroy jacket with imitation fleece on the shoulders, like John Denver used to wear, was also blackened by dirt and the smoke from my hobo stove fires. If I had seen me enter the store, I would have fled out the back door.

I walked slowly back to my car, shocked. I climbed into my pickup, stared at myself in the rear-view mirror, and said, "It's enough." I couldn't go back and live in a desert cave any longer; the insanity of the behavior had become too great to bear any more.

But where would I go? What would I do? I had a few options.

Maybe I could run away to New Mexico, Taos perhaps, and be a cowboy poet. Only I am not a poetry kind of guy: I prefer the rain, not the rainbow. When it came to romantic movies I preferred "A Boy and his Dog" to "When Harry met Sally;" for romantic "chic flick" series on television I liked "Airwolf:" the continuing stories about two men and their mutual love for a highly lethal flying killing machine; on Christmas eve it was always "The Rocky Horror Picture Show" on DVD for me, not "It's a Wonderful Life." I think the ending to "Independence Day," where humanity survives complete annihilation, is a sad ending. On Valentine's Day it is "The Bride with White Hair." I would make a lousy, a shitty poet.

Perhaps I could go live in the Rocky Mountains of Colorado; maybe up there around Alma where I can find a mountain woman with strong hands and a large healthy pair of, um, lungs who raises goats and splits firewood the old fashioned way: get a man to do it. Her fingers would stay warm and supple from milking the goats twice a day, among other things. It's wonderful what clean, thin mountain air does to women; I could make a study of the phenomena. On winter evenings she would play the mandolin and I would play her squeeze box. Maybe own and run a pizza shop on Main Street, next to the highest altitude bar and marijuana dispensary in the continental USA. ("Oh, crap! Some of my dried herb caught on fire! Let's go get pizza!")

I could live a few years in the Marshall Islands raising pearl oysters. I could spend the days fifteen feet under water, sucking air through a hose from a compressor on a floating work shed barge, scrubbing oyster shells with a stiff brush to keep them healthy. I knew someone who could set that up for me. Perhaps find a skinny and lithe island woman to pound kava root for me in the afternoons, and check my bookkeeping.

I was breathless with wonder at what my future could be. The first step of course was obvious. I knew exactly where I needed to be.

I fired up my pickup's engine, put the beast into drive, and headed to the highway. As I pulled onto the highway and headed south, I did not pause to wave "Good-bye" to Barstow. Instead, I imagined an atomic bomb destroying the city as I watched in my rear view mirror: always good to have a happy ending to an epic tale.

The freeway went from two lanes to four lanes, one way. Hugging the edge of the "slow lane," being passed by homicidal sociopaths going three times my speed, I managed to make the correct right-hand lane change and headed west. With shock I found that the freeway grew to six lanes, and I was in the center surrounded by speeding traffic. Traffic all around me hurled past, with a few feet between cars, and I looked in vain for a gap to my right in which I could get into the "slow lane." Terror seized my heart in an iron grip; nervous sweat collected on my forehead and trickled into my beard. People really live like this? All day? For years and years and years? No wonder people no longer act like people.

The desired exit ramp was 44 miles away, and it took me that long to get into the far right lane. I tried to be careful; I tried to be polite; I tried warning my fellow citizens of my pending lane change with the correct turn signal. My coy behavior only seemed to infuriate the soulless mechanical beasts thundering down around me. The relief I felt upon exiting the highway was like a last-minute reprieve from a state-sanctioned execution in some Texas "death row" prison compound.

After a few convoluted turns I came to a quiet neighborhood street and slowed down to a crawl. The house I was looking for didn't have a paved parking spot so I eased my vehicle's front wheels hard up against the curb and then gunned the engine. With a lurch and a hop the pickup came to rest on the front lawn. I killed the engine.

Looked like no one was home. I got out, shaken and damp from the frightening journey, and went to kick the door a few times. No one came out. Looking around I found no chair to sit and wait, so I laid on the ground with my head resting on the doorway's concrete step. Time passed and I fell to sleep.

I woke up, hours later, to see a buccaneer grin staring down at me. My brother spoke.

"I can get a pizza or two delivered here in under an hour," he said. I pulled my hat up off my eyebrows and said, "I'd rather go to a family restaurant for a regular sit-down dinner."

"I like the idea," my brother said. "It's been weeks since someone punched my face."

"And then after we're finished eating. . . ." I said, patting the belt knife at my hip with my right hand. My brother's grin turned sinister, like an amused pirate who just found the cabin in the captured ship where the gold and women were hiding.

"No witnesses!" we said in unison.

It's good to have a brother like that. Everyone should have one.

EPILOGUE ; WHAT HAVE I LEARNED ABOUT MYSELF?

***"You can count on a memoirist being passionate about the subject."* - Mary Karr**

In April, year 2011, I returned to my cave in the Avawatz mountains to clean the area and haul away the trash I had left. It was emotionally injurious to see the changes a mere decade had wrought upon the East Mojave Desert: thousands more people have moved into Sandy Valley, Tecopa, and near-by areas. The spring where I collected water east of my cave has decreased in size to a tiny fraction of what it had been; most of the brush has died. The latest ground water survey in East Mojave Desert shows the majority of historical, long-term seeps and springs have gone dry.

The water below the surface has also decreased sharply, with old wells needing to be drilled deeper, and a new well is being drilled every few months to meet the increased human demand. There are now alfalfa fields producing in the East Mojave Desert where once only creosote and chamisa had struggled to survive.

This is utter madness. This is contrary to the survival of not only most species in the region, but also the humans.

Invasive species, and specifically desert mistletoe, have killed or are killing the remaining mesquite trees in the only area that, a mere decade ago, the mesquite had been thriving: now, all along Salt Creek the trees lay dead, leafless, stark, and grasping towards the sky in their silent death throes while the Department of the Interior sat back and let it happen "because it's natural."

Picnic tables and camp sites have been placed at the western end of Shadow Valley, along with a concrete and plastic building for people to shit in; where conservationists had planted native species on the old dirt road heading into the Pahrump Valley Wilderness, about a third of that new growth has been bulldozed to allow recreational vehicles to easily park at the new camp site--- erasing hundreds of "man hours" of effort to help the desert reclaim the road.

What little water left on Clark Mountain is poisonous; some of it is slightly radioactive.

Chinese corporations have financed many tens of thousands of mineral claims throughout the East Mojave Desert, giving them (via their USA citizen proxies) the right to come in and extract any and all minerals from the public land.

Thinking about these changes at night, as I sat on my "lookout wall" to the east of my cave ten years after my extended stay, I tried to convince myself to not care about the destruction of the desert region. I have no children I know of; I have no horse in the human race to the future. If people with children and grand children are content to see their progeny much worse off in life than they had it, why should I care? But gosh, some how I cannot bring myself to not care. I have grown weary of caring about human suffering, human misery, human sorrow, human loss and grief; yet I still care. Short of death, I have found no other way in which I can bring myself to stop worrying about what will happen to people in the near future.

The East Mojave Desert is warming anomalously by about +0.3 Fahrenheit per decade; it is also getting dryer, with precipitation decreasing by about -0.13 inch per decade. These demonstrable facts are called "liberal lies" by 54% of the United States Congress members. This fact has crushed what ever hope I had for the future of humans and everyone else on Earth.

But gosh, where does my duty to the future lay? If a slave finds comfort only in his chains, surely I would be a fiend if I took the shackles off of him for his own good. I shall be content as I watch humanity suffocate on its own wastes: they do not care, so why should I?

For two days I hauled my abandoned gear to my pickup. Plastic sheets; blankets; plastic buckets; car battery; light bulb and wires; folding chair--- all laboriously taken over the rocky ground and to my vehicle 2.2 miles away. I have left only the books, sealed in a dozen ammunition cans, for another adventurer to discover some day. For two nights I lay on the top of my rocky ledge and grieved over the changes humanity has inflicted upon that which I have for so long dearly loved: the East Mojave Desert.

Stephen Reed Donaldson once wrote that the best way to destroy a man utterly is to take from him something he cherishes, break it, and give it back to him. I will never return to the East Mojave; I could not bear seeing what has become of it.

I have more than enough material to write a decent book about my time and my experiences in the East Mojave Desert. But gosh: I find the actual book to be of no significance at all. It was the journey, the "doing," and not the reporting that motivated me--- the book project was the excuse for fleeing into silence, not the driver.

Now and then, though rarely, I meet someone who is much like I am. We tend to instantly dislike each other more than we dislike the inferior beings we both regrettably must contend with. But there is also some times a knowing smile that passes between us; a form of letting the other person know, "I know a great deal about you." To them I would council not doing what I did. The benefits you might gain may not outweigh the loses. You have spent a lifetime learning how to blend in with lesser beings, learning to emulate their ways: an extended period of isolation may not be itself detrimental, but that is time lost from learning social skills to increase your ability to survive among the as yet unevolved. Also, we need you to survive and soon join us for The Time Of The Great Taking Over, when we finally get to run the planet and the non-odd finally get what they richly deserve.

What have I learned from spending twenty-nine months living alone in the Avawatz Mountain Range, under what many people would consider harsh conditions?

I am convinced that some times unhealthy, irrational behavior is a matter of time, place, and circumstance: there are billions of ways to see and experience the world, and people who see reality differently than most people are still worthy of respect, compassion, and empathy when their behavior is harmless. The world is full of people who fall outside the standard distribution of human behavior, and I strive to always hold in my mind the fact that people are living their own individual lives with their own back-stories far different than mine.

I have learned that contentment is internal. Other than in special cases such as when health care is needed, or when basic needs are absent, no one and nothing can make a person content: the ability is all inside one's own head. Other people can, do, and some times should help make one's life happier and rewarding. Being content is an individual effort, impossible to share.

I learned that it is important to keep one's friends. You might need them someday. And if you're lucky, they may someday need you.

Silence and wisdom come hand-in-hand, a packaged gift: both traits feed upon each other. Growing older often "bootstraps" the process, but not always. Wise people are quiet people: they hold their council until asked to share it. If you wish the sagest of advice, ask the person sitting quietly among the sea of people talking. Wisdom comes from seeing, hearing, listening, and contemplating silently; with wisdom, for the lucky few, comes contentment--- this greatest of life's gifts is never granted to the person whose mouth is constantly working.

Perhaps the most important lesson I have learned is that a person should always be uncomfortable; there should always be some struggle to overcome, some goal to work towards, some level of discomfort and pain to motivate action and perhaps therefore facilitate personal growth. That growth should be towards emotional maturity and towards acceptance of harsh realities that we cannot change and must therefore deal with. The good news is that this is easy to achieve, as it only requires letting go of infantile and therefore obsolete ideals and wishes; the bad news is that far too few people understand just how easy this is to do.

APPENDIX ONE; GEAR IN MY BACK PACK

Ibuprofen, in two separate water tight plastic containers (two, in case one is broken or lost), located in two different compartments.

Magnifying glass, three inches in diameter, used to start fires with sun light; also used for finding cactus needles in feet and ankles and fingers; also used for gold dust prospecting.

Six one-liter plastic bottles, located in different compartments of my back pack in case one side of the pack is crushed (if I fall or sit on the pack).

Four cotton socks. Sore, blistered, injured feet can bring death when hiking in the desert. If you feel a foot chaffing, STOP WALKING!

Copper tube, about 16 inches long, quarter inch inner diameter. Typical plumbing material, the tube is used for sucking water out of cracks, sand, and other hard-to-reach sources of water.

Magnetic compass, Army field unit. Armored, folding, with sight tube and a lanyard.

Assorted shoe laces, more than one dozen.

Sail twine, waxed, and sail repair needles. Carried in a section of bamboo that has been plugged at both ends with cork.

Folding pocket knife, with attached tools.

Magnesium block and steel shaver. Used to start fires quickly; people who have never used these tools should practice with them first before the day comes when they need to start a fire in a hurry.

Tomahawk, stainless steel, 14 inches long. Very sharp on one side of the head, with a sharp pike on the other side. Light weight, the tool was used when I came across dead brush for camp fires; can be used in self defense.

Folding hand saw. In 30 months I used it once, to cut brush out from under my Toyota Pickup truck; the brush had wrapped around the drive shaft.

Man-overboard whistle, bright orange. May be used to signal for help.

Pocket chain saw, with pouch. Carried in case I needed to cut through wood, a dead animal, or my leg if necessary.

Folding needle-nose pliers. Included in the handle: tiny saw, knives, screw drivers.

Two P38 can openers. These are included in every box of "C" Rations, and the Army had tens of millions of them made. They were meant to be used once or twice, then discarded.

Toilet paper, one full roll. When in the desert for an extended stay, it is important to keep your ass clean; use dirt if necessary to remove all moisture from around your anus. Lingering shit can cause chaffing and sores, which invites infections.

Kitchen matches. Stuff these in a plastic bag, then place inside the toilet paper roll's cardboard tube.

Chlorine bleach (sodium hypochlorite) to add to drinking water. I carried bleach in a plastic tube "blank," which are fed in to soda pop bottle machines and inflated with very hot air into liter-size bottles. The "blanks'" walls are extremely thick, and are nearly indestructible. A cup of water (eight to twelve ounces) needs only one drop of bleach, if mixed well, to kill most if not all bacteria. One liter of water should get three or four drops, well mixed, and then left to "air" for about 30 minutes.

Tin can, one end removed. I carry an empty olive can. One can heat food and water in the can, and use it to dig with, and carry water in, and drink from. The desert traveler who does not carry a tin can is a fool.

Cardboard identification card. After folding the cardboard in half twice, I wrote my name, birth date, and Social Security Number on all eight surfaces; this is to make at least one surface readable if wind and rain wears out other surfaces. When law enforcement officers come across a dead human, they get irate when identifying the pieces of skin and bones is difficult.

Spare hat. I do not mind being dead; it's the dying by having my brains fried by the sun that bothers me.

Pen light, skinny enough to clamp between my teeth so that I can illuminate what I'm holding.

Black tee-shirt. This is used as a bandanna, to cover the back of my neck; it is also used to wrap around my head, ears, and eyes at night when trying to sleep.

Spare sun glasses. Some people visit the desert without eye protection; the technical term for these people is "idiots." I need my vision for my old age, so the sun glasses go on my face seconds after the hat goes on my head. Polarized are good; polarized "shooter's glasses" (with semi-transparent side panels) are best. I carried one on my face and one in my back pack; they cost about $130 each, were called "unbreakable," and came with a "life time guarantee."

Soup spoon. Stainless steel, very heavy, hard to bend. Millions of uses if you are clever.

Note book and ballpoint pen. For writing down my last words for my grave marker if my bones are found.

27146624R00151

Made in the USA
San Bernardino, CA
26 February 2019